PROJECT KINGFISHER

PROJECT KINGFISHER

ATHOL MOFFITT CMG,QC,BA,LLB

ANGUS & ROBERTSON PUBLISHERS

Unit 4, Eden Park, 31 Waterloo Road,
North Ryde, NSW, Australia 2113;
94 Newton Road, Auckland 1,
New Zealand; and
16 Golden Square, London W1R 4BN,
United Kingdom

First published in Australia
by Angus & Robertson Publishers in 1989

National Library of Australia
Cataloguing-in-publication data

Moffitt, A. R. (Athol Randolph), 1914–
Project Kingfisher.

Bibliography.
Includes index.
ISBN 0 207 16375 8.

1. World War, 1939–1945—Borneo—Prisoners and
prisons, Japanese. 2. Prisoners of war—Borneo.
3. World War, 1939–1945—Borneo—Personal
narratives, Australian. I. Title.

940.54'72'52

Typeset in 11 pt English Times by
Midland Typesetters, Maryborough, Victoria
Printed in Australia by Griffin Press

THIS BOOK IS

DEDICATED to the heroes of Sandakan: the 2400 Australian and British prisoners of war who endured suffering beyond belief and died at Sandakan, on the marches and at Ranau: to Captain Lionel Matthews, George Cross (posthumous), MC and bar, tortured and executed, for refusing to implicate others; to Dr J. B. Taylor and the native civilians Heng Joo Ming, Kassim bin Amadi and many others who were tortured to death, imprisoned or executed for helping prisoners; and to Warrant Officer Walter Wallace, Major Rex Blow, DSO, Gunner Owen Campbell, Private Nelson Short, Bombardier Keith Botterill, Warrant Officer (later Major) Bill Sticpewich and others who escaped against impossible odds.

AND

ACKNOWLEDGING the Japanese who struggled against the cruelties of others imposed on them and who are represented in my story by Private Takahara and those such as Shoiji, who stole food for starving prisoners, and by the soldier Matsuba, who, when ordered twice to shoot a prisoner, fired and missed deliberately, *and* by those who disapproved of the policies of the Japanese leaders and are represented in this book by Colonel Yamada.

ALSO

WRITTEN so later generations, including, I hope, those of Japan, can calmly and accurately know the enormity of what occurred and why it occurred and was allowed to occur when we and Japan were at war.

ACKNOWLEDGEMENTS

I acknowledge the considerable help given to me by prisoners who escaped from Sandakan: Bill Sticpewich, back in 1946, and in recent years, Rex Blow, DSO, and Nelson Short; and the willing help given me by Sir John Overall, Kt CBE, MC and Bar, and Lawrie Black of Z Special Unit. In my researches, I have had, without exception, the utmost assistance from the staff at Archives (in particular Mark Wagland of the ACT), of the War Memorial (in particular Ron Gilchrist and Peter Stanley), of the New South Wales, Mitchell and Law Courts Libraries, and from employees of Qantas interested in aviation history.

I acknowledge the assistance, both general and on some matters of detail, provided by books written about the Sandakan prisoners and escapes. In some matters their source is the same as mine, namely the Labuan trials. I acknowledge, in particular, the works *From Hell to Eternity* by Peter Firkins, *Escape from Hell* by Walter Wallace, *One Man War* by Hal Richardson, *Three Came Back* by Agnes Keith, *Prisoners of War* by Hank Nelson and *Sandakan* by Don Wall.

I acknowledge the help of many in the preparation of the manuscript, especially Norman Rowe for his suggestions, advice and help otherwise in regard to Chapter 12; and Lionel (Bill) Hudson, Justice Bill Perrignon and Sonia Paul for their help in reading, commenting on and preparing the manuscript.

Athol Moffitt
4 August 1989

FOREWORD

The author is a distinguished lawyer, an ex New South Wales Supreme Court judge, and equally important in the formulation of his views and his standing as the author of a book of this nature, he was an officer with the 9th Division AIF.

Athol Moffitt's background and qualifications for this task are further enhanced by his central involvement as prosecutor in the collaborator trials in Borneo in 1945 and then at the Sandakan war crimes trials held at Labuan. The reader therefore feels a closeness to these events; he or she observes them at first hand. With some readers this book will refresh old, and maybe bitter, memories, but for many others it will be a fresh insight into Japanese attitudes and especially their treatment of prisoners of war in the 1939–45 conflict.

Some will question the justification of recording factually the attitudes and brutal behaviour of Japanese military leaders towards prisoners. They will argue that we must forget past history, that we must live in an environment of world harmony, and that trading relations are now the priority and core of relationships between Australia and Japan.

I firmly believe that it is self-destructive to live on hatred and bitterness, but equally firmly I believe that the events recorded in this book should be published. The barbarity of the Japanese and their complete non-adherence to the Geneva Convention must be understood by the generations of Australians who have followed—and will in future follow—their forefathers who were forced to end their lives on a death march. What more damning indictment of the actions of the Japanese military leaders could be produced than to give the figure of only 6 survivors out of 2400 Australian and British prisoners at Sandakan, the last of them forced to take part in the death marches?

If out of this callously planned and executed carnage there emerges a reasoned thread of understanding—no matter how slight—then the publication of this book has achieved a worthwhile purpose. It has fulfilled the need to make us all, especially the young ones who were not associated with the events of 1939–45, factually and intimately aware of what took place. Hopefully it will give us some understanding of our erstwhile enemies (now our allies and trading partners) and thus enable us to build a better mutual relationship based on knowledge rather than on wartime bitterness or post-war euphoria.

Sir Roden Cutler
VC, AK, KCMG, KCVO, CBE

CONTENTS

Sketch of the author made at Labuan on 9 February 1946 by G. Takase, an artist attached to the headquarters of the 37th Imperial Japanese Army.

OVERVIEW

The Japanese invaded Borneo on 16 December 1941. It had no defence and within days, not only the rich oil fields, but the whole of Borneo fell under the domination of the invader. The first landing was just nine days after the attack on Pearl Harbor, which commenced the undeclared war against the US in the same way as Japan had commenced its undeclared war against Russia in February 1904 with its surprise attack on the Russian fleet in its stronghold at Port Arthur. Following the pattern set by its Nazi Axis partner in Europe, Japan in its Asian mainland wars and then the Pacific war invaded one small, defenceless country after another.

In Borneo and in other invaded countries, Japan professed to have come to liberate the people from their European or American oppressors and to incorporate their country into a sphere of co-prosperity and equality. Six weeks after Pearl Harbor, General Tojo described Japan's East Asia Co-Prosperity Sphere as "a truly grand undertaking . . . which will mark a new epoch in the annals of mankind . . . [in which Japan] will proceed to construct a new world order along with our allies . . . in Europe." Instead of equality or prosperity, Borneo, which had long enjoyed peace, was subjected to an oppressive regime which brought misery and death.

Civilians, including some of the indigenous peoples, were massacred as were prisoners of war in Japanese custody. The most infamous of these attrocities was the brutal annihilation of almost all the Sandakan POWs which occurred over three years and involved very many Japanese.

To the civilians in Borneo it was soon apparent that the Co-Prosperity Sphere was no partnership but a one-way traffic affair in the Japanese direction. The give-away was Tojo's speeches, and in particular his reference to the Co-Prosperity Sphere as one "with Japan serving as the nucleus." In 1943 he declared his determination to retain the Japanese military forces at full strength in the occupied territories, when Japan won the war.

Instead of the promised dawn of a new era illuminated by the rising sun, Borneo was plunged into the darkness of midnight. Oppression, misery and death for which many thousands of different Japanese were responsible, spread throughout the occupied countries. These included those along the entire coast of the Asian mainland from Korea to Burma, and from 1942, the Philippines, Borneo, the Netherlands, East Indies, Timor, New Britain, the Solomons, the north coast of New Guinea and all the other islands west of the line from the Aleutians in the north to the Solomons in the south. Australia and New Zealand, the only countries in the region not invaded, stood tense as the dark cloud of oppression, savagery and death sped south, threatening to engulf them.

Tojo had said early in 1942 that if Australia joined the Co-Prosperity Sphere, Japan would extend "its help and full understanding for [its] welfare and progress . . . but if Australia continues to resist we will show no mercy and crush [it]." It was a promise and a threat reminiscent of those of Hitler in the 1936–39 period. Australia did not believe Tojo's promises, as in the end Europe did not believe those of Hitler. The Borneo experience showed that Australia was right.

What occurred in Borneo generally, and to the Sandakan POWs in particular, provides a sample—in the case of the POWs, a sample examinable under the microscope of the war trials—of the actions of the Japanese in other occupied territories and of their motivations and attitudes. It provides an indication of what would have occurred to the Australian people if their country had been invaded wholly or in part.

The Japanese in charge of Australian prisoners in Borneo boasted of Japanese domination of Australia when Japan won the war. POWs were urged to be more diligent in their compulsory learning of Japanese, so they would get the "good jobs" in Australia after the war. Captain Hoshijima, the Sandakan prison commandant, who lived in a commandeered house overlooking Sandakan harbour, boasted that when Japan won the war he would have a house with the best views of

Sydney Harbour. Colonel Suga, who was in overall charge of the many prison camps in Borneo, declared that when Australia was invaded he would be in charge of prison camps there. The Japanese made some survey of motor vehicles in Australia and concluded there were 808,000 and considered they "could be mobilised for the smooth transportation of materials in the Co-Prosperity Sphere." They were then mainly of US and British manufacture.

The Japanese lost the war, but now own houses and properties with some of the best views and positions along the Australian coastline. Many Australians now voluntarily learn Japanese, with an eye on the better jobs. Australian roads are crowded with motor vehicles manufactured under Japanese control and with Japanese names. The post-war "co-prosperity" trading relations with Japan have many one-way tracks leading to Japan and its interests. The acquisition by Japan of land and commercial interests in other countries has little equivalent in reverse. Japanese personal and public exclusiveness and the regimentation of its company structures discourage or prevent such foreign intrusions, particularly takeovers of Japanese companies or the acquisition of Japanese interests. Before I record what happened in Borneo as a sample of Japanese occupations of the Second World War and before I explore many questions as to why atrocities occurred and examine the part played by the war trials, I will relate the grim end to the story of the Sandakan prisoners of war. The last days before the delayed surrender of the Japanese in Borneo provide some of its darkest hours when humanity ceased to exist. What happened there reveals in stark and conclusive form Japanese attitudes and characteristics. The earlier part of the Sandakan story to be later told and examined in the light of the Labuan war trials also reveals much about the Japanese generally.

The story concerning the Sandakan prisoners there, on the "death" marches and, in the end, at Ranau, is one which ought to be told and recorded for itself, as accurately as possible, as part of history. It ranks as one of the great tragedies of the Australian people. It is a story of the utter darkness which descends when humanity vanishes; it is a story of three years of brutality and suffering, leading to the deaths of 2400 POWs; it is a story of bravery when, in the face of impossible odds, prisoners and civilians displayed heroism, daring and endurance beyond belief. It is a tragedy made worse because the final brutality and the death of some 1500 men could have been avoided by a plan to rescue the prisoners which was unjustifiably abandoned. Out of shame the story of the abandoned rescue was deliberately buried and for nigh on fifty years has been allowed to lie hidden. This part of the tragedy, now to be told from documents formerly top secret and from memories of the past, is equally part of our history.

Thus my story begins at a time just before the Japanese occupation of Borneo ended, and at a time when Japanese cold-blooded and inexcusable cruelty reached its zenith. Conduct such as this, not open to question and most of it admitted, put a stain on the history of the Japanese people, a stain which will be slow to fade unless Japan as a nation and as a people acknowledges this past and shows a resolution to live it down by objective actions which demonstrate, in its place, an unselfish humanity with consideration for and help to the family of nations beyond Japan. However, in post-war years Japan has by uncompromising economic ambition pursued the same goals of domination which it failed to achieve by military means.

More recently an attitude has developed in Japan which tends to regard the atrocities committed by many thousands of Japanese on perhaps as many as a million victims as if they did not occur or to see their enormity rendered insignificant in the context of the dropping of the atomic bomb. If they do think of the findings of the war trials, they appear to regard them as the product of a revengeful victor's justice which did not reveal the truth. In that, as the Borneo examples will show, they were wrong. Unlike the Germans, they have not been prepared to come to terms with what happened in the Second World War. History should accept the trials as revealing what did occur.

1

THE LAST DAYS —ESCAPE OR DIE

> You go now. Go jungle. If you stay you will be mati. All men very short time mati mati.

The grim warning of death was given by a Japanese private, Takahara, to an Australian warrant officer, Bill Sticpewich, on 27 July 1945 at the prisoner of war compound at Ranau in Borneo. Earlier that day, as he passed Sticpewich, Takahara had silently slipped a bottle of quinine and atebrin tablets into his hand and pointed to where some bananas were hidden. Then in the pitch dark of night a hand touched Sticpewich and Takahara whispered the warning.

Sticpewich hurried to Captain Cook, the senior POW, and told him what Takahara had said. Cook called together the two medical officers, Captains Oakshott and Piconi. Despite the warning, escape of the prisoners posed impossible problems. Ranau, a place of great beauty, isolated in the sweltering inland jungle of North Borneo, lies on a plateau some 3000 feet above sea level at the foothills of the 12,700 feet high Mt Kinabalu, but on that day it was a place of death. There in a primitive Japanese jungle compound were a little fewer than fifty POWs, the last of about 2000 who had been in Sandakan prison compound, 150 miles away, some seven months earlier.

Their condition at the end of July when Takahara gave the warning was appalling. Deliberate maltreatment had reduced them physically and mentally to a state of utter degradation. With insufficient food to sustain life, most were five or six stone, some less. Most had no footwear or shirts and were clad in lap laps. Those who could still move about were like spectres or human skeletons with long and matted hair and beards, which obscured their identity. The means of shaving and cutting hair had been taken from them. Some had grotesquely swollen limbs or testicles caused by beriberi. Some had splints attached to limbs, their bones visible due to tropical ulcers. Most were sick with malaria or dysentery or had ulcers of varying degrees of severity. Half were bedridden. Each day men died. The two medical officers, also sick, did what they could without any medicines. Those who could walk were made to work in burial parties or to fetch and carry for the Japanese, who had sufficient food and were robust except for a few who had malaria or dysentery. The prisoners had descended to the level of animals as they struggled to survive and squabbled over the distribution of the meagre food. Some resented Sticpewich, who cooked for the Japanese and managed to eat scraps of their food. The POWs had inadequate shelter in the hut which they had constructed. Those with dysentery had to sleep on the ground under the floor. Hygiene was non-existent. There was little water for washing. An evil stench permeated the quarters and the prisoners.

Sticpewich was prepared to undertake the great risk involved in escaping from a remote place surrounded by jungle, where assistance sought from natives involved real risks of being turned over to the Japanese. Recapture meant certain death. The Japanese, who by now greatly outnumbered the dwindling number of prisoners, were obsessive and vigilant about escapes and vigorously pursued any who were missing. It was many miles over difficult mountain trails to the coast, an impossibility for debilitated men without any source of food.

The condition of the prisoners was such that Captain G. Cook and the medical officers Captains J. Oakshott and D. Piconi considered there was none fit to escape. Earlier there had been rumours that the Japanese intended to shoot the surviving prisoners, but despite the warning they still clung to the hope of surviving where they were. For Oakshott, who had no footwear and a large ulcer on one foot, escape was not possible. Cook and Piconi were more fit and Sticpewich tried to persuade Piconi to come with him, but none of the officers would join the escape. Their decision was influenced by their sense of duty to the dying men in their charge. One prisoner, Private Herman Reither, although ill with dysentery, was prepared to go and Sticpewich was prepared to take him. Cook told Sticpewich of a spot where he (Cook) would bury the prisoners' records and any final message. He farewelled the two men and wished them good luck. Later the records could not be found. It seems they fell into Japanese hands and were destroyed.

The next day, 28 July, Sticpewich waited until he had prepared the Japanese meal and then, under darkness, the two men escaped past the wire. They adopted the wise course of hiding under jungle cover within the compound area for a day while the Japanese searched for them along the jungle trails beyond the compound perimeter. From their hiding place, they could see some of the Japanese having their faces slapped because of the escape and the search party go out and return. Then at night, the two men melted into the jungle.

28 July 1945, when Sticpewich acted on the warning, was just eighteen days before the Japanese general surrender and nine days before the atomic bomb was dropped on Hiroshima, but by then it was abundantly plain to all, the Japanese included, that Japan had lost the war. The Allies had complete air and naval superiority. US fleets of planes bombed the Japanese home islands unopposed. Tokyo was all but wiped out and other cities and installations destroyed. Japanese shipping was virtually non-existent. Even the smallest shipping upon which communications between the Japanese Islands depended had been destroyed. When Takahara gave his warning, it was just three days after the British–US Potsdam proclamation called on Japan to surrender.

After some days in the jungle, Sticpewich took the chance and sought the help of Dihil bin Ambilid (later nicknamed

"Godihil"), who hid the two escapees from the searching Japanese in his hut in the jungle. The Japanese searched the hut, but did not discover the concealed men. Three miracles combined to preserve Sticpewich. At two moments critical to his survival, Takahara and Godihil, each dedicated Christians, came to his aid and Godihil happened to be aware that Australian commandos had recently penetrated this jungle area and was able to put him in touch with "an agent", one of the natives recruited by Z Special Unit (colloquially known as Z Force), which led to his recovery and survival. Reither died two days before help arrived. The official history of the operation of the Z Force, known as AGAS III, which in early August entered the Ranau area, records that on 8 August a "native named Gimbahan" brought a message from Sticpewich, and on 10 August they picked him up "in a very weak condition." He told the Z Force officer, Flight-Lieutenant Ripley, of the earlier escapes of four other POWs from Ranau, who may still be alive in the jungle. Z Force mounted a search for them. The four other POWs had escaped from Ranau on 7 July, some three weeks before Sticpewich.

The prisoners at Ranau were those who remained of the original Sandakan POWs. In 1942 and 1943, a total of about 2750, 2000 Australian and 750 British, were transported from Singapore to construct for the Japanese in Sandakan a military aerodrome, but by late 1943 some 300 officers and NCOs had been moved to Kuching. Between late 1943 and May 1945, 1100 died in Sandakan under its commandant, Captain Hoshijima. In all, just over 1000 left on two death marches, one in January and the other in late May 1945, from Sandakan to Ranau, but fewer than 450 survived the marches. Just under 300, left behind at Sandakan when the second march left, died or were shot. Seventy-five of them were taken on a third death march and disposed of. None survived. By late July 1945, those who had reached Ranau were reduced to that last fifty or so.

Some escaped during the first march, but none survived. Some escaped in June 1945 during the second march. These included five who escaped together and one on his own. Of the group of five, four perished, but the one remaining (Gunner Owen Campbell) and the man on his own (Bombardier Dick Braithwaite) miraculously survived after weeks in the jungle. One was picked up by Z Force and the other made his way with native help sixty miles to the coast and was picked up by a US torpedo boat. Each of these two men, at some time, was alone in the jungle without food for some five days. Braithwaite ate fungi from the trees. These two were the only survivors of those who escaped during the second march. After years of fortitude and hope in the face of brutality and death, they did not need to be told in the end that to remain in Japanese custody meant certain death. They saw escape into the unknown and hostile jungle with nowhere to go and little chance of survival as preferable.

The last days of the war at Ranau for the handful of the Sandakan prisoners still alive and the awful alternatives of death or escape were recaptured recently (1988) for me by (Private) Nelson Short, one of the four who escaped from Ranau, the only one now living who completed the second march. By the time that march arrived at Ranau on 26 June 1945, the prison compound had been moved some kilometres into a concealed jungle valley, because of Allied air raids on Japanese positions at Ranau. The new area had two atap huts and a wire compound for the prisoners. The Japanese occupied the huts which were outside the wire. No provision had been made or shelter constructed for the prisoners. They were left after arrival to do this. When the survivors of the second march arrived, they found that only six of the 250 survivors of the first march were still alive, five Australian and one British. In all, fewer than 200 were still alive from the 1000 who had left on the two marches. Despite their condition, those prisoners who could walk were assigned to carrying work for Japanese units in the area and to other labouring tasks around the compound. They were repeatedly beaten, often for no apparent reason. In the period of two weeks from their arrival until 7 July, when the four escaped, about sixty died. In the further three weeks which elapsed until Sticpewich escaped, many more died. With numbers declining daily, no more than rough estimates could be made by Sticpewich and Short.

Short's decision to escape and the spur to it, typifies the mental and physical state of these men, all then close to death. He was ordered by a Japanese, Suzuki, to get a bucket of water. Short was then about five stone and could see he would soon die like the others dying at four or five a night. With difficulty, he struggled with the bucket up the steep and slippery slope from the creek, spilling it as he went. When delivered, it was about one-third full. He was set upon and bashed about the head by Suzuki and as a result his eye was opened up. He shows that mark today, forty-three years later. This was the incident which made up his mind for him. As he recalls, "That was it. If I stayed I would die and be again bashed before I did; escape and death in the jungle could not be worse." He knew the penalty for a failed escape would be an agonising death. Earlier, a prisoner who had escaped from Ranau and was recaptured was chained to a post in the open for all to see, beaten and starved and died a lingering death after some days. Another prisoner was shot and killed while attempting to escape.

Short revealed his intentions to a friend from his march, Anderson, who informed him that two other prisoners from the first march were planning to escape that night. These men, Bombardiers Keith Botterill and Bill Moxham, were by now the last of the 470 prisoners who had left Sandakan on the first march, the other four having died in the previous two weeks. They too realised that to remain meant they would soon share the fate of their 468 comrades of the first march. Short joined them in the escape plan. He persuaded Anderson to join them, although Anderson was very sick with dysentery and "did not think he could make it." The four men spoke to their officers who shook their hands and wished them luck.

These four men went into the unknown jungle with little to hope for. They knew little of the war situation or that it would soon end. All they could see was unopposed Allied air activity in their area and earlier at Sandakan. Their survival depended on food. They did not know which natives would help them and which would turn them over to the Japanese. However, Botterill and Moxham knew that hidden in the jungle off the trail and outside the wire there had been a rice dump in a hut to which they had carried rice when they had been in the other compound area. As the men crept through the wire and past the Japanese, they had the cover of a pitch-dark night and heavy rain. They held hands in order to keep together as they searched in the jungle for the rice hut. They found it! They broke into it. It still had rice in it!! They took as much rice as they could carry. They had little else than their tattered clothes and their packs. Importantly, they had between them instruments for survival—a billy necessary to cook rice, a magnifying glass to light a fire and a jack-knife to take thin shavings from dry bamboo to start a fire which would not smoke. The thread on which hung the survival of these determined men, in physical and mental extremity, was very thin indeed.

Loaded with the rice they walked all night along the trail, and as dawn broke they fell down exhausted in long grass. Realising they were still in danger, they soon pressed on, leaving the trail on the ridge and forcing their way through the jungle down to a river at the bottom of the mountain. There they hid for three days until the intensity of the search for them died down. They cooked rice.

Moxham had a map, so they decided they would try to get to Jesselton, for fear of dying where they were. Jesselton was some eighty kilometres away by a jungle trail over high rugged mountains, a journey which in their condition was impossible. With Jesselton as their target, they climbed back up the mountain to the trail. They crept past what Botterill knew had been a sentry post, but it was deserted. They went some distance and then exhausted, they left the trail again and found a small deserted hut. Short was just outside it, when an armed Japanese soldier appeared some distance away. He mistook the bearded near naked Short for a native. In Malay, he called out to Short for a match. Short, in Malay, replied he didn't have a match and threw himself into the jungle and rolled down the hill. Later, when he crept back, the Japanese was gone.

The four men hurriedly moved on to seek a better hiding place. On the way, they suddenly ran into a native, Barega, carrying a bunch of bananas. Short asked, "Friend?" Barega replied, "Yes, bad Japanese here—I will come back and find you a place to hide." He gave them the bananas. He might have come back with Japanese troops but they sensed they could trust Barega. They waited for him in a nearby empty hut. An unarmed Japanese private walked into the hut. In English he said pointedly that four prisoners had escaped. They replied that they all had malaria and a Japanese officer had gone to get medicines. The reference to an officer put the Japanese private off his guard. He grunted and hesitated. Then he asked for food and whether they had any watches. Just then there was the sound of an Allied aircraft. Their practice was to strafe any building. The Japanese fled into the jungle for cover and the prisoners ran in the opposite direction and into Barega.

Barega hid them in a jungle spot and with his parang quickly provided some cover for them. Several days later he moved them to a safer hideout, where he had constructed a shelter. Anderson was now so sick, he had to crawl to it. There they stayed for some weeks. Anderson died and they buried him in a shallow grave. Although Barega supplied them with food, the three survivors became weaker. Botterill and Moxham were desperately sick. Botterill had his twenty-first birthday there, but he was too sick to remember. All had beriberi. Short felt he was dying.

When these men were near to death, after six weeks in the jungle, a native told them that men had come out of the sky. These were the Australian paratroops, including a medical officer, who on 18 August, three days after the surrender, were dropped to reinforce the tiny Z Force in the Ranau area to search for and provide medical aid for any escaped POWs still in the jungle. Some time later, Barega brought a note signed by Flight-Lieutenant Ripley AGAS III (Z Force) which read: "The war is over. If you are well enough, make your way to us. If not, wait until we come and get you." The three men wanted to set off, but Barega said, "Wait, you are too weak." After three days, although aware that the men were getting worse each day, Barega came and said, "lekas" (come quickly). He explained that the Japanese in the area had not surrendered and had sent other natives to get them and hand them over to the Japanese. The hiding place was only a few miles from the prison perimeter. Barega's natives came to help the men and, with torches, lit the way for them to move on at night. On the way, they met native agents of AGAS III coming to them. It was 24 August. Later the Australian soldiers of Z Force appeared. The first one was nicknamed "Lofty" because he was some 6 feet 6 inches tall, but he seemed to the escaped prisoners to be a 7 foot giant. Short was four and a half stone, and the average weight of the men was less than five stone. The three men cried and so did some of the rescuers towering above their countrymen who looked all bones. Botterill and Moxham were carried on stretchers, but Short insisted on walking, helped along by his rescuers. Botterill was close to death and they thought he would die.

The three men and Sticpewich were too sick to be moved from Z Force base in the jungle for three weeks. Then on 18 September came the moment of their dreams. They were on their way home to the outside world! There was overwhelming joy and relief as they were carried on horseback over rough trails to a jungle air-strip. Moxham's plane crashed on take-off and he suffered head injuries. They took with them on the Auster aeroplanes to Labuan, Anderson's kit bag and a Japanese rifle given to a native to kill Sticpewich, but instead given to him. They also carried with them memories which would haunt them for the rest of their days—memories of the countless mates whom they had seen die and of their own three years of horror. As I discerned from Short recently, they would never be able either to forget or forgive. Clean beds and tender medical care in the Labuan army hospital seemed unreal. Providence had plucked them from the shadow of death.

The warning of Takahara proved correct. None of those who remained when Sticpewich escaped survived. What happened to them was known only to the Japanese. Their accounts varied. One account which I had before me at the war trials, was contained in a statement made by Fujita Masuo, a civilian interpreter attached to the Japanese prison compounds at Sandakan and Ranau.

> . . . a party of over 10 POW were carried up the hill to the cemetery and did not return.
>
> I think they were all killed. Included in the party were Captains Piconi and Oakshott, perhaps Captain Daniels, Captain Cook and others whose names I cannot remember . . . There were no POW left after this incident.

Other accounts confirm, as he surmised and as the Japanese accepted, that all were shot. The Japanese officer in charge of the Ranau POW compound admitted at his trial that thirty-three—the last of the POWs—were shot in three groups, being of five (the officers), seventeen, who were too sick to walk and were carried to the cemetery and there shot and buried in two graves, and eleven, marched along the trail and shot individually. The stethoscope of Captain Piconi was found alongside the graves.

The Japanese, in admitting the killing of the last of the prisoners, falsely gave the date for shooting them all as 1 August and hence just two weeks before the general surrender. All of the Japanese prisoners who were held in the same compound at Labuan were uniformly able to remember the same exact date. Fujita, the civilian, gave the lie to it. He said the date for the shooting of the last and smaller group which included the officers, was 17 August, which was two days after the general surrender. He gave the date of escape of Sticpewich correctly, ie 28 July, and he said the prisoners were shot ten days before the Allies dropped leaflets on Ranau. This is officially recorded as 27 August, which fits the 17 August date given by Fujita. There is also some confirmation from Short who said he heard machine gun fire from the compound direction and that this was after he was told the men came out from the sky, which in fact was just after the surrender. Some of the Japanese documents themselves suggest that 1 August as the date all were shot was a concoction. The Japanese issued death certificates for prisoners who died. Fujita said that when a prisoner was shot, the certificate showed he died of illness. Some gave dates with regard to the shooting of some of the officers, which were not consistent with other evidence, and others gave dates later than 1 August. The Japanese at the Ranau compound disregarded the leaflets and claimed later that they had believed they were propaganda. It is clear that they ignored the general surrender and killed off the last of the ten or so prisoners, including the officers, probably as Fujita suggests. When they ascertained that the prisoners who had escaped were still alive, they pursued them in order to kill them. It may be that the three massacres occurred on different days. As will appear, reports of AGAS III (Z Force) confirm that the last of the prisoners were shot after the general surrender.

It is clear that the reason for the Ranau killing of the last Sandakan POWs in captivity was to prevent them falling into Allied hands and hence to ensure that there would be none left to tell the world or some tribunal what had happened at Sandakan, on the death marches and at Ranau. The massacre of the last prisoners, including those carried to the place of execution, could offer no threat to the Japanese already defeated and no encumbrance to those at Ranau, who remained there to surrender. The suppression of news of Japanese atrocities, the ruthless actions against escapes and the starvation and elimination of prisoners, as will be seen, was in accordance with Japanese policy.

The Japanese must have thought, and with good reason, that none of the few who escaped in June and July 1945 would survive. In each case sick and emaciated prisoners had escaped into a hostile jungle in Japanese controlled areas, remote from help and apparently with little food and no source of supply. No doubt with the execution of the last prisoners, the Japanese expected there would be no one left to tell the dreadful story. It must have been with disbelief and horror that they learned, just as or after the war ended, that three prisoners who had escaped over six weeks earlier, were still alive just a few miles away. It must have been a matter of surprise and anguish for the Japanese when in late 1945 Sticpewich appeared with an investigation team and moved through the ranks of the imprisoned Japanese and identified those later charged with war crimes.

When imminent defeat was obvious self interest could have led some Japanese to show compassion for POWs. This however was not the motive behind Takahara's warning Sticpewich. His sense of humanity, derived perhaps from his Christian faith, had led him earlier in 1943–45 to show some guarded kindness to prisoners at Sandakan. From those times he had been on friendly terms with the likeable Sticpewich. The action of Takahara not only led to the escape of Sticpewich, but was the key to the rescue of the other three POWs, and hence to the only survivors from Ranau. His action therefore enabled the horrors of Sandakan, the death marches and Ranau to be told at the trials and revealed later to the world.

When the roles were reversed and Takahara became a prisoner, Sticpewich did not forget his kindness and the action which had saved his life. In late 1945, I was engaged in the military government of North Borneo as a captain attached to the Australian 9th Division. Near the end of December while at Brunei, I received a signal to report to Labuan as I had been transferred to HQ 9th Division to act as prosecutor in the war trials concerning Sandakan POWs to commence on 1 January 1946. I found on arrival that on my first assignment to act as prosecutor in the trial of Captain Hoshijima, the Sandakan commandant, Sticpewich was to be the only oral witness for the prosecution. The other survivors were too sick to be brought back from Australia. Days passed and there was no Sticpewich. Then two days before the trial, he arrived, but still his first priority was to search the Japanese compound at Labuan for his "mate", and there he found Takahara to whom he took presents and food. Rear Admiral Earl Mountbatten, Supreme Commander South East Asia

Command, was in Labuan at the time. He heard the story. Takahara was on the next plane home.

I will later return to the trials and the part played by Sticpewich, but move ahead to relate the tragic end to this story. Before he left Borneo, he went back along the death march trail to aid the team who searched for and located the bodies of his fallen comrades. When he returned to Melbourne, he remained in the army and was promoted to Major, no doubt for his magnificent efforts in Borneo. He who had survived the hazards of Sandakan, a death march, Ranau and a jungle escape, did not escape the hazards of the Melbourne streets. He was knocked down by a car and killed a few years after the war ended.

2

BORNEO AND THE OCCUPATION

Borneo is one of the largest islands in the world and is one of its great jungle wildernesses. It has long been a land of mystery and known to many only as the home of the "wild men", the orang-utan and the white rajahs. Most Australians know in a very general way that the Australian 7th and 9th Divisions were engaged in successful wartime operations there and that many 8th Division POWs never returned from its jungles.

Beyond this, little of Borneo or its history is widely known. Accordingly, in this chapter I will deal with its recent past, up to and including the Japanese occupation.

The first European involvement in Borneo was in the late seventeenth century when the Dutch made agreements with the sultans in the south of the island to gain exclusive trading rights for their colony in nearby Java. These sultans were beginning to enjoy greater influence as the formerly powerful Sultanate of Brunei, which had long held dominion over the whole of Borneo and of the Sulu Archipelago, appeared to be in decline.

The British had not shown any interest in colonising Borneo, until in the nineteenth century the increase in piracy, slavery and the instability caused by frequent revolts against the Sultanate of Brunei were considered as threats to Britain's trade routes to China and to the free trade of her possessions at Penang and Singapore. As a consequence, Britain became involved in the northern part of the island and ultimately became the governing force in Borneo.

In 1841 the Sultan of Brunei ceded Sarawak to an English adventurer, Rupert Brooke, and made him a rajah in return for Brooke's assistance in suppressing a rebellion. Five years later, in response to a plot to kill Brooke, a squadron of the British Navy was sent to Brunei and having been fired upon, bombed the town and occupied it. Sarawak was then made unconditionally independent of the Sultanate and in the same year Labuan, the small island in Brunei Bay, was ceded to Britain and became a crown colony.

The north-east of Borneo, later to be called British North Borneo (Sabah), was the subject of a complicated series of agreements and leases granted by the Sultan of Brunei followed by assignments in favour of a succession of private individuals and companies. After a number of failures, title passed to a chartered company—the North Borneo Company. The charter was granted by the British Government on condition that it had the power to control its foreign relations, direct some of its operations and make some of its appointments. Its ports were to be open to the British Navy, slavery was to be abolished, local customs observed and the rule of law was to prevail.

By treaties in 1888, British Borneo, Brunei and Sarawak became British protectorates. In 1891 Britain and Holland agreed to establish a common boundary between their two areas, Dutch-Borneo having by then become a Dutch colony.

By the late nineteenth century fundamental changes had occurred in Borneo under British influence. There was freedom and equality before the law, there was freedom to deal and trade and there was an equality of treatment of the different racial groups.

On 24 September 1941 a constitution was introduced in Sarawak which put an end to the absolute rule of the Rajah. His power passed to the Council Negri which consisted of nominated leaders of the various groups in the society. This constitution required the consent of the Council to any new law. It was an important step towards democratic self-government. On this day the centenary of Sarawak was also celebrated, and amid the gaiety and jubilation in the streets of Kuching there was neither thought nor realisation that on the coming Christmas Day the town would fall to the Japanese, and that the peoples of Borneo who had lived in peace with each other for over fifty years and who had posed no threat to any other country, would suffer oppressions, tortures and massacres far worse than any in their long history.

* * * * *

On 16 December 1941 the Japanese landed on the north coast of Borneo and before long had occupied the whole of the island with little or no opposition. Borneo was a Japanese priority for occupation. It could be taken without delay and its location was strategically important to the Japanese military forces because of its proximity to Singapore, the Philippines and the Dutch East Indies, all then still unconquered. The Japanese war machine, bent on conquest in Asia and the Pacific, was hungry for oil and Borneo had massive and readily accessible reserves. The initial unopposed landing took place at Miri in Sarawak, one of the central oilfields in northern Borneo. In an instant, the Miri oilfields, those at nearby Seria in Brunei and the refinery at Lutong in Sarawak which served both, were in Japanese hands.

Without delay, the Japanese rounded up and interned all the Europeans who had not escaped. A few, such as medical staff, were released to carry on essential services. Even non-Europeans soon fell under the ruthless discipline of the Japanese army. The regime was particularly cruel to the Chinese, most of whom were descendants of Chinese families which had settled in Borneo centuries before. The Japanese were ruthless and demanded subservience from all the inhabitants of Borneo, some of whom they set against the others. It has been revealed in later years that whatever plans Japan professed to have had for the independence of some occupied territories brought within the Co-Prosperity Sphere, its intention all along, in respect of each of the three northern states of Borneo and Malaya, had been to make them part of Japanese territory under Japanese rule with a Japanese Governor-General stationed at Singapore. These territories rich in resources were to have made Japan a prosperous country. The talk of co-existence, co-prosperity, equality and the prospect of independence was a lie from the beginning.

To exploit the resources of Borneo and to build essential military installations the Japanese resorted to using slave labour, often imported from other occupied countries. Javanese labourers were forced to construct wharves to serve the oil pipeline from the oilfields to Brunei Bay and many of them died. As the locals of nearby Brunei put it to me in late 1945, there was a life lost for every pile driven during the construction—and there were hundreds of piles. The Javanese were used elsewhere in the region as well and the fortunate survivors were eventually repatriated after the war ended. Prisoners of war were transported from Singapore to build the military air-strip at Sarawak and were treated little differently from the war slaves of twenty centuries ago who were forced on by floggings and who were regarded as expendable by their masters.

Originally, European civilians were interned near their place of arrest, but later most British and Dutch were moved to Kuching, the capital of Sarawak. The men, the Roman Catholic priests and the women and children were held separately in three camps. Over one hundred Dutch and English Catholic nuns were imprisoned with the other women and children. Some prisoners of war, British, Australian and Dutch were also held in Kuching, each in separate compounds.

The interned civilians and prisoners of war were ill-treated, underfed and humiliated. The official attitude was that Europeans were to be despised as inferior to Asians. Those in charge of civilian men and women, and prisoners of war, implemented this policy by exercising their absolute discretions to insult, beat and torture their captives, often accompanied by outbursts of uncontrolled anger. They responded cruelly to those who breached regulations or to those whose behaviour failed to reflect the required degree of humility in the presence of their masters. Those who complained about ill-treatment were often further punished for making a false accusation. It was taken as axiomatic that Japanese were humane and incapable of any wrong. Sometimes a complaint led to torture until there was an admission that the complaint was false or until some humiliating compromise was reached. The wise and the experienced bore adversity without complaint.

All the internees were put to work on either the most menial tasks or the most sustained heavy work without regard to their sex, their past way of life, their strength or their abilities. The living conditions were mostly appalling, often insanitary or otherwise unhealthy. Many died from a combination of overwork, exposure to disease, lack of proper medical facilities, lack of proper or sufficient food and ill-treatment. Whatever may have been the difficulties of food supply in other areas and at other times, no such difficulty existed in Kuching which could warrant the starvation rations imposed on the internees.

In order to impress the local people that Europeans were inferior and servile, POWs and interned Europeans were often to be seen in public places in their straitened circumstances. This same policy was evident when in August 1942 POWs were transported from Singapore to Korea and for two days were paraded through the streets of Seoul in a starved, emaciated condition and in tattered clothes to contrast sharply with the robust and well turned-out Japanese soldiers who marched beside them as their guards.

The Japanese used many other devices designed to bring to an end all respect for or loyalty to Europeans. The use of English (and I assume likewise Dutch in the Dutch area) was prohibited. Steps were taken to make Japanese the second language to Malay. Wirelesses were banned and severe penalties imposed for any breach. The people were given the Japanese version of their continuing victories. The use of European and local currencies was banned. Those who kept or used them were severely punished. Despite this these currencies were secretly stored and later used when Japanese currency became unacceptable.

In Brunei there were competitions for the writing of plays

and poems praising the new order with the prize a trip to see "beautiful Japan and its beautiful ways". One winning play, written by the Malay who organised the competition, had a plot in which a young Malay joined the Japanese army and in the end won the heart of a beautiful Malay girl. Unfortunately, by the time the prize came to be collected, available air or sea transport to Japan was becoming a matter of some difficulty and so the prize winner had to settle for a trip to Kuching. I found a further example of Japanese propaganda in Brunei in late 1945 when I was shown Japanese matchboxes with the covers depicting an overweight, besotted and cowering Churchill being kicked in the buttocks by a Japanese soldier.

Some of the young Malays and Chinese who were personally ambitious, took positions of authority in the new order. Some did so because of nationalistic feelings encouraged by Japanese propaganda. Others, who were duped in the earlier stages, were later enlightened by what they saw. However, all those who took office, even imported Japanese civilians, were under the immediate direction and control of the Japanese military forces. In the law and order and the justice fields, it was the kempei-tai who were in firm control and who ruthlessly applied their arbitrary, cruel and intimidatory practices. These military police introduced Malay and Chinese recruits to their methods and promotions were for efficiency and enthusiasm in applying them. Some of them eagerly accepted the new power and authority and were attracted by the status they achieved in their office under the kempei-tai. They willingly tortured and beat their fellows with sticks to make them inform on others or to confess. The justice meted out by the Japanese, in which at times their recruits participated, involved arbitrary punishment including death, sometimes for no more than expression of anti-Japanese sentiments on private occasions. Intimidation and ruthless example were the instruments used to procure an obedience to orders and to the Japanese will in those places where it could be exerted.

I did not know in 1945 how the informer system worked

but learned this in later years. The kempei-tai set up a dual system.[1] In each village there was a Malay, native or Chinese informer. The system was set up by the Japanese calling on the headman for a list of all villagers. Many men or women selected at random were separately asked whether he or she would work for the Japanese. The nature of the work was not revealed. The informer was selected from those who were willing to work for the Japanese. The duty of the one selected was to report what was happening in the village, including any anti-Japanese or pro-British actions, attitudes or statements. Refusal of duty after selection, or the revealing of one's identity as an informer meant arrest and torture or death. The duty was only to inform directly to the kempei-tai. This was done when, every few days, a member of the kempei-tai dressed in Malay clothes visited many houses in the village, including that of the informer. It was, of course, obvious that the visitor was Japanese, but the absence of uniform allayed fears and by visiting many houses villagers did not know who was the informer or whether there was one. A similar system applied in the towns and in the work places. Each of the many Japanese companies employing local people had an informer similarly selected. His or her duty of informing extended to informing on other informers who talked. Informers who proved to be a risk, talked or failed in their duty, disappeared.

Some, the Japanese failed to tame or intimidate. These were the Dyaks, particularly the Ibans and the Muruts, who were less accessible in a country where distances were measured by the number of days' walk—and sometimes the distance was a week or two. The burning of long-houses and the killings which were standard reprisals for failure to obey Japanese commands, led reformed headhunters to headhunt again, but now for heads of Japanese. Brutality extended to the native villages irrespective of the ethnic groups living there. Where anti-Japanese activity was suspected, villagers including children and women with babies were assembled and shot. Accordingly many became willing recruits of Z Force, which had infiltrated the interior. The Dyaks claimed many

Japanese lives with their silent blowpipes and the rifles supplied to them. Some thousands, however, fled to the Sulus in the nearby Philippines to escape the brutality and many there joined the US guerillas.

The British had understood these people and had integrated them into the community while leaving them free. With headhunting banned and almost unpractised, justice was a co-operative affair, much of it being directly administered by head men with British guidance. These people became loyal friends. The Dyaks, as I found them, were the lovely people of Borneo, who lived the free and simple life in their long-houses alongside the swift streams in the beautiful jungle.

Those prisoners of war or civilian internees who escaped from confinement camps attracted the particular anger of the Japanese. This, as we shall see, resulted in a confrontation at Sandakan prisoner of war camp when there was an attempt to compel each prisoner to sign a document asking that he be shot if he attempted to escape. The consequence of a failed escape attempt was being shot out of hand, but the Japanese were inconsistent and this did not always happen. In addition to the desire to intimidate, the Japanese appear to have strongly resented the fact that prisoners should wish to escape from them. The same resentment seems to have arisen when persons fled from capture in the first instance or resisted the Japanese arrival.

Shortly before the Japanese landing in Borneo, a group of civilians fled from Miri into the interior. Some European husbands remained behind and were eventually interned, and some survived. The party which escaped included their wives and children, as well as European men and missionaries. After a long journey through the interior, they reached the Dutch area of Borneo. Long after the occupation had commenced the Japanese learned of the escape. A Japanese force was despatched to the area and after engaging in a battle, shot the surviving men. The women and children were taken prisoner. Two months later the women were tortured and all were then put to death. Included in those killed were missionaries, their wives and children, and even a baby.[2]

Japanese reprisals following any uprising or actions against their occupying forces were fearful. Moreover the reprisals were not only against those responsible, but also against suspects not involved, and often against others simply by way of example or out of frustration or revenge. The Japanese reaction to a revolt in Jesselton (now Kota Kinabalu), in British North Borneo (now Sabah) provides the most extreme instance in Borneo of matters earlier referred to. The revolt, which was mainly by Chinese, resulted in the death of about forty Japanese. This, of course, would be a serious matter for any occupying force, but the Japanese response was violent and sustained in the extreme, extending in many directions against many innocent people. It continued into the following year and to many areas way outside Jesselton. First, a number of villages were bombed and their people machine-gunned. In Jesselton the kempei-tai rounded up a large number of people and tortured them to gain information and confessions. There were summary mass executions of a large number of Chinese, many on mere suspicion and without trial. The searches, tortures and mass killings continued in villages on the mainland and extended to some small adjoining islands thought to be hiding suspects or guerillas. On the islands of Mantanani and Dinawan, nearly all the inhabitants, mainly Suluks, were wiped out. All Mantanani women and children were tied together and machine-gunned. Later some women and babes-in-arms who had escaped to the mainland, were seized by the kempei-tai and six weeks later were executed. Lieutenant Shimizu, who was responsible for the Mantanani massacres, was tried in Singapore in 1946 and sentenced to death.

It is impossible to say how many were executed in response to the Jesselton revolt. In late 1945 I saw documents which included one local estimate of about 1000 people. E. F. L. Russell's later research indicates that 189 Chinese died at the mass execution at Jesselton, several hundred died while imprisoned there from torture, disease or starvation and 310 perished in the Mantanani massacres. In addition, there were those who were killed at Dinawan and in the mainland villages.

The attitudes and activities of the Japanese in Borneo do not sit comfortably with what Premier Tojo said in the course of a speech he made about a month after Borneo had been occupied. He said in general terms which were applicable to Borneo:

> Japan is now vigorously proceeding with the great task of establishing the sphere of common prosperity in Greater East Asia . . . The basic policy of establishing the Greater East Asian Co-Prosperities Sphere . . . [is] to enable each country and people in Greater East Asia to have its proper place and demonstrate its real character, thereby securing an order of co-existence and co-prosperity based on ethical principles with Japan serving as the nucleus . . . It is truly an unprecedently grand undertaking that our Empire should establish everlasting peace in Greater East Asia with a new conception which will mark a new epoch in the annals of mankind and proceed to construct a new world order . . .

Looking back and leaving aside the prisoners of war and European civilians, I have often wondered what the many thousands of the formerly free indigenous peoples of Borneo who were coerced, brutalised and killed, would have thought of Tojo's remarks and the high sounding words of those who proclaimed the ideals of the Co-Prosperity Sphere. The words and the promises of Tojo to small nations and to their peoples were as empty as those of Hitler.

3

THE AUTHOR LOOKS BACK —1945 DIARY

Upon the Japanese general surrender in August 1945, the whole of Borneo came under the military government of the Australian army. Proclamations to this effect had been issued as the Australian forces landed and gained control of various regions. General Baba who was GOC of the *37th Imperial Japanese Army*, the occupying Japanese force, declined at first to surrender and had to be persuaded by his superiors in Japan to do so. There was a tense period during which the Japanese in many areas failed to recognise the surrender. It was not until 10 September that General Baba eventually surrendered to General Wootten, Commander of the 9th Division.

Formerly an artillery officer, I arrived in Borneo soon after the general surrender. I was then attached to the 9th Division and in this capacity performed various administrative and legal functions in the military government principally in Brunei, Sarawak and Labuan. From this position of advantage, I learned a great deal about Japanese conduct during the occupation and the conduct of the people of Borneo under the Japanese. I met many Malays, Chinese and Dyaks and I talked to them about events during the occupation. At the official level I actively investigated crimes and interviewed those from whom I could gather evidence. I examined voluminous files of investigations and statements taken by others. In 1945 I was responsible for decisions to prosecute and I personally prosecuted crimes committed by local people during the occupation. In early 1946, I acted as prosecutor of Japanese war crimes at Labuan.

In all of those prosecutions I was able to probe the details of the events and to observe the dispositions and motives of the people involved. Every day I meticulously recorded at some length, what I had learned and my reactions to those revelations in a diary. I kept duplicates of the transcripts of some trials. It is this diary speaking from the past which has enabled me to write with some accuracy about the period, to draw certain conclusions and to speculate about Japanese attitudes and policies during the occupation.

* * * * *

In late 1945, Lim Soo Kiat stood before a military court in Miri, Sarawak. By force of a proclamation, the court applied the laws of Sarawak and exercised the powers of its courts. The charge was of treason under the Sarawak penal code.

Lim Soo Kiat was born in Singapore of a Chinese father and a Japanese mother. In 1933, two years after Japan invaded Manchuria, he went first to Kuching and then to Miri where he settled and gained employment at the oil company as a tally clerk on the wharves. He was then already aged forty-seven. Later, as operations in the new fields at Seria expanded, he was employed in the equipment stores where he gained an intimate knowledge of the machinery used in the oilfields and in the refinery. He had been educated in Tokyo, spoke fluent Japanese and also had a Japanese name, Ogawa Saburo. None of this was known, even to those who worked alongside him over these nine years. He appeared, at least to me, to be Chinese.

At about the time of the attack on Pearl Harbor, when it seemed inevitable that these undefended oilfields would be attacked and seized by the Japanese, key machinery used in the refinery, pumps used on the oilfields and vital small parts of other large machinery were collected and crated and shipped to Singapore, where they were hidden. A ten ton truck and its Malay driver were also taken on the ship to make the deliveries in Singapore. Details of the parts and their location for reinstallation were carefully documented. This was done by four employees expert in the equipment field. One was Lim Soo Kiat. The operation was secret and the documents and all copies were sent to Singapore, or at least that is what the authorities thought. Although not proved at the trial, it is highly likely that Lim Soo Kiat had a copy or details of at least a part of them. Unwisely, the driver of the truck who knew where the equipment was hidden in Singapore returned to Miri.

By 9 o'clock on the morning of the Japanese arrival in Miri, Lim Soo Kiat was seen in consultation with Japanese officers. Later he appeared in the uniform of a Japanese officer complete with samurai sword and took on his Japanese name. Ten days later, all the drivers were lined up and Lim Soo Kiat pointed out the driver who had gone to Singapore with the equipment. Under threat of decapitation, the driver disclosed the location of the equipment. The interrogator was Lim Soo Kiat. When Singapore fell, the driver was flown there and pointed out the secret location of the equipment and within a few months the crates were back in Miri. The evidence was that Lim Soo Kiat helped the Japanese to reconstruct the machinery.

It was no function of the trial, or myself as the prosecutor, to enquire into what destruction there had been of the oil installations and refinery before the Japanese arrived or how effective any destruction was, but there is little doubt from contemporary records that before the Japanese arrived, orders were given to fire some of the wells and to blow up some of the buildings and installations. In other areas, where Dutch Shell operated, sensitive parts were removed, so that they could be more conveniently destroyed. It is clear that in North Borneo parts removed were not destroyed and that they later fell into Japanese hands. To have initially regarded Singapore as a safe storage place is understandable, but it is more difficult to understand why, when the fall of Singapore was imminent, the parts were not destroyed. It is more surprising because the European oil staff at Miri were ordered to Singapore so that the Japanese couldn't use their expertise. Nonetheless, the parts brought back from Singapore because of the action of Lim Soo Kiat could scarcely have been reinstalled had the installations been completely destroyed.

Although Lim Soo Kiat had been guilty of cruelty and like offences during the occupation, the trial was confined to the major matter of treason. In court he was a cringing, almost pathetic old man whose only concern seemed to be what the people of Miri, many of whom had been victims of his domineering cruelty, would do to him if he fell into their hands. He had been in custody since Miri fell to the Australian army. This provided him with protection from those who would probably have cheerfully killed him. He admitted helping the Japanese and it became obvious that the last thing he wanted was to be acquitted and freed. The evidence was called, the charge proved and he was sentenced to life imprisonment in accordance with the laws of Sarawak. He seemed unconcerned, but almost demanded that he have a secure vehicle to transport him from the court to the gaol. The request for transport was refused. As the Malay police also showed concern, their number was increased and they were ordered to fix bayonets and march the prisoner through Miri to the gaol. They arrived without incident. In retrospect, it is not without interest to reflect upon the reason why the Japanese saw fit to plant a spy in the Borneo oilfields as early as 1933.

In the months following the end of the war, Miri was a troubled place. The purpose of my visit there in November 1945 from my post at Brunei, was to help set the court system in motion by the trial of a few selected cases. Law and order was in danger of collapsing. Densely populated Miri had been the industrial centre of Sarawak, with an economy based on the oil industry. When the war ended, the oil installations and the town were in ruins. Many were left homeless and destitute and there was massive unemployment and a serious shortage of food. Moreover, resentment ran high against the Japanese and any local inhabitant who had helped them in their cruelties or was even suspected of doing so. Some of the latter were in custody and some were at large.

This resentment was fuelled to flashpoint by the mass funerals of twenty-eight hostages who had been shot by the Japanese. When the Australians entered Miri, the Japanese retired some nine miles into the jungle, taking with them hostages of different races. Then, after the general surrender, they retreated further into the jungle and shot them. When the Japanese from Miri surrendered, they confessed to Captain Neil Steen and others that the hostages had been shot. On Steen's orders, they identified the place of the mass burial and were then compelled to dig up the decomposed bodies and transport them to Miri. There was a day of public mourning for the re-burial services. Speeches were made by an Australian padre, a Moslem haji, an Indian and a Chinese. When I arrived a few days after the service Miri was a tense, angry place.

We had information that there had been some rioting in Malaya because there had been delays in dealing with those who, under the Japanese, had tortured or exploited their fellows. In consequence, a decision was taken by the senior legal officer at Labuan to extend my operations beyond the State of Brunei into nearby towns in Sarawak, where I would bring to trial in each a selection of a few serious cases. The local law was applied to the cases tried by an army officer exercising power under martial law. I was the prosecutor. The former procedures of Brunei and Sarawak were applied and three leading citizens (of different races) sat as assessors and expressed their opinions on the case, although responsibility for the decision rested with the presiding officer.

Another case tried in Miri in this way was of charges against a Chinese who had been recruited by the kempei-tai. The accused man applied their torture methods to extract confessions which he was often left to do on his own. The evidence, as an example of his conduct, was that he repeatedly beat one suspect with a thick stick until he collapsed unconscious, revived him with water and then repeated the process, and that he did this over some days. He denied the man food, who as a consequence became a physical wreck and contracted beriberi. The accused man did not deny what was alleged about his conduct, but sought to justify his actions by saying it was the Japanese method of gaining confessions and was no different from the American "third degree" methods. He then admitted he had beaten over twenty people for the Japanese and claimed in mitigation that he had been good to many "friends" by using his influence so they were saved from the beatings of the kempei-tai. To show their appreciation, they had made him "gifts" of money and food. He was found guilty and sentenced to a term of imprisonment.

The accused in this case also seemed to welcome the conviction, rather than being set free and left to the attention of the Miri mobs. He also sought motor transport to the gaol, but was marched there under armed guard. Troubled Miri could see that law was being enforced by the military government, participated in by their leaders.

* * * * *

I went to Brunei seven weeks after the Japanese general surrender. As well as the garrison force, some officers of the military administration had been there since the surrender. I was told by the colonel in charge that I would be the legal adviser to the State of Brunei. That seemed simple enough, for there was not then and had not been earlier any lawyer there.

Brunei had been severely bombed, and when I arrived the central area of the town, including warehouses, public buildings, the legislative assembly, a church, schools, shops and clubs, was a mass of rubble. Along the waterfront there were still about thirty Japanese vessels which had been sunk or destroyed. Otherwise, the dwellings, including the vast kampongs built out over the river, were largely intact.

I took up quarters in a house just beyond the bombed area. There was one large bomb crater in the garden. The house was suitable, as it was opposite the building set up as a temporary court and not far from the temporary police offices. The room I took was unoccupied. There was Japanese stationery still strewn over the floor and there was a pin-up of a geisha girl still on the wall. As I wrote in my diary,

I wondered where my Japanese predecessor in title then was.

I had a Chinese boy in spotless white to look after me. We had an excellent Chinese cook and another to wait for us. He even served from the correct side. In the cool of the evening on the day of my arrival, we sat on the verandah and watched the assortment of people passing by. The Chinese women looked neat and gay, the Malays were in highly coloured clothing and their children eternally chattered in high-pitched voices. There were several Sikhs wearing orange turbans. There were Dyaks clad in only red loin cloths. It looked as though peace had been restored to Brunei, despite the devastation—but, as I soon found, there was much for me to do.

The next day I surveyed the legal work before me. There were extensive files covering investigations into criminal matters made by a US team and later by some Australian Army personnel. They told a dreadful and depressing tale. On my later assessment, there were forty or more serious cases where there was sufficient evidence to take some action. There were many more which needed further investigation or the collection of evidence in satisfactory form. Some concerning Japanese crimes would have to be dealt with at 9th Division Headquarters in Labuan. As to matters to be dealt with in Brunei, questions would arise, I could see, as to what law was to be applied to crimes committed just before, during and after the Japanese occupation. The law would have to be the law applying in Brunei at the relevant time—but what was the law? There was available a set of statutes and proclamations of a state of emergency issued in the name of the Sultan as nominal head of Brunei when war was imminent, and there were the proclamations of martial law by the 9th Division. How were the charges to be framed? How were cases to be dealt with in the absence of persons with legal training, other than myself, who would have to be the investigator and the prosecutor? On that first day, the head of one who had been only a fledgling barrister at the New South Wales Bar before the war and who had given up law for gunnery in the artillery, spun a little. Stan Monk looked in on me.

"You need a break, old man. Come and look at Brunei."

Captain Stan Monk was an English officer who had been at Brunei as a Civil Affairs officer from the day the Australians entered Brunei and had carried the main burden of the military administration there, including acting as a magistrate, although he had no legal training. He was to be an endless source of information to me in the months ahead. He took me on a tour of Brunei town and its outskirts and showed and told me some of the things that had been done to get the place working again. There were some twenty licensed shops, but black-marketing, although under attack, was a problem because there were severe food shortages and rationing. Administrative services were operating, with Malay and Chinese staff. A Malay police force had been recruited, but this was posing problems because they were either totally inexperienced or had been police under the Japanese. Later some were dismissed on my recommendation when their past activities were revealed. Two rubber plantations had been put back into operation, giving employment to local people, including in particular 150 Javanese. There were still 800 unemployed, displaced Javanese in rags and without any source of sustenance. The army fed them and issued each with six yards of cloth.

Monk took me out to see the derelict former palace of the Sultan. This is the account I recorded in my diary:

> We went along the road to visit the Sultan's palace. It is about 1½ miles out and on a beautiful field overlooking the whole expanse of the river and the river kampongs. Although not bombed, it has many bullet marks and is virtually falling to pieces. It is a gaudy cheap place on the Indian style with tall stone pillars and a stone fence round the entrance leading to the banquet hall. Long grass has overrun the paths and there is a musty smell and hollow sound on entering. All furniture is gone, except the throne stripped of its tapestry. Inside there is only the banquet hall and the harem's rooms on the ground

> floor. Above the women's rooms is a kind of catwalk from which the rooms could be looked into, no doubt so the Sultan could check up on his womenfolk. At the back are the grimy servants quarters much like a josshouse. As we went to enter, a swarm of bats flew around, so we viewed it from without. Visiting the old palace reminded me of "Rebecca" and the return to the old mansion overgrown with weeds—where thoughts of people and things that have been past came to mind.
>
> No doubt, here was a place of much superficial pleasure and many intrigues, for the sultans of Brunei have a reputation of intrigue, and it is alleged that several wives have died by the gentle art of poisoning. I picked up a little bottle—could either have been perfume or poison for some eastern lady.

I later visited the temporary palace of the Sultan on a formal occasion in December. I described in my diary the room in which we were received and the events which followed:

> It was a long room closed off from the rest of the house by a circular wooden wall with holes in the form of stars carved at the top. Some of the art treasures were really beautiful—beautiful gold carved swords and all sorts of eastern ornaments—a large brilliant bronze statue of something of a cross between a tiger and a Chinese devil, but the arrangement and the taste was cheap. Between all these things you would find a one shilling Australian canteen mirror, a cutting of a modern car from a U.S. magazine pasted on the wall and green or red frosted balls hung down in gaudy fashion inside the stars cut in the wall.
>
> We all sat down to little tables interspersed with the upper class Malay gentlemen . . . Running around amongst the people was the Sultan's 17-year-old daughter, a big loose type of girl with a skirt about two inches above the knees and colour on her lips, a thing [then] unknown amongst the Malays, except the Malay prostitutes.
>
> After a while, Royalty appeared in the shape of 5 feet nothing and in English morning dress complete with tails—in

meeting the guests a bow extending from the hips was made and a hand, which was more like a day-old mullet was extended—it did not grip or move. His hair was carefully oiled and the top of his skull shaved for about 4 inches in diameter, for the purpose of ventilation, as we were told later. He had a long moustache, waxed and curled in almost a complete circle and he laughed like a schoolgirl. The Sultan is 32 . . . We ate a little food, but it was terrible—I picked up one slice of a slippery kind of sweet, had a bite and it was awful. It looked and tasted like jelly made from the Brunei River. I would like to have silently slipped it into the vase alongside me, but the Haji opposite was watching me—I was a fool and a martyr and ate the rest of it. Meanwhile the band was playing—they played one Malay tune and then got on to the "Isle of Capri" and "Alexander's Ragtime Band" (at about half the correct tempo).

After staying about an hour, we left the presence of His Royal Highness and returned to a decent meal.

* * * * *

In the three months to the end of 1945, in Brunei and parts of Sarawak such as Miri, Marudi, Limbang and Lawas, my review of the many investigations earlier made by others, my own investigations and my contacts with people in the course of trials and otherwise, taken together, provided me with a mirror which enabled me to look back, I believe with some clarity, to the conduct and attitudes of the Japanese and of the local people during the Japanese occupation. Then in the first two months of 1946, when in Labuan I acted as prosecutor at the Japanese war trials, I had a similar insight into the Japanese conduct in relation to the prisoners of war.

What appeared in the Miri case concerning the recruitment by the Japanese of local people who were cruel to and exploited their countrymen, was repeated again and again in Brunei and other places, usually with some sinister variation. As the Japanese encouraged them, they became arrogant and insolent. The attitude of many who were recruited by the Japanese police was voiced by one who declared that the British would never return and that he learned the superior way of the Japanese and that he would be like them. Another at Limbang, whom the Japanese often left alone to do their work, used starvation and other cruel devices to obtain information or confessions. He boasted that he had complete power under the Japanese, that he could kill if he liked and that he had now learned new things and had absorbed the Japanese spirit. He was intelligent, received promotion, studied Japanese and went to a special police training course in Kuching. Because of his obvious eagerness and intelligence, he was originally recruited to our police force, but was later dismissed and charged. At first he denied everything, but when he saw the evidence against him, he protested, falsely, that the Japanese had forced him to act as he did. Another in the Limbang police force was also dismissed. He had beaten and ill-treated a Chinese suspected of participation in the Jesselton revolt. He eventually confessed, but explained that the Japanese had said to him, "You can beat him if you like," and that he had hit the man because he wouldn't confess.

At times, the Japanese in Borneo, as they did in other occupied countries, decapitated captured airmen. A Malay sent out from Brunei to capture and bring in a wounded US airman shot and killed him, and on his return, boasted of what he had done.

From time to time investigations provided evidence about war crimes, which at this time were outside my province. One was concerning a chief Japanese police officer and the recapture of a European who had escaped from internment. He was hidden in a village and his presence was betrayed by a native who told the Japanese of the village in which he was concealed. Another Malay ran ahead and warned the European to flee. However, he was too sick with malaria to walk and was recaptured by the Japanese. Natives had to carry him. The Japanese police officer had the man's hands tied above his head and he was then suspended by a rope to the ceiling. He wasn't given any food or water except a little smuggled to him. He was dead in three days. The police officer was told by the natives that he was a Christian and should be given a Christian burial. This was refused. A Dyak stole the body and buried it in a spot which he marked and later told US Intelligence about it. I passed on this material to the 9th Division section which was investigating Japanese war crimes. I suggested he be put on the list of war criminals being investigated.

One of the most common offences that came to my attention was informing on Chinese and Malays because they were suspected of being British spies or because they were known or believed to have British sympathies or to have uttered pro-British statements. To be so accused often resulted in imprisonment, torture, beatings, and sometimes death. Some, who did favours for the Japanese, including informing, were given lucrative concessions, and thereby acquired considerable wealth, freedom and power under the Japanese.

There were some cases where local persons in authority engaged in anti-British and pro-Japanese propaganda. These cases raised some legal difficulties and, anyhow, were, on our approach, low in priority compared with cases where injury or death was caused to others. However, the case of a very senior Malay official, pre-war and head of the education system in Brunei, was brought to trial. He became the head Malay for propaganda in Brunei under the Japanese. He was acquitted, I think reasonably. His anti-British activities were extreme for one who had been so senior an official, had seen service in the army in Malaya and had been decorated. He had made, for example, many public speeches in extreme language against the British. He was tried in Brunei before a senior officer sent from Labuan—I acted as the prosecutor. He was not guilty of any cruelty to any of his fellow countrymen and he claimed, probably correctly, that he was subject to the close supervision and direction of Japanese military officers. When the Japanese were about to enter Brunei, British officials, including the Resident, left Borneo and the Malay officials in the British administration were left to carry on. He made a speech to the head officials telling them to carry on as best they could until the British returned. I thought then, and still do, that the case, both in law and in fact, involved difficulties. The three local assessors considered he should be acquitted and the presiding officer acquitted him.

*　　*　　*　　*　　*

In mid-October 1945, I undertook an expedition lasting about a week into the Dyak country in Sarawak, in order to persuade them to resume their former trading relations with Brunei, particularly the supply of hill rice which had been brought to an end by the Japanese occupation. I was accompanied by a British army medical officer and an Indian medical sergeant who were to treat the Dyaks suffering from malaria and dysentery in the area.

These Dyaks (the land Dyaks) were the former headhunters of Borneo and inhabited the interior. In Sarawak they lived in the regions of the mighty Rajang and Baram rivers which ran from the Dutch border to the China sea, and the rivers such as the Limbang, which flowed into Brunei bay. The Dyaks who lived near the upper Limbang river or its tributaries pre-war, were an important source of rice (hill padi) for Brunei, and now that hostilities had ended, Brunei was in desperate need of their produce.

On the way up the Limbang river, we called at the town of Limbang presided over by a Malay district officer. I discovered that he was commandeering the limited supplies of rice brought down the river by the Dyaks and was paying only half the fixed price. He was using some for his family and friends and despatching the rest to the black-market which was selling it at many times the fixed price. The practice was stopped, the district officer later suspended and after an enquiry, dismissed.

We proceeded by boat up the river from Limbang for about a day, and the next day, with Dyak guides, set out through the jungle. This was one of the areas into which the Japanese, who refused to surrender, had retreated. My diary records our trek through the jungle and arrival at the long-house where we stayed for the first night.

> It wasn't long before we were in the mud and slush—most of the narrow native track being under water. It was beautifully shady because the jungle growth kept out the sun—everything was moist and dripping and everywhere grew beautiful ferns and staghorns and long monkey ropes. We crossed several streams by means of narrow log bridges—this was often difficult as the logs were sometimes a foot or more under the muddy water. From time to time we came to a stop while the leading boy cut the jungle growth away. We came to a swamp and got up to the thighs in water—could not get any further so took another route which brought us out on a slope. A boy climbed a tree and called out—a voice in the distance replied. Some time later two perahu arrived—one remaining hidden while the first came forward. The Dyaks took this precaution and were armed with rifles, as they thought we were Japs. Our baggage was taken by perahu and we were shown a tortuous way across the swamp. And so we came to the kampong called Mankassin—a long-house with a population of about 90, nestling in a pretty spot alongside the narrow swiftly flowing Lubai. By this time we were wet through with perspiration. We entered the long-house, which was some 120 ft. x 40 ft. and built on sticks some 20 ft. off the ground. Inside the house is divided by a wall down the centre. On one side there are a series of doors to the 9 or 10 rooms, each of which houses one family. In each room is a fireplace and a mat on which to eat and sleep. A ladder runs up to the high roof, the rafters acting as a storeroom. Each room has a window to the next house—like the backyard fence in other countries—and sometimes a door instead. On the other side of the house is the street, which is like a large room where people sit and talk, keep their prize-fighting cocks, dogs and cats (usually tied up by the legs of a night). If there is an overflow, people sleep there.

We were greeted by the penghulu (head man). I found my Malay sufficient to enable easy communication. As a courtesy and witness to our goodwill, we left our rifles just inside the entrance to the long-house. My diary records one particular impression:

> The men wore loincloths and the women only sarongs low on their hips. Nearly all the women had good figures and the young ones could match any girl. The young were naked.

To cool off, we swam naked in the crystal waters of the swift stream, and before long some of the girls also stripped off and joined us a respectable distance away. We used the head man's quarters to change and to sleep, but whenever we did so, women at the window of the adjoining quarters watched with giggling interest. They were an unself-consciously free and happy people. It was hard to understand how fierce they had been to the Japanese, but the enemy had made the mistake of interfering with their way of life. A meal of chicken and rice was served to us on nice plates along with some of the local brew. The head man and his wife just sat and watched. We were seated on clean mats specially provided and had a bowl in which to wash our fingers.

While I talked with the penghulu, who was willing and anxious to resume trading relations with Brunei, including the supply of rice and to have other Dyaks elsewhere do the same, the medical officer looked at the problem which had brought him there. He found considerable malaria and dysentery. He took appropriate measures, including the supply of some medication. He was then besieged by almost everyone, including the young, who acquired imaginary pains to procure some medicine.

Later, thirteen blackened Japanese skulls were taken down from the rafters. Some still had some hair on them. Two holes were bored in the top of each, through which there was rattan by which the skull could be held. There was straw hanging out of the eye and mouth sockets. I queried the identity of one who had some gold in his teeth. The head man said he was the Japanese doctor from Brunei. When asked why he was killed, he replied, with a twinkle in his eye, "He didn't give us any medicines." I, with a corresponding twinkle in my eye, translated for my doctor comrade from Brunei.

In the evening, there were festivities with all the Dyaks assembled in the common area of the long-house. There was dancing with the skulls, and exhibitions of strength and agility. The frivolity was aided by the consumption of a local alcoholic brew. First, the young Dyak women decked in special, coloured sarongs and ornate silver belts, but otherwise naked, did a dance to the former head-hunting song, but with new words. It was a slow dance with swaying bodies and a skull held by each. The words on my Malay translation ran something like, "You were one proud people who thought you could rule free people, but look at you now—your blackened skulls dangling in the dust for dogs to lick." As they sang the last words, they dipped their arms in unison so the skulls touched the floor. Then the men did a vigorous dance with many yells. The dogs were attracted by the skulls and got mixed in with the dancers. Finally, young naked boys, amid great laughter, seized the skulls and tried to imitate their elders.

The penghulu said to me, "What about you Tuan?" It was almost a royal command. By a sudden inspiration, my comrades and I did the hokey-pokey dance, which was then popular in European circles. It was an instant success. The Dyaks needed little persuasion or training to join in. The highlight was the enthusiasm with which the Dyak maidens performed the part, "You put your front side in and you put your back side in and shake it all around."

Tired after a long day, I slept in my sleeping bag on the floor of the penghulu's room and opened my eyes in the morning to see a set of eyes and bare breasts peering at me through my mosquito net.

After that we moved on, staying a night in each of four different long-houses, which were a substantial distance apart. In some cases we were taken by the Dyaks in their long perahu down the swiftly flowing Lubai, and at others were escorted by them over obscure jungle trails. The perahu were some thirty feet long, carved out whole from a tree and, when loaded, had a free-board of about one inch. They were no more than two feet wide and glided through the water easily and silently. I described part of this journey in my diary:

> The river ran swiftly through the shade of the jungle. As we rounded the bends, we could see new scenes of intense green foliage, the hills rising steeply above us. Over the water hung huge orchid bushes with long green creepers hanging down. A few were scarlet and white in colour. Most of the trees were covered by staghorns and ferns. Many orchids hung down at the end of the monkey ropes. Birds called and occasionally we saw highly coloured birds like kingfishers, with large yellow bills. Many black spider monkeys raced across the trees and once we saw a crocodile . . . The Iban paddlers told us that various noises were either deer or wild pigs, but in the undergrowth we could not see them. From time to time we had to cut away the undergrowth, or a boy would have to get out and push away the logs banked up by the flooded stream.

In the four long-houses we visited, in all forty Japanese skulls were produced. There was a total male adult population of about ninety Dyaks, and they said they had lost only two men in these encounters. The area we visited represented but a small section of the Dyak population, who had been active against the Japanese. As a sample, it shows the considerable success of the Dyaks generally in Sarawak in their encounters with the enemy.

The Dyaks initially used blowpipes and parangs (long swordlike knives). One given to me was about two feet long with a handle of bone beautifully carved into the shape of a head with human hair. Later, they used captured Japanese rifles and arms supplied by Z Force. The blowpipes were about seven feet long with a spear at the end. We practised with one and were able eventually to spit out the darts and hit an object the size of a playing card some twenty or thirty feet away. These weapons, with their lethal poisoned darts, were effective in thick jungle where the presence of the Dyak would not be known unless the dart found its mark. The Dyaks in one long-house warned us to be careful of the Japanese still at large and said that some of them approached the house during the night and then fled. They had killed a Japanese only ten days earlier and said there was evidence still of the presence of others in the area. They alleged there were approximately 400 still in the interior, some in their region.

I found that along the Limbang, Baram and Lubai rivers, the hatred of the Dyaks for the Japanese was matched by their warmth for the British. There was no doubt about the warmth of their welcome to us in our week's visit to them. A leading Dyak of the Baram river who acted as an assessor at a trial at Marudi, expressed his affection for the British and his admiration for the British system of justice which left his people free but allowed them to participate in government. He told me that there was an enormous welcome back planned for the white Rajah. Dyaks along the whole length of the great Baram river were being organised to get together a fleet of decorated boats to provide the welcome. At the time I spoke to him, there had been no announcement concerning the return of the Rajah, but later it was announced that he had ceded his office to Great Britain.

*　*　*　*　*

In November 1945 I went to investigate the murder of a Javanese in Lawas, a small town on the Lawas river, which runs from interior Sarawak into Brunei bay. Only one officer and wireless operator were stationed there. I discovered that two Tagals, members of a primitive tribe, had been escorting the Javanese, who was to have been repatriated. However they took his head in order to bury it alongside the recent grave of the father of one of them, so the Javanese would be his servant in the hereafter. In order to re-establish authority and discourage head-hunting, they would end up being locked up for a short period so others would know that this kind of thing was not acceptable.

On 14 November 1945, which was almost three months to the day since the war had ended, a Murut runner arrived in Lawas with a message written on toilet paper which asked that a signal be sent to 9th Div HQ as follows:

Arriving with 327 Japs., 15 NOV—Many sick—No food —Blow.

The note also said that the party would arrive at 3 p.m. on the next day and that it consisted of 317 Japanese plus ten others: four Japanese women, one child, one Chinese girl, four Japanese envoys, and four Australians. It finished:

Sorry for notepaper, but I have no other—Blow, MAJ.

The four Australians were two officers and two sergeants, members of Z Force. The Japanese envoys had been with them to persuade these Japanese to surrender, as all others had.

15 November happened to be a Malay holiday in Lawas. At 2 p.m., when festivities for the holiday were already under way, involving the Malay, Chinese and other people of Lawas, the Japanese prisoners arrived. During the occupation the Japanese and in particular the officer in charge had been very sadistic and cruel to the Lawas people. Accordingly, the arrival of a long single line of some 300 of Nippon's proud warriors in two groups, each with one bronzed Australian stripped to the waist at the front, and one at the rear, was greeted by a hysteria beyond imagination. Most of the Japanese looked quite fat and healthy, but some looked as if they were dying on their feet. One, nicknamed "the Rajah", was carried high by two Japanese. One of the Japanese was a little woman carrying a baby. I learned later that her husband had been a civilian but in the last stages of the war, he had joined the army and both he and his wife had fled with the other Japanese. The other three Japanese girls were prostitutes. The Chinese girl was a nurse, whose status was doubtful. She said she was forced to go with them, but later said she did not wish to be separated from her "friends".

The Japanese soldiers were loaded on to three barges which had come from HQ at Labuan. First, however, those on the "wanted" war criminal list were separated from the others. It was a long list and ten were located. Three kempei-tai were put aside with them. I had a close look at this group and some were fat and looked sadistic. One, who had been identified, looked particularly brutal. He was alleged to have placed a large number of Indians in a locked house, fired into it and then set it alight. The head of the kempei-tai, who was amongst the group, was a big powerful looking man with a ferocious black beard. He was truculent when ordered into a barge. The envoys and women were left until the next day, because of the inadequacy of the water transport.

The Australians, after some weeks in the jungle, enjoyed the hospitality provided by the locals, which included plenty of samsoo. The story from here is best told in the words of my diary, dated 15 November 1945:

> I met and became good friends with the 4 S.R.D. lads and a finer group of men I have never met—happy, carefree, kind and wild. The chief was Major Blow, a tall good-looking chap with an easy manner and wicked smile on his face. He was captured with 8th Div. and escaped about two years ago from Sandakan, Borneo (most of his friends were murdered there later). He somehow managed to escape to the Philippines where he joined and fought with the U.S. guerilla force for about two years and was there promoted to Major. Then, early this year he landed with S.R.D. in the centre of Borneo. The other officer, a grand fellow with a large silky beard, no shirt, yellow skin and a smile had a blowpipe as a walking stick. The 2 sergeants were individuals of the first water. One, Sgt. Butt, famous with the S.R.D., is a serious-minded lad in one way, but seems to know everybody in the district. The other is a wild man—a young fellow who came in with an evil looking black beard—looked like a pirate.
>
> They stayed with us for the night—and what a night—and set off in the morning.
>
> From them we got the story of the Jap pursuit. They were sent in about a month ago from Lawas, it then being believed the force was small. They were sent because they knew the country and people—they used a handful of Muruts to act as spies and runners. After seven days from Lawas, they caught up with the Japs, who fled and then started a

ridiculous chase of 350 or more Japs armed with mortars, browning machine guns and some 300 rifles by 4 Aussies. A chase for ten days across some of the wildest country in the world—a chase after the war was over . . . They soon found the force was larger than [expected], but that didn't make any difference. There were a few engagements and about 20 Japs were killed. At one time, the serious sergeant was ambushed while he had his rifle apart cleaning it—the Japanese fired a machine gun at him, but he dived into the jungle—it was lucky they missed him. Along the track were signs of Jap brutality—sick, some still just barely alive, left to die on the track—they passed some 30 dead on the way.

Finally they caught up with the Japs, who were on a small hill across an open padi field. Four Aussies v. 350 Japs. The envoys were sent across and after much argument, the Japs decided to surrender, and in the pouring rain the last of the Japs surrendered to these Aussie lads in the wilds of Borneo, a week's walk from the nearest white man. The Japs were disarmed and their arms destroyed. Then started the long trek back. 15 they left behind in a field hospital as they were too sick to come. They broke into two parties of about 150 each—a white man in front and one at the back. Imagine the prestige of the white men as this procession passed through the native villages—they all expressed amazement at these miracle men, who tamed so many of these dreaded soldiers who had beaten them, stolen their crops and burned their houses.

They kept them moving, starting at first light and continuing until dark. Many of the Japs found it hard-going and lost spirit on the way, and one went off his head, but came to when he raced up a hill and fell flat on his face on a rock. It was wild mountainous country, with many hills, cliffs, rivers and washaways and the usual late afternoon and night rains. Even inside the houses where the whites slept at night, you needed two blankets—they were 3,000–4,000 ft. above sea level. The Japs slept in the open with their own army shelters.

I am sure the lads never ill-treated the Japs, but they said the conduct of the Japs showed they were really only animals. The officers, when they had the sick parade in the morning, would give their own men who could not stand up a mighty kick, or who could not hold their head up a hit across the face. No man would help another who fell down or was too sick to walk, and they had to be ordered to help each other. The Aussies made them carry 3 or 4 who could not walk, and when the Australians were round the bend out of sight, they would beat them to make them walk. Once one was missing and the Japs said he died, and the sergeant went back and found him hanged on a tree—"You have no friends in the Jap army". Another the Japs beat to death. When they arrived at Lawas, only one was being carried. He was known as "the Rajah" (riding on his elephant)—his spirit was such that he refused to die. He was thin and his legs looked paralysed. The Japs beat him over the head to kill him, but still he lived—I saw his face, which hardly looked like a face any more—his head was battered and his cheeks were swollen up into his eyes—a bluish mass of pulp. I can understand now what is said about the brutality of the Japs to our people when this is what they do to their own people.

The other 3 told me the quiet sergeant was kind and helpful to the women—when they fell down in the mud and slush and couldn't go any further and the Japs didn't worry—he would go back and lift them up and take them by the hand and encourage them by telling them it wasn't far—and so they took spirit. They said if it hadn't been for him, some of them would never have reached here.

There were the funny sides too—one party came to a swiftly flowing stream which the Japs refused to cross. He had about 100 and they just sat down—without saying a word, he walked down near them and let go a stream of owen gun rounds over their heads—they quickly took to the water.

Night was a cause for celebration—we and the S.R.D. lads were invited out to makan. I kept off the samsoo, but 2 of the S.R.D. lads got very bright on it. However, we made up for it on our return and two bottles of whisky were produced. Suddenly, one of the S.R.D. who had disappeared, returned with the 3 Japanese girls—a most amazing sight—not very beautiful to look at, but there was something novel about it all. It was not fraternization, but simply a desire on somebody's part to create an unusual experience—I could understand the angle of these S.R.D. lads—lots of fun, but no harm in them. The girls, of their own accord, saw that we always had water for our whisky, etc. and turned on their Jap dances—one sang while the others danced. After a while we sent them off and continued our party.

So ended an eventful day.

16th November, Friday

We saw S.R.D. off in the morning—somehow, our friendship came naturally, and I felt that they thought the same. They had been a month without seeing a white man on a difficult and tiring job, and we opened our home to them.

When I made this diary record in Lawas, I did not then know that six weeks later I would have my activities switched to the war crimes trials. Although Blow had told me a little concerning his escape and that of his companions who escaped with him, it was only later that I learned the fuller details. Likewise, although I had a considerable general knowledge of the operations of Z Force, I needed to consult the unit's recorded history in the archives to gain more detailed information.

Z Force had operated successfully in various theatres of the Pacific war. The operation which ended in Lawas on 15 November 1945, when the last of the Japanese were handed over to the 9th Division, was the washup of the military operations of that force. The history of Z Force in the SEMUT I and II operations reveals that a Japanese, Fujino Tai, mustered 578 Japanese and took them on a march which commenced from near Brunei at about the time of the general surrender. On that surrender, aggressive action by Z Force ceased, but Fujino Tai, then in the Limbang river area, ignored all requests and warnings and commenced pillaging. Two unarmed natives were shot. The Japanese advanced up the Limbang River in September and although the Australians were withdrawing, they were fired on and eventually retaliated. The Japanese force continued to advance, ignoring leaflet drops and envoys. Consequently orders were given to prevent any further advance. By the 15 October, the Japanese reached Trusan river between the Limbang and the Lawas rivers, where they were captured by the four Z Force members, Muruts and envoys earlier referred to. These Japanese envoys carried letters from GOC *37th Japanese Imperial Army* ordering surrender. As the history put it:

> After considerable discussion, the Japanese force surrendered, was disarmed, escorted to Lawas on the West of Brunei bay and handed over to the AIF.

It added that of the 578 Japanese that set out from the Brunei area, 220 were "accounted for" directly or indirectly "by SRD up to the time of the surrender." These figures about confirm the 327 whom I saw arrive at Lawas. It omits the human detail I heard and then recorded.

The Z Force's achievements in Borneo were remarkable. It was an Australian operation, with British, Dutch and US participation. It commenced its operations well before the seaborne landings in Borneo by dropping an advance guard secretly into the interior of the island near the border of Sarawak and Dutch Borneo. In a short time, an airstrip was constructed from bamboo poles in the middle of a large ricefield in a fertile valley. The first Auster crashed, and the next day the strip was increased by eighty yards. Thereafter planes landed without incident. Headquarters were established nearby complete with rest quarters, a hospital, administrative offices and a wireless post.

The function of the operation was threefold—to provide an intelligence service in advance of and in aid of the seaborne invasion, to provide a guerilla force and finally, to provide a force to attack Japanese inland posts from the interior on "D" Day (the day of the seaborne landings). The Japanese were not aware of the plans and it seems even of the very existence of the force as the attack on "D" Day took them completely by surprise.

The native people of the interior were recruited and armed by rifles "on loan" on strict terms. It was important that there be no attack until "D" Day, except against any Japanese patrols. There were some, but none of the Japanese ever returned from any of these patrols. There was some initial doubt in the minds of the leaders of Z Force as to the degreee of co-operation they could expect from the people of the interior, on the view that they might be reticent to help because of fear of Japanese reprisals. They indeed had taken place in the past, and natives had been killed. Their doubts were soon resolved, as part of the history of Z Force puts it:

> When the party was inserted, it was uncertain whether there were Japanese in the area, and the natives' attitude and probable reception was an unknown factor. However, within five minutes of landing, one party was met by natives carrying a white flag, and the moment they recognised the party as white men, they sent runners to villages from 20 miles around, and by nightfall over 500 people had come in to help the party find storage, storepedoes and other stores.
>
> The natives were delighted to see the party . . . at the same time they were very nervous about Japanese reprisals if they helped the party. 14 natives had already been taken prisoner, and were killed by the Japanese for helping American airmen who had been shot down.
>
> Major Harrison [the commanding officer] immediately assembled all chiefs from an area up to three days walk, in order to overcome these fears, and to make them realise the potential strength of SEMUT. This conference was successful and from that time on, unlimited native support was received in this area, without any further misgivings on their part . . .
>
> After receiving one further stores drop at Bareo, the main H.Q. was moved eastward to the Sarawak-Dutch border behind Kabak. By now, native deputations were coming in from up to 12 days' walk away, and the party leader was spending approximately eight hours a day talking to these people and conducting interrogations. Everywhere, their request was for arms; and the time for talking had passed and

> SEMUT I was now about to prepare for action . . . SEMUT I was able, during the latter part of April and May, to supply some 300 rifles and provide instructions in their handling. By the end of July, over 1,000 men were under arms, some of them equipped with captured Japanese weapons.

The intelligence system of Z Force proved invaluable to the landings. Native agents penetrated coastal areas, including Brunei and Beaufort and reported Japanese preparations and dispositions. The identified targets were later effectively used by the RAAF on "D" Day. There were attacks on the Japanese in inland towns and many garrisons were wiped out. Every Japanese at Trusan, Sundar, Lawas, Bole and Loembis were killed. After these "D" Day attacks, Z Force, with the native recruits using rifles, parangs and blowpipes, ambushed the Japanese retreating from coastal areas. The Japanese had made little preparation for such an eventuality, but Z Force had. When natives, acting as scouts, warned of Japanese approaches, food and people were hidden in the jungle, so that on arrival at long-houses, the Japanese could find no food and no people to coerce. Native trails were hidden or diverted to add further to their confusion. In this way Z Force was able to capture many Japanese in a successful guerilla operation.

The attack on Lawas on "D" Day warrants some further mention. As stated, all the Japanese there were killed in the surprise attack. The cruel and hated senior Japanese officer earlier referred to, was induced by a ruse to leave his quarters and walk down the path, where he was shot by a Z Force agent lying in ambush. He had occupied the residence of the former European district officer to which he forcibly took, as his mistress, a young attractive Chinese girl, who was the adopted daughter of the then interned European district officer. The story, as I was told by a Lawas Chinese, was that earlier the girl had been raped, as evidenced by her screams, and that just after the Japanese had been shot she walked down the path with a cup of tea for the Z Force agent. The residence was the one that we occupied and in which we had our party with Major Blow and his three comrades. It stands on a cleared hill overlooking the town of Lawas and commands a beautiful view over the river and beyond to a towering range of mountains somewhere near the border of British North Borneo and Sarawak.

* * * * *

Little did I know on that day in November 1945 when I met Rex Blow, the first prisoner to escape from Sandakan (June 1943), that six weeks later I would meet Bill Sticpewich, the last prisoner to escape (July 1945).

It was on 29 December, when I was back in Brunei, that I received a signal from HQ 9th Division at Labuan to report there to act as prosecutor at the court martial Japanese war crime trials to commence there on 1 January. I had returned to my beloved Brunei for Christmas. We were by then in luxurious quarters—in the pre-war government residence which had not been bombed and was on a hill with fine views over the Brunei river. I had enjoyed a sumptuous Christmas dinner cooked by an excellent local cook, attended the Sultan's Christmas party and when the signal came, had just finished prosecuting a collaborator case, which by coincidence concerned Sandakan. The man charged was a local man who erected the Japanese flag over his shop when the Japanese army entered Brunei and then joined the naval invasion force for Sandakan to provide the Japanese with local knowledge.

Then on New Year's Eve I went to Labuan. I changed my mansion and my Chinese boy for a humid tent at Timbalai, Labuan, just five degrees from the equator, with a snake in residence under the floorboards. It would have required demolition to eject him, and as he appeared to be small and probably not poisonous, I let him be. Nearby in a large but oppressively steamy tent, the Sandakan tragedy was replayed with many of the actors appearing in person. As a pre-war Sydney barrister of just one year's experience, I sensed a great challenge as on 8 January I stepped onto the stage where the then unknown events at Sandakan and on the death marches were to be revealed. My first task concerned the story of Sandakan itself with the trial of the Sandakan prison commandant.

I prepared my cases and wrote my diary late into the night. My apprehensive co-tenant snake used a small hole in the floorboards to slide to safety when I appeared. I respected his presence by tucking my mosquito net in on all sides of my stretcher bed. Despite all the challenges, I managed at times to get a little intoxicated. Liquor was rationed, but curacao and sugar inserted into coconuts and allowed a little time to improve, acted as a supplement. I was younger then and had a good constitution. It was fortunate for us both that I did not step on my co-tenant when I came home to my tent late at night from the mess.

My young turbulent mind was fired by anger at the enormity of what I learned and saw. Just the same I tried to distinguish between the various Japanese who were in the parade which passed before me on the strength of the evidence or their personal demeanour. How could some who were fresh faced, pleasant looking young men, who were, as was I, recent university graduates and who if together at university would have been friends, participate in the way they did in the mindless destruction of their helpless fellow men in ways which could not advance the Japanese war effort? I made friends with the leading Japanese defending officer, a friendship which was reciprocated. We talked at times on many things.

From that time in January 1946, as my diary reminds me, until the present, I have tried to understand why these things, which occurred not in the heat of battle but extended over so long a time, could happen and be allowed to happen and how the victims were able to endure them. How could this ultimate breakdown in human relations, involving so many people on either side, endure not for a day or a month, but for years? I could understand not taking prisoners and aerial bombardments extending to civilian areas. I could understand revenge immediately following battle casualties on either side. I could understand killings out of fear or lack of trust. I could not perceive any reasonable national or personal justification for the protracted ill-treatment and then killing of the Sandakan POWs any more than there could be any possible justification for the systematic exterminations carried out by the Nazis.

Before I provide a detailed description of the trials, I will sketch in some of the background necessary to come to an understanding of how and why the atrocities at Sandakan, on the death marches and at Ranau occurred. The only Sandakan prisoners to survive the end of the war were the six of the eight who escaped in June 1943 and the six who escaped in June–July 1945, apart from those officers and NCOs who were transferred to Kuching in September 1943 and most of whom survived. It was only the last six to escape who could tell the story of the hell of Sandakan in 1944–45, on the death marches and at Ranau after the marches. However, even what any one of those survivors had seen or knew was limited and the more so by reason of the separation of the prisoners at Sandakan and on the marches. The trials put together material from many sources, including the initial interrogations of Japanese and their later evidence and cross-examination at the trials. From this source the story as a whole appeared. However, for some years there had been some restrictions on access to material which might identify prisoners with gruesome events. This was presumably to prevent anguish to relatives. Sticpewich, who by reason of his particular position in the prisoner organisations, his special prison duties and special relationship with the Japanese, did have a wider knowledge of events, died a few years after the trials.

It was only in later years that investigative writers revealed what had occurred to the Sandakan prisoners. The source of the Sticpewich version of events, of necessity depended on the record of his evidence at the trials. I personally heard much of what Sticpewich knew and what others related when memories were fresh. I observed and questioned the Japanese at the trials and recorded my reactions in my diary and I now seek to add to the story and put it together as a whole. It is my purpose to write the story in a general way, to examine the Japanese part in these events and to ask why these things occurred, rather than to record the details, sometimes horrifying, of what occurred in particular incidents to individuals or named prisoners, except where necessary to describe or illustrate the generality.[1]

4

THE STORY OF THE SANDAKAN PRISONERS

The total number of POWs sent by the Japanese from Singapore to Sandakan in 1942 and 1943 was about 2750, 2000 of them Australian and 750 British. They provided the labour force for the construction of two military airstrips carved out of the jungle some eight miles out of Sandakan. After the fall of Singapore, the Japanese embarked on labour programmes, dividing up the very large group of prisoners and sending them to different areas. The first was "A" force, which consisted of 3000 Australians and was sent to Burma. Soon after "B" force of just under 1500 Australians, which included 145 officers under Lieutenant-Colonel Walsh, was sent to Sandakan, stopping at Miri on the way. This occurred in June 1942. This force was increased in 1943, first by 750 British who had come from Singapore via Jesselton, and by "E" force of 500 Australians sent from Singapore, which stopped on the way at Kuching and then staged at Berhala Island at Sandakan. The British arrived in April 1943 and the Australians of "E" force left Singapore in March 1943, arrived at Berhala Island on 15 April and were transferred to the mainland compound at Sandakan on about 5 June 1943.

Originally the three groups were kept in separate compounds. The two Australian groups were kept apart, so friends suffered the frustration of not being able to communicate. After a while, one group was lined up at a distance from the other, so they were able to see each other and shout greetings. One group had their hair shaved to prevent interchanges on working parties. Searches were made and writing utensils taken. Then the Japanese transferred some of the officers from Sandakan to Kuching. One group of seventeen was moved in June 1943. The senior officer, Lieutenant-Colonel Walsh, was among them. All these things were done, it seems, to counter the possibility of the prisoners setting up some organisation which might threaten security. In September 1943 after the "Sandakan incident", to which I will later refer, all but a few of the officers and NCOs were removed and sent to Kuching.

The selection of the Australians to go to Sandakan was to a degree left to the Australian forces. A number of units were involved and some men volunteered to go. Reasons varied. Some sick or wounded went, having been wrongly led to believe the facilities would be better in Borneo. Others thought that island life away from Singapore would be better or less boring. Some, such as Rex Blow and Miles Gillon, thought Borneo, being closer to home, would offer a better chance of escape.

The prison compound was at the site of an experimental farm, some eight miles from Sandakan and only a few miles from the airstrip. The work was heavy and unremitting. There were beatings and some brutality, but initially conditions were otherwise tolerable. The prisoners were allowed to arrange concerts and there was an occasional fishing party. At an early stage however, the commandant and project engineer, Hoshijima, then a lieutenant, emerged as a super efficient but ruthless and cruel man. There were inadequate supplies of medicine and food and as a consequence the number of sick soon increased. The ration of food for men engaged in such hard work was meagre and was less than that which the guards, who did not labour, received. The ration for the sick was substantially reduced. Major F. A. Fleming, then in charge of "B" force, complained to Hoshijima and referred to the international convention concerning the treatment of the sick. Hoshijima's reply was "We know nothing of international conventions. You are under the Japanese Army." The ration issued to the prisoners was shared so the sick got a little more.

The increase in the number of sick caused difficulty in supplying adequate labour for the airstrip work. Therefore the sick were forced to work. At times Japanese guards made inspections and often kicked men on their bandages to see how sick they were. Medical staff often substituted for these men in the labour force, but this produced its own problems in the care of the bed patients.

There was little equipment of the kind required for the work and progress on the project was slow. As the Japanese southward thrust started to stall, the need for the airstrip became greater. The delay was a source of frustration for Hoshijima. With fewer fit prisoners and slower progress, brutality increased. There were mass beatings and cut rations for all. Often officers were beaten for the imagined shortcomings of their men. In late 1942 Hoshijima erected a punishment cage. It and its use and the brutality inflicted on those sentenced to the cage and the resultant deaths, will be referred to later. Cruelty increased when Formosan guards were added to the Japanese complement. They were even more brutal than the Japanese, but Hoshijima never interfered.

The commandant's frustration and ruthlessness were graphically revealed in early 1943 by his warning to the prisoner reinforcements. Short, who arrived at Sandakan compound, via Berhala, in April 1943 with "E" force, recalls the "welcome" of Hoshijima:

> You will work until your bones rot under the tropical sun of Borneo. You will work for the Emperor. If any of you escapes, I will pick out three or four and shoot them. The war will last 100 years.

The determination of the prisoners to meet the uncertain future is typified by the address of Major F. A. Fleming in Sandakan at Christmas 1942. It included:

> Let us resolve tonight, to go on with our heads up and our eyes straight to meet whatever may be our lot in the same

> spirit as the old A.I.F. fought and won an undying tradition . . . Let us be ever ready to help the weaker amongst us, to assail not those whose footsteps may stumble and whose will may falter as the road becomes rougher, let us serve this force and each other with good spirit and all our ability. Tonight I dedicate myself anew to this Force. I pledge myself to continue to serve you to the end to the limit of my powers and in the interests of you all. That is the pledge I give to you and is a pledge I ask of you in return . . . And finally, gentlemen, when the going is tough and the way is rough, if the conditions become more difficult, as indeed they may, when the burdens seem well nigh unbearable, let us hear a voice say "even these things shall pass". Yes, gentlemen—"even these things shall pass" and in the Almighty's good time we shall return again to Australia—to our homes, to those whose thoughts are always with us and who wait for us.

If at that time there had been thoughts of escape from Sandakan, that was not the occasion to express them—Hoshijima was present and could speak English.

The escapes and the Japanese attitudes to them and their discovery later in that year of an underground and intelligence organisation involving prisoners inside the compound and civilians outside it, had far reaching effects on the treatment of the prisoners and may have contributed to what occurred in 1945. A number of books have been written about particular escapes.[1] In order to understand the story of Sandakan and the trials, it will be necessary to look at the escapes as a whole and in a wider context.

The chance of escape to some neutral or Allied zone was equal to the chance enjoyed by the convict Buckley in his attempt to walk to China from the New South Wales penal colony. With Japan firmly in control in Asia, the East Indies and adjacent Pacific regions, there seemed to be little option but to ride out the unknown future in confinement. To add to the problem, the prisoners were cut off from news, and lacked knowledge of where to go, if they did escape from the compound. They had no way of knowing if there was some safe escape route or some area of guerilla activity. Some escaped in 1942 from the Sandakan compound before it was fully wired and tried to sail to Australia, but were captured in Sandakan harbour.

However, by late 1942 work began on the setting up of an intelligence system involving some prisoners headed by Captain Lionel Matthews and local people, including Malays and Chinese, headed by Dr J. P. Taylor, an Australian civilian working at the Sandakan hospital. Some former members of the North Borneo Constabulary were also involved. It was this organisation which, in 1943, set up the supply, from outside the camp, of parts which could be used by the prisoners to assemble a radio receiver. Parts were also supplied for a transmitter. The receiver became operational shortly after the Allied victory at El Alamein on 23 October 1942. The first war news received by the radio was of this turning point in the war. It was a great boost to prisoner morale. The news was in contrast to the Japanese accounts of their victories and the exaggerated or invented claims concerning the bombing of Australia. On one occasion, a prisoner had managed to slip into the guard house and switch the amplified Japanese propaganda broadcast to Radio San Francisco. Unfortunately, it did not remain on that frequency for long. News sheets were smuggled out to Dr Taylor who sparingly passed on news by word of mouth to selected persons. For security reasons, the use of the radio was limited and, when not in use, the set was buried.

The organisation was also used by Dr Taylor to supply the prisoners with much needed medicines and medical equipment. Moreover, since there was still some trading by small craft between Sandakan and the Philippines, including Tawi Tawi, the closest of the larger islands, the organisation was able to establish communication with US and Filipino guerillas there. This became a possible escape route and a possible line of communication with Australia.

Escape, with but a remote chance of success, was further discouraged by Japanese threats to shoot those attempting to do so and to make reprisals against others. The Japanese often made threats in order to intimidate, without any intention of carrying them out. However, the Japanese gave total discretion to individual officers and soldiers to enforce their policies and this led to inconsistent and unpredictable responses to situations. Therefore threats could never be confidently ignored. Some who attempted to escape or were recaptured were shot. One starving prisoner who had crept under the wire and was stealing vegetables in the prison garden was shot and killed at short range. Some who escaped and were recaptured were tried and sentenced to imprisonment at Outram Road Gaol in Singapore.

In September 1942 not long after the arrival of the first group of prisoners at Sandakan, Hoshijima issued an order that each prisoner sign a document asking to be shot if he escaped or attempted to escape. There were extra guards and there was a machine gun covering the parade. A table was set up in front of the parade and on it were the papers for signing. Lieutenant-Colonel Walsh, the senior officer present, was called on to read the document. This he did and then jumped on the table and shouted: "I for one will not sign". He was dragged from the table and taken outside the wire and there tied up in view of the parade. Hoshijima organised a firing squad. In the tense situation with the machine gun trained on the prisoners, another POW officer intervened and the statement was changed to say that if the prisoners attempted to escape, they knew they would be shot. The prisoners chorused that it was under duress, but that they would sign the amended document, and Lieutenant-Colonel Walsh was released. At his trial, Hoshijima did not deny the substance of events, including the binding up of Walsh and the organisation of the firing squad. He claimed that an error had been made in the drafting of the document by use of "we" instead of "I" and that the Japanese did not understand that Europeans only liked to sign on behalf of themselves and not for everyone. He said this was the correction made and that all then signed. He said that the machine gun and the firing squad for Walsh were essential for security, because there was a difference of opinion amongst the prisoners.

The first prisoners of the Sandakan force to escape successfully were the eight who, despite opposition from some of their officers for fear of Japanese reprisals, got away from Berhala Island in June 1943 and reached Tawi Tawi where they joined the US and Filipino guerillas. The former Sandakan quarantine station on Berhala, a small island at the mouth of the Sandakan river, was used as a Japanese prison camp, first for Sandakan civilian internees who were later moved to Kuching, and, later in 1943, as a staging camp for 500 Australian prisoners of "E" force transferred from Singapore to supplement the Sandakan workforce. It was under the control of Hoshijima as the Sandakan POW commandant. Of the eight who escaped, seven were from "E" force at the staging camp. The eighth was a prisoner from "B" force, Warrant Officer Walter Wallace, who had escaped from the mainland Sandakan prison compound with two others at the end of April 1943. The other two sought help from Malays who handed them over to the searching Japanese. They were severely beaten and shot. Wallace was hidden by a Chinese family and, through the underground he communicated with the prisoners on Berhala and arranged to join them in an escape bid. The underground arranged water transport for him to Berhala and later for some of the group from Berhala to Tawi Tawi.

One of the seven from "E" force to escape was Rex Blow, whom I met in 1945. I did not see him again until he visited my home in Sydney in 1988. Having heard that I had prosecuted Hoshijima, he wrote to me in early 1988 and said in his letter:

> As soon as we saw that bastard [Hoshijima], we held a meeting of the escape club and agreed unanimously that there was no future for us under that guy. He just looked evil. I was very lucky to escape his wrath the first time we met—he lined us up for an inspection. I was carrying a handgun, a compass and part of a radio. No chance to offload them. All I could do was try to make a bit of a hole in the sandy soil and put the groundsheet on top and spread my clothes over them. Miles

Gillon [who later escaped with the Blow group], who was standing next to me said I went a funny kind of green. Luckily all they were looking for was writing equipment so we couldn't correspond with those already on the mainland.

The group who escaped comprised Captain Ray Steele, Lieutenants Rex Blow, Miles Gillon and Charles Wagner, Sapper James Kennedy and Privates Rex Butler and Jock McLaren from "E" force and Warrant Officer Walter Wallace from the mainland compound.

Wallace had arrived at Berhala prison compound some days before the others were ready to go, but was able to communicate with them outside the wire, when they were on a working party. Until their escape, he was fed by the prisoners from inside the compound. The seven men from "E" force escaped from the compound the night before the force left Berhala for the mainland. The eight men then hid on Berhala for some days before their move to Tawi Tawi.

For tactical reasons, the escape from Berhala was in separate groups, but on the same night. Some went by dugout canoe-type craft, hiding by day in the shelter of tiny islands. The journey took some ten days. Others were hidden in a small trading vessel. All reached Tawi Tawi eventually where they were reunited, had a warm welcome by the people there and joined the US and Filipino guerillas. Butler and Wagner were later killed in action. The others served for various periods with great distinction in Tawi Tawi and Mindanao. Individual members were periodically promoted.

Some were repatriated to Australia at different times in 1944. Blow and McLaren remained until 1945. In Mindanao the Japanese had a high price on the heads of Blow and McLaren and published photographs of them in news bulletins. Steele, then a major, returned to Australia to report on the Japanese atrocities in the prison camps. Captain McLaren and Major Blow, as they had then become, joined the Borneo Z Force in early 1945. A sense of adventure must have been combined with courage in Blow, because when the war finished he worked with the British Army and the British Government in charge of a fast small armed vessel, pursuing pirates in the waters he knew off the east coast of Borneo.

The reports of Japanese conduct in the Sandakan prison compound, brought to Australia by Wallace and Steele, of course only included information derived directly from the compound, which was up to April 1943, and as was known to Wallace. Although the determined and cruel disposition of Hoshijima was evident early and although prisoners had been harshly and cruelly dealt with in 1942 and 1943, no one could have imagined what was to happen in the next two years.

The courageous service of these eight men was recognised. All were mentioned in dispatches, two posthumously. Blow received the DSO and bar, Gillon the DSO and McLaren the MC and bar. Wallace received the US Bronze Star.

In July 1943 the Japanese learned of the underground organisation, from which flowed devastating consequences for those connected with it. Indirectly, it affected all prisoners in some way. By a quirk of fate, the discovery led to some being imprisoned in Singapore and some transferred to Kuching, so they were not at Sandakan in 1945 when all in custody there perished.

The discovery by the Japanese was not due to any fault of those who aided the escape of Wallace to Berhala and then of the eight from Berhala. A Turkish civilian who was aware of some of the activities of the organisation tried to blackmail a member of the organisation and, when rebuffed, went to the Japanese. The kempei-tai were called in. Under torture there were disclosures by civilian members of the organisation, which in the end implicated Captain Matthews as head of the organisation. As a result of the discovery of notes passed from the compound, the radio receiver, and a diary kept by Lieutenant Wells,[2] other prisoners were subjected to the torture procedures. Lieutenant Wells was one. Under torture he revealed the whereabouts of some radio parts, but concealed the existence of the transmitter and did not implicate others. Matthews was tortured over a long period but with great endurance and heroism remained silent and did not in any way implicate anyone else. There were intensive searches of the prisoners and the compound.

Prisoners suspected of involvement in the underground were thrown into the punishment cage and kept in these harsh and cruel conditions for many days. The investigation on the civilian side was thorough and brutal and continued at Sandakan until late 1943. Some died as a result of the torture, harsh treatment or deprivations during their long imprisonment. A few managed to avoid arrest by fleeing to other areas of Borneo and survived there until the end of the war.

Towards the end of 1943, those considered to be implicated were transported to Kuching where the interrogations continued until the trials in early 1944. A large number of prisoners and civilians stood trial before a military court in Kuching. The material presented to the court was largely what was alleged to have been said by various prisoners and civilians under torture, as reported by interpreters.

Matthews and eight civilians were convicted and sentenced to death. They were executed in Kuching on 2 March 1944. Matthews was posthumously awarded the George Cross. He had already been decorated with the MC and bar for valour early in the Malayan campaign and later in the last days of the defence of Singapore Island. In a statement by Dr Taylor which I had before me at the trials, he commented on Matthews' bravery and devotion to duty. He referred to how Matthews procured the radio to get news of the outside world to Sandakan, and how he co-operated in getting medical help for sick prisoners. As Dr Taylor put it:

> His sole care right throughout this time in the camp and in his period of imprisonment was for the welfare of those around him, both Australian POWs and Asiatics. His bearing throughout imprisonment and his conduct at his trials was that of a very brave man. I considered him a most courageous officer . . . he upheld the highest traditions of an Australian officer.

The Japanese who were brave in battle and admired bravery in their enemies, are said to have commented on the courage of Matthews. They accorded him the honour of a military funeral at which senior prisoners and Japanese officers attended wearing decorations.

After the war, Matthews' body was moved to the war cemetery at Labuan. The Australian War Graves Commission exhumed the bodies of the civilians who had died for helping the Sandakan prisoners. They are buried now at the "Heroes Grave" in Kuching. The Memorial over the grave says:

> IN MEMORY OF EIGHT GALLANT MEN OF ALL RACES WHO LOYAL TO THE CAUSE OF FREEDOM RENDERED ASSISTANCE TO ALLIED PRISONERS OF WAR AT SANDAKAN CAMP AND WERE EXECUTED IN KUCHING ON 2ND MARCH 1944 AND ALSO THE FIVE WHO DIED IN PRISON FOR THE SAME REASON
>
> EXECUTED:
>
> JEMADUR OJAGER SINGH; ALEXANDER CLARENCE LEONARD FUNK; SERGEANT ABIN; ERNESTO LAGAN; HENG JOO MING; WONG MOO SING; FELIX AYCONA; MATUSUP BIN GUNGAU
>
> DIED IN KUCHING PRISON:
>
> SOH KIM SENG; AMIGO BIN BASSAN; KASSIM BIN JAMADI; P. C. KASIA; SIDIK BIN SIMOEN

A large number of prisoners and civilians of all races received varying sentences from twelve years down to six months served in the infamous Outram Road Gaol in Singapore, where some died. Lieutenant R. G. Wells received a sentence of twelve years, as did Dr Taylor. His wife was sent to internment at Kuching. They survived and were reunited after the war and lived in Sydney. He was awarded the OBE. This man of outstanding courage who did so much to help the Sandakan prisoners, particularly the sick, was a usual guest of honour at the dinners of the "Old Sandakans" (the officer survivors of Sandakan and Kuching) where I, also a guest, had the honour of meeting him.

At the end of September 1943, when investigations at Sandakan were almost complete, the Japanese, without prior notice, moved the officers and some NCOs from Sandakan to Kuching. Some 200 were transferred. Some prisoners had already died. Reconstruction of numbers is difficult, but on my 1946 information about 2390 remained at Sandakan in

October 1943. Only a very few officers were left at Sandakan. Captain Cook, assisted by two others, was in charge of prisoner administration, and three medical officers remained as well as several padres. The intention of the Japanese was obvious. The underground organisation was destroyed and the prisoners were deprived of leaders. A serious consequence was that the number of medical officers and staff was greatly reduced in proportion to the number of prisoners who remained at Sandakan at a period when hospital cases were rapidly increasing.

The collapse of the underground put an end to any escape plans. There had been a group of six preparing to escape to Tawi Tawi with outside assistance. One in this group was Sergeant A. M. Blair, the Northern Territory member in the Australian Parliament, but without the underground this escape was no longer possible. There were no further escapes from Sandakan. The next successful escape was not from Sandakan, but from the second death march. Thus, the only person ever to escape successfully from Sandakan compound was Wallace in April 1943.

From October 1943, the conditions of those who remained at Sandakan deteriorated badly. The Japanese were on the defensive and the need for the airstrips increased. This demand was soon to become even greater as US sea and air dominance was established. With the work incomplete and delayed, the Japanese took out their frustrations on the prisoners and brutalities increased. Much of what occurred will never be known, because only six of the 2390 survived. Forced to concentrate on their own labours, they did not see most of what happened to others. For these reasons nearly all of the detailed evidence of ill-treatment which could be given at the trials and has later appeared in the accounts of investigative writers, relates to the period before October 1943 and not the worst period from October 1943 to May 1945, when cruelty and death were rife. It is in this period to May 1945, where little detail has been revealed, that 1100 prisoners died at Sandakan. To this should be added 288, some of whom died at Sandakan or nearby in the period May to June 1945.

The breaking up of the intelligence and escape organisation had other consequences for the prisoners at Sandakan after October 1943. No longer did they have any wireless receiver. They were now cut off from information from the outside world. All they had were Japanese versions of continuing victories. It was only from late in 1944, when they could observe changes in aerial activity, that they were able to speculate about changes in the war situation.

Following the US victory in the sea battle of Leyte Gulf in October 1944, Sandakan was constantly bombed by the Allies. Work by the prisoners on the airstrip continued, but it was mainly to repair bomb damage. Some prisoners were killed in the bombings. The Allies soon had air superiority in the region and Japanese communication by sea with Sandakan in a practical sense was at an end. By the end of 1944, with the air strips no longer operational and work on it at an end, the exhausted prisoners, many of them bedridden, were now a liability to the Japanese. They were put to vegetable growing.

In January 1945, HQ of the *37th Japanese Imperial Army* at Jesselton issued an order that 500 of the fittest prisoners were to be moved to Ranau. Even by Japanese standards there was not that number fit and only 470 left on the march. Even so, some with beriberi or serious ulcers were sent. Some key prisoners, including officers, who were more fit, were kept back.

The move was combined with the evacuation of a regular Japanese army unit, the *2nd Battalion 25th Independent Mixed Regiment*, unconnected with the prisoners. This unit was to go to Jesselton, which was some distance beyond Ranau, where a new compound for prisoners was to be established. The prisoners and the Japanese were divided into groups, each of fifty prisoners and fifty Japanese, with a Japanese officer in charge. Groups moved about a day apart. The prisoners were to be used to carry ammunition and stores.

The distance to Ranau is about 164 miles. The route for most of the way was by jungle trails. In the early stage, it was through swamps. January was the wet season and it rained every day. Often the men were in mud up to their knees. After this, the march was over rugged mountains, at some points the trail being some 6000 feet above sea level. In the mountainous areas, there were long climbs, one for a whole day. At times prisoners had to go on hands and knees with Japanese loads on their backs. There were steep descents into river valleys. The trail was rough and slippery and through some of the wildest country in Borneo. The mountain ranges are those in which Mount Kinabalu rises to its towering height. Some of the prisoners had no boots. Rubber footwear provided by the Japanese proved useless and was discarded.

Along the trail there were rest houses at intervals, but the shelter was not sufficient to provide cover for the prisoners. Food and medicines were totally inadequate. Many with beriberi, malaria, dysentery or ulcers struggled on, forced on by beatings with sticks or rifle butts, when they slowed down or stopped. In the end, many fell down and could not go on. They were shot by Japanese moving at the end of their group.

Some of the later groups halted for some days at Paginatan, some twenty miles short of Ranau. This was supposed to enable the prison camps at Ranau to be made ready, but when the prisoners arrived, some rough huts had been built at the edge of the jungle, but there were none for the prisoners.

Of the 470 prisoners who left Sandakan, only about half reached Ranau. Most of those who did survive the march were sick and emaciated. The Japanese selected from the survivors of the march those whom they considered fit and put them to carrying rice from Paginatan to Ranau. They went back this twenty miles over the high mountains on the same trail, carrying heavy bags. Many died on these journeys or as a result of them. How they died or whether they were shot is not known. Hygiene and medicines for the prisoners at Ranau was almost nil. Many died there due to exhaustion from the march, or from rice carrying or from various diseases. When the second march arrived at Ranau in June 1945, there were only six alive from the first march; five Australians and one British. The 470 who left Sandakan five months earlier had been selected as the fittest!

Meanwhile, between January and June 1945, the death rate of prisoners left behind at Sandakan rapidly increased. The prisoners were dying of starvation or of illnesses caused or exacerbated by the atrocious conditions. By March of that year, the prisoners were dying at the rate of ten a night—300 in one month. It was no longer possible to make sufficient coffins. Surviving prisoners buried their dead companions naked in mass graves.

In mid-May 1945, Hoshijima handed over command of the camp to Captain Takakuwa. At the same time, HQ Borneo ordered that Sandakan compound be closed and moved elsewhere. Two weeks later, on 29 May, the second death march left Sandakan for Ranau under Takakuwa. On 27 May, there was a massive aerial and naval bombardment of Sandakan. The orders for the march to Ranau and the closing down of the Sandakan compound had preceded the bombardment, but what the Japanese construed as a prelude to a landing influenced the way Takakuwa implemented his orders and conducted the march.

When the march started, there were only 824 POWs still alive. About half were hospital cases, many of them on stretchers. One Japanese assessment made before the march was that of the 824 POWs, only one-third would be capable of surviving the march and told HQ so. 536 set out on the march. Some used sticks to walk. Some weighed about six stone. When those who were to go were assembled, they were ordered to carry the stretcher cases into the open. Then all the buildings, including the hospital, were set alight and destroyed. The POW records and the remaining medical equipment and supplies were burned in the fires. The few medical officers left were taken on the march. As those on the march moved off under guard, they saw the burning buildings and the 288 stretcher cases left out in the open with a few guards staying behind in charge of them. None of the 288 survived.

When the prisoners were told to assemble to move out

of the compound, they were not told they were to go to Ranau. In the absence of the 1943 intelligence system they were unaware of the war situation, but because of the naval and air bombardment of Sandakan on 27 May, they reasoned that the war had turned against the Japanese. False rumours spread amongst the prisoners that the Allies had landed at Sandakan and by some that the war had ended and that the prisoners were to be marched to Sandakan township to be handed over to the Allies. Incapacitated men, some hobbling on sticks, joined the march believing their rescue was at hand. Some sick took the view that if they remained where they were, they would be picked up in time.

When the prisoners reached the road, to their dismay, they did not turn to the left into Sandakan, but to the right. They were on their way to Ranau and, for nearly all, to death. Takakuwa in command was no less ruthless than Hoshijima.

As none of the 288 prisoners left behind at Sandakan survived, little is known of what occurred to them. I was unaware of their exact fate at the time of the trials. Following the earlier pattern of illnesses and death, many of the bed patients, in any event, would have been near to death and most could not have survived long, left exposed in the open without medical attention. From accounts of natives in the Sandakan area given to members of Z Force, or later collected by an investigation team and from bodies and other discoveries on the Ranau route at the Sandakan end, it seems there was a third death march of some kind of about seventy-five prisoners who were marched into the jungle where they perished or were shot. Presumably, they were the last of the sick prisoners still alive some time after the second march left and the buildings were destroyed.

Much of the detail can never be known of what occurred in the various groups on this march to Ranau, the worse of the two marches. Many of the sick gave up heart when the march turned right to Ranau and lasted only hours or days before collapsing and being shot. A fourteen day but light rice ration was issued to POWs at the start of the twenty-eight day march and in the end POWs tried to survive from what they could get from the jungle. One group caught a python, a great delicacy. The Japanese had an extra ration of rice issued to them which was carried on the march. They also had some medical supplies, but the POWs had none. There were some medical aid posts set up on the route, but on Takakuwa's orders only the Japanese could use them. As with the first march, the prisoners were divided into groups of fifty. The procedures concerning disposal of prisoners were now more highly organised. There were special squads who shot all who could not go on. At first POWs were shot only when they could not go on. Eventually, each morning before the march continued, the Japanese decided which prisoners were unfit to continue. They were then ordered to stay behind. A rotating system was used so nearly all guards did some killing.

Two POWs escaped during the second march and survived. One was in a group of five who escaped during the confusion of an Allied air raid. They managed to seize some of the Japanese reserve rice thrown down in the haste to take cover. Some time after the escape, two were shot and two died. Only gunner Campbell survived. After weeks in the jungle he was picked up by Z Force. The other survivor was Bombadier Braithwaite, who escaped on his own. At one stage he was confronted by a Japanese soldier whom he killed with a branch of a tree. After further incredible experiences he was assisted by some natives to the coast where he was picked up by a US patrol boat.

Of the 536 who left on this march, only 183 reached Ranau. In some groups, such as the one Short was in, only eight out of the fifty arrived. At Ranau these 183 were held with the six who remained from the first march in a primitive compound in a new location in the jungle, under conditions already described. Most did not survive long at Ranau. With the guards in the end outnumbering the POWs, there was little chance of escape. There was a ruthless determination that none of these dying men escape. Those who attempted to escape were shot or as a lesson to others, tortured to death. Four escaped in one group and three of them survived and finally so did Sticpewich. Some time after his escape, the last thirty-three POWs, were shot. They included the medical officers and Captain Cook, the POW commander since mid-1943.

The Japanese at Ranau, including those at the POW compound, did not surrender or lay down their arms until some weeks after the general surrender on 15 August and ignored the leaflets dropped to them telling of the surrender. When they did, there were no Sandakan POWs to hand over. The Australian army had to scour the jungle in search of POWs who may have escaped. When all was done, there were only six.

The records and the means of identifying POWs were destroyed in the Sandakan fires, despite protests. Japanese records concerning the POWs thereafter were virtually non-existent. The Japanese made out death certificates in respect of prisoners and some were preserved. Most were false. They always gave some nominated sickness as the cause of death. The dates on some were false. The identity of POWs who had been at Sandakan and what had been their fate, at least originally, depended on the memories of those who had left Sandakan two years earlier and of the few who escaped. In the months following the end of the war, as the story of Sandakan emerged in indefinite terms, the press around Australia was inundated by pathetic requests of parents and wives for information concerning the many POWs who were missing. The bodies of many about whom enquiries were made lay in mass graves in Sandakan, Ranau or strewn unburied alongside the jungle trails.

No greater inhumanity could be inflicted by one nation on another than that which Japan inflicted on Australia in Borneo. What occurred was encouraged by the policies of higher command in Japan and in other ways was aided and abetted by Japanese leaders. Sandakan, the Burma Railway, Bataan and Nanking have cast a stain on the history of twentieth century Japan which will not easily fade.

5

THE TRIAL OF THE SANDAKAN COMMANDANT

As the New Year of 1946 dawned, I began to prepare for the prosecution of Captain Hoshijima, the commandant of the Sandakan prison compound. I was to come later to see this trial as a tense and moving drama contested at length and with great vigour—a drama which revealed both the tragic struggle of the POWs to survive and the appalling conduct, in essence equivalent to the massacre of over 1100 men, on the initiative of one man. This was the trial of a crime without parallel in Australian history.

There were four charges already defined for me, as summarised in my diary: "cruelty, cruelty by confinement in a cage resulting in several POW deaths, starvation and denial of medical attention causing deaths and forcing sick men to do heavy work."

The file contained fifty sworn statements, most of them dealing with cruelty and nearly all covering only the period up to 1943 when the officers were moved to Kuching. Sticpewich, who was being flown from Australia, was to be the only witness for the prosecution and the only one who could cover the later period in any detail. As I recorded in my diary of 2 January 1946:

> It is a difficult case . . . It is easy to prove cruelty, but 1,100 died during Hiroshima's time and 1,250 within two months of his time . . . The defence to the vital charge of starvation and lack of medical attention is obvious—that the Allied bombing

> sank all their ships—that ship was the only method of supply and that Hoshijima, as a mere captain on the spot, could not help and was not responsible for the tragedy, that rice was cut out by H.Q. 37 Jap. army.

In substance, Hoshijima had said just that in his interrogation. He had claimed the deaths were largely due to the prisoners being deprived of rice, which was their staple diet and that he had done his best to provide substitutes. There was no doubt HQ had issued the order cutting out the prisoners' rice ration. This order was issued to the army quartermaster at Sandakan, who was not under the command of Hoshijima. There was no doubt that HQ had also issued the orders for the death marches.

Some matters in the general statement of Sticpewich suggested that the basis of Hoshijima's claim and likely defence was false, but, as the days passed, there was no Sticpewich. As I anxiously waited, I recorded in my diary in reference to the expected defence:

> . . . however I am sure [it] is not the truth—but the evidence we have is far from watertight. There are two possibilities still—Sticpewich, when he arrives in person may be able to answer several vital questions and secondly, some of the Jap quartermasters may give a lead to Hoshijima's part. I will ferret them out and see what I can get.
>
> Drinking party again tonight . . .

As I worked on, I wondered what Hoshijima would look like and what kind of man he would be. I saw him for the first time on the morning of the trial which was held in a large tent set up in a coconut grove fronting Timbalai beach and looking out over the China Sea. The court martial was constituted of three officers, Major Greville (presiding), Major Briscoe and Captain Davis. Major Briscoe was a British officer. The others were Australians.

The name of the commandant, Captain Hoshijima Susumi, was called. From the moment he was marched into the court by the Ghurka guards, it was apparent that he was an impressive man with a domineering personality. About six feet tall, a powerful athletic looking man, he towered above his diminutive guards and the Japanese defending officers. He clicked the heels of his well polished boots, saluted with military precision and gazed intently, even defiantly, at those who were to try him. The corners of his mouth were slightly turned down to reveal the face of a determined and cruel man, characteristics to become apparent from the evidence presented to the court and from his demeanour before it in the many days of the trial. Throughout the trial there was no relaxation of his set and steely look. At times he wore a sinister set type of smile.

The charges were read and to each he gave a loud response of "not guilty". In legal essence, all the charges were war crimes of criminal inhumanity to prisoners of war. The defence did not challenge either the competency of the court or the legal validity of the crimes charged.

As prosecutor I was assisted by an instructing officer from Staff HQ of the 9th Division. At the same time there was a second adjoining court martial trial in a similar adjoining tent with Lieutenant Ray Balzer, who in civilian life was a young New South Wales solicitor, acting as prosecutor.

The Japanese had four defending officers, all Japanese. They served both courts. They were headed by Colonel Yamada. He was highly qualified, being a pre-war graduate of Cambridge and Osaka Universities. During the war he had served in the Japanese Army as a lawyer. He spoke excellent English. Apart from his legal training, he was a well educated man of considerable charm. He and I were always opposed as advocates in the major trials in which I prosecuted, but we were on friendly terms, as are opposing members of the Bar in Australia and elsewhere. He was dedicated to the task of defending his countrymen, a task which he performed with ability. I often detected worry and strain on his face, as the cases against the men he was defending unfolded. I described the others:

> The other three are also graduates of Tokyo and lawyers.

> Two are small and typically intellectual Japs. The third is the fierce bull type of Jap—looks quite clever—has a face set without change of expression. He was a judge in Japan before the war. These three are sitting in as defence counsel, but actually only the bull one and one other are on the case.

The duty of a prosecutor in such a case as Hoshijima's was greater than merely to produce evidence sufficient to support some finding of guilt in the matters charged. The occasion of the trial, as I saw it, afforded me the opportunity of establishing the full extent of the responsibility Hoshijima in fact had for the deaths of the prisoners in his charge and later. The principal, or at least initiating cause of those deaths appeared to be the starvation of the prisoners leading to their physical collapse and the contracting of diseases exacerbated by the denial of medicines. The matter of any punishment to be ordered by the court and any confirmation of it at higher levels could only be determined satisfactorily if the full responsibility of Hoshijima was properly and clearly established.

There were some special provisions in the Australian War Crimes Act which facilitated proof of guilt due to the special circumstances in which war crimes may have been committed (such as where witnesses were killed), but it seemed to me as a lawyer that, at the end of the case, the determination of guilt and the imposition of any penalty, particularly the death penalty, ought to be solidly based on proof of matters of substance by clear direct evidence.

The court was open in the sense that there were seats at the back where anyone could come and observe, but I never saw any person in civilian clothing in the court, except the Australian Minister for the Army, the Hon. Frank Forde, who paid a fleeting visit during the trial relating to the first death march. There did not appear to be any journalists present at any time. In this respect, the trials at Labuan stood in contrast with some court martial war crimes trials held openly in Malaya in court buildings in towns or cities and especially with the later Tokyo war trials, which were held in the utmost glare of publicity. The few reports of the results of the Labuan trials, which appeared in the Australian press, were meagre in the extreme. I suspect they were taken from reports made by me in summary form for circulation and information within the 9th Division.

While awaiting the arrival of Sticpewich, I busied myself with interviews and obtained statements from various Japanese who had been in Sandakan, one not within the prison organisation of Hoshijima. The most important was a statement by Lieutenant Arai, the head quartermaster of Sandakan. His declaration was so critical that I had him go through it several times and assent to it and put his initials to alterations which he had suggested. He did not understand the Hoshijima defence and that what he said destroyed it. At the trial he made a partial attempt to, but did not succeed in disowning what he had said and signed.

Sticpewich arrived on the Sunday before the trial, set to commence on Tuesday, and after he had visited his "mate" Takahara, we set to the task. I felt that his evidence, particularly when aided by what Lieutenant Arai had stated, should destroy Hoshijima's claims and defence and establish that he was the one directly responsible for the starvation and hence death of the prisoners in 1945.

Sticpewich was "the answer" to my prosecutor prayers. I described him in my entry of that Sunday night, 6 January:

> Sticpewich arrived today, so all is well . . . He is the typical Aussie—fairly rough, but hail fellow well met with a ton of resource and personality in a rough way . . . He got on the right side of the Japs and can speak a lot of Japanese—being very handy as a carpenter and good at fixing machines, he made himself invaluable to the Japs. He had the run of the camp and got a little extra food from the Jap leavings. He also poked his nose into things and can now tell us all sorts of things as to what food they had and what medicines they had, etc. At the same time, he was a member of the secret organisation run by that hero Capt. Matthews . . .

Later work with Sticpewich over the next three weeks

confirmed those impressions, with some additions. He was a member of the later committee headed by the senior prisoner, Captain Cook. From 1943 to 1945, this committee received reports from prisoners and made complaints and requests to Hoshijima. He had a remarkable capacity to supply statistics of prisoner deaths, rice rations, the location and the amounts of rice stored and dates. They turned out to be substantially accurate when tested against admissions later gained from the Japanese or the failure of the Japanese to challenge them.

The case proved against Hoshijima on the starvation question holds the key to the ultimate fate of the Sandakan prisoners. It was not a case of men starving and dying of illnesses because they were cut off by the war situation, as is sometimes assumed and as the Japanese tried to maintain. The truth is that men need not have died and that they were deliberately and systematically denied available food and medicines long before the Allied invasion of Borneo. The story of the trial and the deliberate conduct of Hoshijima, there revealed, has never been written. It should now be recorded in some detail.

The central point of the prosecution case, proved beyond doubt, was that Hoshijima was directly responsible for the death of at least those prisoners who died at Sandakan in 1945 until mid-May 1945, when he handed over his command to Captain Takakuwa, and for the weakened and sick condition of the remainder who died or were shot in the following three months on the second march or at Ranau. Three months before the HQ order which cut out the prisoners' rice ration, Hoshijima had unofficially done so. He continued to draw it from the Sandakan Q store with the Japanese ration. The prisoners' rice was stored at the compound and some was used by the guards, while the POWs starved. Then he acquiesced in and promoted the making of the official HQ order in April 1945, completely cutting out the prisoners' rice ration.

Despite a vigorous defence, to which I will later refer, all these matters were clearly made out, in the end being supported at many points by the admissions and evidence of Hoshijima himself before and during the trial. As a more experienced lawyer, I re-read the transcript of the trial and I believe that the foregoing account is beyond doubt the truth that lies behind the Sandakan tragedy. Whatever may have been his motives and whatever other factors intruded, Hoshijima, when the labour of the prisoners at the airstrip was no longer required, embarked on a systematic course of starving them, so they fell victim to illnesses for which medicines although available were withheld. Rice had proved to be an essential part of the diet necessary to sustain the strength and health of prisoners. At earlier periods, such as in 1943 and early 1944, when they were doing heavy work on the airstrip project, their strength was largely sustained by a reasonable, but moderate, issue of rice, with supplements at times of meat and fish. Despite complaints, the ration for sick prisoners was always less and inadequate.

From mid-1944 there were official reductions made in the prisoners' rice ration and the Japanese provided "substitutes" (of vegetables), which never took the place of rice in sustaining strength. Anyhow, what the prisoners received was in fact less than the ration entitlement. In 1945, these "substitutes" degenerated largely into watery foods, principally tapioca. Moreover in 1945 the supply of meat (usually only entrails) and fish virtually ceased. Consequently most prisoners rapidly lost weight, some of them many stone. According to Sticpewich, apart from bed patients, there were a hundred or more in the Australian section who were not sick, but who weighed between five and six stone. There was no evidence concerning what happened in the separate British section, as there were no survivors to give evidence, but the death rate there on percentages was higher than in the Australian section. Hoshijima, in evidence, conceded that at times in 1945 about half the prisoners were bed patients. According to Sticpewich, those who lost weight rapidly became subject to beriberi, dysentery and malaria. Rice, the staple food which had formerly sustained the prisoners, had been taken away.

There had been orders in June and September 1944, issued by HQ, which reduced the prisoners' rice ration but this would not have been life-threatening had it reached the prisoners. At the same time, there was an equivalent reduction in the Japanese rice ration, which had always been more generous than that of the prisoners. However, the ration for the prisoners and the Japanese was issued to the compound in bulk, leaving the Japanese to make the division. They took theirs first and the prisoners got only what they left. The order from HQ which completely cut out the rice ration to the prisoners (but not to the Japanese) in Sandakan, was not made until April 1945.

The evidence of Quartermaster Arai, supported by the Japanese in the Q store within the compound, and Sticpewich, was that the division of rice and other rations, such as meat and fish, was left to the Japanese in the compound and was under the ultimate control of Hoshijima.

The evidence of Sticpewich was that after 10 January 1945, work ceased on the airstrip and no further rice was issued from the compound store to the prisoners. The prisoners, over a long period, had saved a small number of bags of rice to cover an emergency. Some they had in their own store and some was held as a credit in the Japanese store at the compound. In January and February 1945, the prisoners drew on their credit, but this provided them with only three ounces per prisoner per day. The Japanese took the balance of their credit to use on the marches. Thereafter, the prisoners used the last of their meagre savings at two ounces per prisoner per day. The Japanese witness, who had worked in the compound Q store, confirmed the evidence of Sticpewich and said, "The POWs in January 1945, in my opinion, were not getting enough rice, taken with other things, to keep them alive." He confirmed that no more rice came out of any Japanese store for the prisoners after February. That which came from the store in February was part of the POWs' credit from the past. The same Japanese witness confirmed that between March and May, the prisoners only had in all five or six meals of fish. The Quartermaster Arai however had said that the ration issued in bulk was sufficient for the prisoners to have fish once or twice a week, and further that, from

January until the April order cutting out rice, the compound still received the prisoners' ration of about eleven ounces of rice per prisoner per day or had authority to draw on their reserves. Thus, from January to April 1945, eleven ounces of rice per prisoner per day was received by Hoshijima for the POWs—in total a very large quantity— but not given to the POWs. This is the key to the Sandakan POW deaths.

Sticpewich, who worked outside the wire and was almost daily around the Japanese quarters, said the Japanese in 1945 still had fish and abundant rice almost every day with food left over after each meal. This was despite the fact that the Japanese ration had been reduced in 1944 and again in 1945. The Japanese were eating the food of the starving prisoners! In any event, having regard to POW numbers—there would have been in the order of 1500 prisoners after the first march left in January—the compound must have accumulated many bags of the prisoners' ration issued to it, but not distributed to the prisoners between January and the end of March.

Sticpewich gave evidence, with confirmations at various points from various Japanese witnesses, of the large amounts of rice stored at the compound in late 1944 and in 1945. The Japanese claimed that rice was stored in one of the areas to protect it against air raids and was not under Hoshijima's direct control. On the evidence of Sticpewich, there were at various times in 1945 about 1000 bags under Hoshijima's house and not less than 1200 bags in all, in several other places. After the bombing of Sandakan started, Hoshijima had moved his residence from the house overlooking the harbour to the greater security of a house at the compound with the protection of a large "POW" sign nearby. In February, when rice was still being issued to the compound for the prisoners, but was not being received by them, Sticpewich saw 900 bags under Hoshijima's house. The Japanese evidence was that Hoshijima had the key to this store and that rice for the prisoners was issued from this store.

At his interrogation, Hoshijima conceded that while he was commandant, some 800 prisoners had died. At the trial, he amended that figure upwards. Asked by the interrogator why so many prisoners died, he said, "First there were no supplies of quinine and other medicines, second the rice change to tapioca was no good for Europeans." Having said no Japanese (at the trial he amended that to one) at the compound had died, and, asked the reason for the difference in the death rate between the guards and the prisoners he replied, "Possibly because the Japanese had medicines and medical treatment." When asked about rice, he referred to an earlier rice cut by HQ in June 1944 and volunteered that he made a special trip to HQ at Jesselton and complained about the shortage of food and medical supplies for prisoners and that he "wanted them to have more solid food." Of course, at that time he was relying on the prisoners as his labour force. He was later to concede he made no such complaint when there was another cut in late 1944 when the work at the airstrip was almost at an end or in April 1945.

The evidence made it clear what must have occurred. The work on the airstrips, which in late 1944 had tapered off, had completely ceased by early January 1945. Thereafter, although the rice ration was still being issued for the prisoners, it was being withheld from them. Feeding the prisoners and the maintenance of their strength and health, were no longer of interest to Hoshijima. The evidence was that in the two years and three months to the end of 1944, only a few prisoners, in the order of one hundred, died, but that from January 1945, the death rate rapidly accelerated and then skyrocketed in March, when 300 died. A great many deaths were due to beriberi, which is notoriously connected with malnutrition and vitamin deficiency.

It was in April, immediately after those March deaths occurred and when, on Hoshijima's admission, many prisoners were bed patients, that HQ cut out rice to the prisoners and Hoshijima not only did not protest, but supported the decision in the way the evidence disclosed. This evidence was set in train by the signed declaration, which I had obtained from Quartermaster Arai, while I was awaiting the arrival of Sticpewich. Arai's statement was that he suggested to HQ that the prisoners' rice ration be cut out, but that before doing so he discussed it with Hoshijima. He recalled that Hoshijima "could not decide for himself" and that "we wired HQ asking if it was alright", and that Hoshijima had said to him that although the substitutes were not as good as rice, "if it was alright with HQ, it was alright for him." Arai conceded that at the time he and Hoshijima discussed cutting out the rice, there was enough rice then in Sandakan to feed all the Japanese there until October 1945 (two months after the war in fact ended).

In his defence, Hoshijima sought to vary what he said at his interrogation by blaming the interpreter. He conceded the interrogator, Captain Russel Brereton (later a NSW Supreme Court Judge), had fairly conducted the interrogation. The weakness of Hoshijima's claim was that he spoke English very well and that in his presence the English translation of what was said was given aloud as it was typed and that he then signed the document and raised no objection. His great ability with Japanese-English translations was demonstrated at his trial by his willingness to object and his constant arguments on translations with the interpreter during my cross-examination.

Blaming the lack of rice for the deaths would be helpful, when he anticipated he could rely on the HQ orders reducing and then cutting out the rice ration. However, it had the completely opposite effect when it was proved that the great rise in deaths preceded the HQ order and was soon after Hoshijima had unofficially completely cut out the prisoners' ration. His defence based on the war situation and HQ orders was gone.

At the trial he did a somersault and said the lack of rice had nothing to do with the deaths. He then sought to blame the shortage of medicines. When asked, he denied knowledge of the cause of beriberi. Questioned by a member of the court about his university qualifications in chemistry, he acknowledged the connection between beriberi and food deficiencies and that his earlier answer had been false. He also conceded that prisoners lost a great deal of weight in 1945. He did not deny some were only five stone.

The case against Hoshijima on the denial of available medicines was equally strong. Dr Taylor, the civilian doctor at Sandakan hospital, gave evidence that just before the war he laid in a store of quinine which would have supplied the whole of British North Borneo for two years. Before his arrest in 1943, he had spoken to Hoshijima and offered to make a supply of quinine available to the prisoners, but Hoshijima refused saying he would get some. Thereafter, Dr Taylor had, until his arrest, surreptitiously sent quinine to the prisoners through the Matthews organisation. Hoshijima denied that Dr Taylor ever made such an offer, but said he had accepted some medicines from him. Later he conceded they went to the Japanese. He claimed this was because their supply had not arrived from Jesselton. He said that after Dr Taylor's arrest, other doctors at the hospital had given him some medicines, but that he had a discretion as to how they were divided between the Japanese and the prisoners.

Sticpewich gave evidence that on at least two occasions, to his knowledge, a substantial number of boxes of Red Cross medical supplies had been received at the compound. On one occasion when he was doing carpentry repairs on the verandah of the Japanese RAP, he saw Red Cross parcels being opened by the Japanese and put into their cupboards and that on this occasion the prisoners received only a few bandages and minor items. Because he could speak Japanese, he was asked by the Japanese in the RAP to translate the directions in English on the labels. He gave evidence that the Japanese guards, earlier and in 1945, were selling quinine to prisoners for possessions such as watches and their reserve money. Hoshijima denied any of these things happened. However, the Japanese from the compound Q store declared that US Red Cross medical cases were opened and used as required by the Japanese and that they were still using them in 1945, and that Hoshijima must have known this.

In his evidence, Hoshijima claimed that the medicines received by him from Jesselton and the Sandakan Hospital were fairly divided by him between the Japanese guards and the prisoners in proportion to their numbers, as were the food rations. This was in the teeth of his explanations of the prisoners' deaths at his interrogation that the disparity of deaths was due to the prisoners not having quinine and other medicines and that the Japanese had not died because they had medicines and medical treatment. Having disclaimed that answer when he gave evidence, the same obvious question still remained—why, if he had treated prisoners and Japanese equally in relation to medicines and food distribution as he claimed, did the prisoners get so thin, and why did over 1000 die while only one Japanese died? There was no answer, but he tried one—the prisoners could not stand up to the tropics as well as the Formosans and Japanese, they worried about being prisoners, and in 1945, grew anxious about the prospect of being released. Owing to this and other similar answers which were against reason and against the evidence of other Japanese, the credibility of Hoshijima, in the end, was nil.

The evidence also disclosed that prisoners were forbidden by Hoshijima from buying food from the natives under threat of severe penalties to both parties. In 1945 when the prisoners were dying of starvation, a delegation from the prisoners' committee, of which Sticpewich was a member, went to Hoshijima and proposed to him that an arrangement be made for the supply of food by the natives. If this were properly organised, the British and Australian Governments, then or after the war, could pay the natives for the food supplied. Hoshijima refused the request. It became clear from some answers in my cross-examination of the civilian Japanese Governor of British North Borneo stationed at Sandakan, that in 1945 the natives were pro-British and that there was some food available from this source. Hoshijima denied any such proposition was put to him. There was no reason for Sticpewich to have invented this evidence.

It also appeared, from evidence which the Japanese, perhaps foolishly led, that in 1945 in other Japanese units at Sandakan, there was a significant number of deaths (but minute compared with prisoner deaths) due to malaria and dysentery. This was so in all units other than the Japanese at the compound, where there was only one death (due to dysentery). This was consistent with the guards being better off than the Japanese elsewhere, having had an abundant supply of food and medicines at the expense of the prisoners. No guard died from malaria and they had quinine to trade to the prisoners, who died in hundreds from malaria. The evidence established each of the three cruelty charges. As I have foreshadowed, I will refer for the most part, in a general way only, to the evidence of brutality given at the trial, although only the details[1] of the evidence can convey its reality and its severity extending as it did over three years, with the result that in the end prisoners were worn out, sick and dispirited.

In the work parties, there was a galley slave system which savagely and relentlessly forced the stronger and the sick alike on never-ending heavy work, often in adverse climatic conditions for long hours. Starving prisoners were caged, beaten and tortured for buying food from natives or stealing it from the store, or taking vegetables from their garden. Sick men were driven to work, both on the aerodrome and in the garden. Cripples were beaten with their crutches to make them work harder. On one occasion, all sick who could walk, doctors, orderlies and cooks, except two or three, were sent to the aerodrome to work, leaving 300 bed patients virtually without attention. Some of the sick had to be assisted there. Hoshijima saw them at the aerodrome. Food cuts for the whole compound were used as punishments for offences committed by one or two prisoners.

There was considerable evidence given by the officers which established that such brutality was operative in the less tense period prior to their removal in 1943. It covered all kinds of particular acts of brutality to individual prisoners, including officers who were often punished for what the men did. It extended to systematic group flogging for the alleged wrongdoing of an individual in the group, such as laziness and sometimes for no given or apparent reason. The evidence was that at times Hoshijima participated in these brutalities, was often present at them, but never interfered or reprimanded a guard. He employed four men as beaters to flog the men with sword sticks and to direct them to work harder and harder at the aerodrome.

For other individual breaches of regulations, whole parties of fifty or sixty would be lined up, made to stand to attention then bashed on the back, face or anywhere else with sticks, hoes, rifle butts or canes. Some were deliberately kicked in the testicles. They then were made to stand looking directly at the sun without hats or shirts, holding their hands, sometimes with weights in them, straight out in front of them. This procedure sometimes lasted for more than an hour. Officers were treated the same.

Two men had their eyes knocked out, one having his eye gouged out by Hoshijima himself. Many men had teeth knocked out or jaws broken. Hoshijima saw many of these beatings and never tried to stop them. In fact, as he admitted, he did a lot of the beating himself. His favourite trick was to make an officer stand to attention and "king hit" him. After knocking him to the ground, the victim would be kicked to his feet. Hoshijima would repeat the performance two or three times.

The case of Corporal Darlington, a cook, is a typical example of Japanese brutality and attitude. He objected to a guard washing his underpants in one of the cooking utensils. The guard beat him and he retaliated, hitting the guard on the lip. Four guards then set on him. He was made to kneel in a most painful position for an hour on a sharp triangular piece of wood with a similar piece behind his knees to prevent him relaxing. In this position he was beaten by the guards with sticks. He was kicked in the crutch. His arm was broken and he was rendered unconscious, bleeding from the head, face, arm and legs. His arms were tied and he was placed in the small cage unconscious. There he remained for forty-eight hours with only a glass of water, his broken arm tied behind his back. Witnesses said he was delirious with pain. Hoshijima admitted he was present, saw it and did nothing to release him until the next day.

Despite the lack of witnesses in respect of 1944–45, Sticpewich was able to give a surprising amount of detailed example evidence, which established a continuation and escalation of the systematic brutality. He saw a great deal of what occurred in and around the compound area, and from some limited visits to the airstrip, several as a relieving member of a work party, he saw sufficient to establish that the earlier pattern of beatings there continued. Sticpewich, although on good terms with the Japanese, was himself bashed in the face and had a tooth knocked out because some carpentry he did for a Japanese was considered not to have had the proper authorisation. His evidence revealed numerous injuries from bashings at times with rifle butts. These included broken limbs, lost eyes and loss of hearing in an ear.

A punishment cage was built at the compound in 1942. It was 4 feet 6 inches by 5 feet 6 inches and about 4 feet 6 inches high. Men could not stand up and could not lie down properly at night. The floor was bare boards and the walls were two inch sticks two inches apart. It was exposed to the weather and mosquitoes. To get into it, the prisoners had to crawl. In this cage terms ranged from a few days up to thirty days. A larger cage was built later and some persons were sentenced to long terms and served most of their time in there. The evidence referred to twenty specific cases of confinement in the small cage, but there were many others. The POWs had no blankets and wore only lap-laps. They were given no food for anything up to the first seven days and then only limited food. They were made to sit directly to attention all day, being taken out and beaten if they relaxed. They were allowed to go to the latrines only twice a day and had to urinate through the bars. They were taken out twice a day for exercise, which consisted of "push-ups" and being beaten with sword sticks when they could not raise themselves. Often men had to be carried back to their cage. Sick men and men with hands tied behind their backs were put in the cage. On one occasion there were seven in this tiny cage for four days. One man actually died in the cage as a result of his treatment. His weight fell from twelve to six stone in fifteen days. He did not die from disease. He was put in the cage on Hoshijima's order. Two others were taken out to die and did die within a day or two of release. In all, about fifteen died because of this treatment or at least their deaths were considerably accelerated by it.

Much of what Sticpewich said of the cage treatment was confirmed by the declaration of a Japanese guard. One cage was near a swamp where there were "millions" of mosquitoes. Prisoners were not allowed to have their mosquito net when in the cage.

Hoshijima, after caging a number of prisoners for getting into the vegetable garden at night, called a parade and warned that the next prisoner who did so would be shot. A few weeks later a prisoner who was found there was shot at short range and killed. Hoshijima further admitted most were sentenced to the cage by him and that there was no trial.

The case of a borrowed light globe indicates the typical attitude of the Japanese to regulations and to the welfare of prisoners. An Australian medical officer, Captain Piconi, had occasion during the night to perform an abdominal operation for a burst ulcer which suddenly became urgent. For adequate light he borrowed a powerful globe from the guard house within the compound. The patient had been injected and Piconi was about to begin the operation, when he was seized for firstly taking the globe without permission, and secondly for failing to obtain prior permission to perform the operation from Hoshijima, who at that time lived away from the compound. He was beaten and made to stand with outstretched arms for some hours, while the patient waited.

After the case on the denial of food and medicines had obviously gone against Hoshijima, his original defence at interrogation was not applicable. However, he struggled on with inconsistent and unbelievable explanations as to why so many prisoners fell sick and died, and he fought doggedly on every issue and scrap of evidence. He often took the defence out of the defending officers' hands and made long speeches, very often not in answer to questions. He spoke at length about Japanese history. He referred to the great Japanese victory against Russia when the Russian fleet was sunk and the Russian sailors were rescued and given rest in hot springs and later repatriated. When the Japanese prisoners were returned to Japan, they were ordered to commit hara-kiri, which they did. He instanced this as showing the Japanese attitude to prisoners of war, but hastened to say that this was not his own attitude and that he did not believe in hara-kiri. He, of course, was alive. This was in contrast with Colonel Suga, the officer stationed at Kuching, but in charge of all prison camps in Borneo, who committed suicide at Labuan. Hoshijima, at one stage of the trial, was able conveniently to say that if any Japanese was responsible for what happened at Sandakan, it was Colonel Suga. But the case against Hoshijima was that what he did was of his own volition and that there were no relevant superior orders; whatever he said about Japanese history was irrelevant.

In the course of my cross-examination of him, he had constant long arguments with the interpreter as to the correct interpretation into Japanese of my questions and the correct interpretation of his answers in Japanese into English. He had elected, as was his right, to give his evidence in Japanese, despite an ability with English sufficient to enable him to have these debates. Of course, his continual arguments distracted the cross-examination and gave him more time to answer questions. In a trial which took about nine hearing days, his evidence took four and a half days, only one day of which was on cross-examination, including his arguments on interpretation.

Subject to minor concessions in cross-examination, he denied most of the allegations of brutality, even those the subject of multiple evidence on the 1942–43 period and even although he had made some admissions and an apology about some of these matters during his interrogation. However, he did concede that he ordered the building of the cages, that he ordered Australians to be caged and that at times the guards beat Australian prisoners. While he admitted that at times he hit Australian prisoners, he said this was only with a single blow with his open hand. He denied any prisoner had been injured or lost an eye. He explained that the punishment of prisoners in the cage and the hitting by guards (whom he admitted he never reprimanded) and by himself was only as a last resort, after the prisoner concerned had been warned many times. He said no British prisoners were punished because they were very good and obeyed regulations. The 750 British were in a separate compound and there were no British witnesses to say otherwise because they were all dead.

He agreed that one prisoner had died in the cage, but said this was from a sudden attack of malaria. Earlier, he had defended his decision to prohibit men in the cage having the mosquito nets, by saying the regulations did not prohibit what he did, the men were being punished and anyhow there were no mosquitoes. One explanation he had given for the many deaths was the absence of quinine.

Near the end of the trial, Hoshijima applied for an adjournment on the ground he was not well due to an attack of malaria. After examination by a doctor, the trial was adjourned for two days. As I recorded in my diary on 16 January:

> Just at this stage, Hoshijima had a sudden turn of malaria—the Court adjourned—surely irony when this is the man who denied medicines to POWs dying of malaria at 6 to 7 a day. I am sure the way the Court referred to the adjournment must have hit something in the Japanese defending officers.

Hoshijima spent considerable time in repeating in general terms how kind he was to prisoners and how he told his guards to be kind to prisoners and not punish them except as a last resort. In the context of the evidence and the objective facts, such evidence could impress no one and only served to destroy his credibility as a witness. During the work at the aerodrome, Hoshijima rode on a white stallion known to the prisoners as "Hossie's horse" to supervise the work there. At the trial, he heaped praise on himself for killing even his beloved horse to help feed the prisoners. However, the evidence of Sticpewich was that when the work at the aerodrome ceased, the horse was no longer needed and was left tied up and became thin, as did the prisoners when no longer required for work. When the horse was killed, the prisoners only got the head, feet and entrails with the heart and liver removed.

The defence called a large number of witnesses, some in high positions. The Japanese apparently had high regard for Hoshijima and concentrated more fire power on his defence than on any other trial at Labuan. However, amongst the parade of witnesses there were some who, in their signed declarations or interrogations, had earlier implicated Hoshijima in some respects in relation to ill-treatment and of some prisoners being put in cages and denied food. The stock answer in almost all of such cases was they did not really know the things which they had said. When pressed, they said they must have imagined them.

Some high ranking persons were called to give evidence of shortages in Sandakan or that Hoshijima was not involved in the decision to take prisoners to Ranau, and had suggested removal to a closer place. As the case made against Hoshijima was of withholding supplies given or available to him and, as the prosecution accepted that the orders for the marches were given by HQ and did not allege Hoshijima was responsible for the orders or the marches, this class of evidence did not answer the prosecution's case.

These witnesses included the Japanese civilian Governor of British North Borneo, Kumabe Tanuki, stationed at Sandakan. They also included Colonel Takayama Hikoichi, a staff officer on General Baba's HQ at Jesselton. Their evidence in fact worked against the Japanese. The former Governor, as did other witnesses, agreed that in 1945, the natives were pro-British and had some available food, a matter relevant to the prisoners' proposal to Hoshijima to save them from starvation.

I described the entry of the Japanese Governor as "an old bald man with a long white beard. He bowed from the hips three times as he entered the Court." I made a sketch of him in my diary. There must have been something in the demeanour of this old man, who had held such high office in Borneo and had earlier been Japanese ambassador to Iran and earlier Spain, for under his sketch I wrote, "Now very humbled, but I think inwardly full of hate."

The evidence of Colonel Takayama, not relevant to the charge against Hoshijima, opened up other questions. His evidence was that he had gone to Sandakan to see the condition of the prisoners and that Hoshijima had said they were not fit to march to Ranau and had suggested a closer destination. My diary entry described what then occurred:

> He at once put himself in a bad position, for two or three weeks after this, the sick men were ordered to go on the march on which so many died. Either he was responsible for not telling H.Q. of the condition of the POWs as was his duty or somebody at H.Q. knowing their condition was responsible for ordering the march. After much quibbling he said the decision to order the march was made by Gen. Baba and that he talked to him about the condition of the POWs first. He sweated terribly as he was forced to put himself or the General in. He then said he didn't tell Baba the POWs were too sick to go. Up till now all the Japs have been most careful not to incriminate the General. No doubt the Colonel will not be popular tonight.

Even at this stage of the trials, I was concerning myself with questions of ultimate responsibility for what occurred to the Sandakan prisoners, for I then added:

> I don't know the future of Baba and his staff officer, but on the U.S. principle applied in the Philippines with the General there—General Baba is responsible for acts of his officers and troops, if his attitude of non-inquiry and non-concern for the POWs amounted to acquiescence in the crimes or criminal neglect of his duty. In addition there is gradually mounting little pieces of evidence that he was directly involved.

When the evidence finished, Colonel Yamada and then Hoshijima at length addressed the court repeating some of his earlier evidence and making some additions. One addition was remarkable. He referred to Captain Cook, the senior POW officer in 1944–45, and to an alleged conversation between them in English:

> Just prior to my leaving Sandakan, both of us had a farewell

> dinner, in which afterwards we agreed to maintain our friendship in future. We exchanged our home addresses. Captain Cook also said, as this was the last chance, "Do you know what your nickname is?" I told him I did not. He told me my nickname was "Trump". I asked him whether he was talking about cards. He told me that was not the meaning, but the real meaning was that I was good and a man of righteousness. I remember that this was on the night of 22nd May [1945].

Captain Cook was not available to give his version of a farewell at a dinner if there was one. On 29 May, a week later, Cook left Sandakan on the second death march and was murdered by the Japanese just before or just after the war ended. Hoshijima was not a party to the murder, but the absence of Cook, the officer in charge of the prisoners, was convenient, as was the absence through suicide of Colonel Suga.

The court found Hoshijima guilty on all four charges and sentenced him to death by hanging. As the sentence was passed, Hoshijima stood as he had done when charged, without sign of emotion. He saluted, clicked the heels of his still highly polished boots, made a precise about-turn and was marched away.

The sentence was confirmed and, on the warrant of General Sturdee, he was hanged at Rabaul on 6 April 1946. He was defiant to the end. It was reported that, as his arms were about to be pinioned, he sunk his teeth into the hand of the provost and drew blood. As the provost released the trap, he said, "This is for the Aussies you killed at Sandakan."

6

THE FIRST DEATH MARCH TRIALS

Problems even greater than those at Hoshijima's trial arose at the trial concerning the first death march from Sandakan to Ranau, owing to lack of witnesses and admission evidence of what had occurred. There were only two prisoners from this march alive to give evidence. As the prisoners were separated into nine groups, eight of fifty and one of seventy, there was no prisoner who could give any direct evidence of anything which occurred in seven of the groups. As prisoners were forced to keep moving in single file, what either of the two survivors could say, even about his own group and what happened to those of the group lagging behind, was limited. He could say little of what occurred to those who dropped out and whether they were shot or died of illness and, if shots were heard, who was responsible. An additional problem was that they were not well enough to be brought back to Borneo to give oral evidence. Their evidence was given by short sworn declarations.

Eleven Japanese, four captains, five lieutenants, a warrant officer and a sergeant, involved in the march, were tried together. Each of the eight officers was in charge of a group, and the warrant officer was second in charge of a group in which the officer in charge had later died from causes unconnected with the march. The ninth officer, Captain Yamamoto, was in charge of the whole march and moved ahead of the first group. The sergeant and the warrant officer were charged because there was some evidence of their involvement in the shooting of prisoners. Proof of the case against each of the accused, other than the leader of the march, Yamamoto, was difficult because the criminal responsibility of each turned on what could be proved to have occurred in the group under his command.

There were two alternate charges against each of the accused. The first was the murder of numerous unknown prisoners of war in their charge. The second and alternate charge was compelling prisoners of war "in their charge to march on long forced marches under difficult conditions and when sick and underfed, as a result whereof many died" (the "forced march" charge).

The evidence in support of the murder charge was very limited. There was specific admission evidence of the shooting of prisoners in the last group, which implicated the officer in charge of the group (Captain Abe), the sergeant and Yamamoto. There was some evidence from one survivor (Botterill) who in an earlier group witnessed the shooting of six prisoners on the trail when they could not go on. He said he saw the "sergeant major" shoot four of them. This was taken to be the warrant officer. Botterill and the other survivor (Moxham) each gave evidence of men falling behind, never being seen again and of shots heard to the rear. The latter evidence was not sufficient to provide the proof of murder by the officer in charge of the group needed in a criminal trial. The case which could be pressed against seven of the officers charged was only the "forced march" charge. The resulting deaths made this in effect a homicide charge.

The specific evidence of the killing of prisoners in the last group, which implicated three of the accused, became available somewhat accidentally. The seventy prisoners in this group were British. None survived the end of the war. The Japanese officers in charge of all the groups, other than this one, were members of the same unit, the commanding officer of which was Yamamoto. They had been together in that unit for a long time, extending back to combat service in China. At all times, at the interrogations and at the trial, they presented a uniform account, which included that no prisoners were shot and that they all died of illnesses. However, Abe, in charge of the last group, was from a different unit. In his interrogation, he said that before the march commenced, Yamamoto gave him an order to kill any prisoners who were too ill to travel or when "there was no other course available", and that Yamamoto also said he expected many to die on the march and that he would take responsibility for killing the prisoners.

At his interrogation, Yamamoto, no doubt dismayed by these disclosures, conceded that he gave Abe these orders. He added that Abe was not one of "my men" and that "if he had been one of my own company commanders, I would never have given the orders to kill POWs, as I would not subject my own men to such a responsibility." He added: "I pitied Abe in having to carry out the orders." He denied any such order was given to his officers, but said, "I instructed my own men that under no circumstances should any POW be left behind at a rest house. No matter how sick a POW, he was to be brought on." In the end there were admissions by other accused in the last group that some prisoners in that group were shot.

In addition to the assertions by the officers in all the other groups that no prisoner was shot, they said, and uniformly repeated at the trial, that when such prisoners were unable to go on they were helped along by the Japanese to the rest houses where they died and were buried. The evidence of the two survivors, despite its limitation for other purposes, gave the lie to the universality of the Japanese claim. Their evidence of men falling out and not being seen again, of some shootings on the trail and shots being heard and of bodies from earlier groups being strewn along the trail, pointed to the uniform story being a conspiratorial lie. The survivor in the seventh group saw many bodies along the trail and smelt others. Sticpewich coming on the same trail in the second march some months later, counted the remains of some thirty-five bodies and identified Australian uniforms along the trail. They could only have been from the first march. Prisoners were not allowed to go near bodies and could not say how men died and whether they had been shot.

Although not sufficient to provide proof against a specific Japanese in a criminal trial, the evidence of the two survivors supported by a great deal of circumstantial material and what some of the survivors of the march, who later died, told Sticpewich at Ranau, leaves little doubt from a historical point of view that the general pattern of the march was that if men could not go on, they were shot along the trail. This view is supported by the admissions of Yamamoto in respect of the last group. It is hardly likely, particularly in view of the evidence of each of Botterill and Moxham of the shootings in their groups which were under the control of officers of Yamamoto's unit, that the order to kill (which he admitted he gave to Abe even before the march) was not also given to the other officers who admittedly were told that no prisoner must be left behind, whatever his condition.

The case on the alternate charge of forced marching of sick and underfed prisoners causing many deaths, was that day after day each group continued the march at a high speed, with which the prisoners in their condition obviously could not cope, and that the sick and dying were not allowed to stop, and eventually could go no further and died. This case was clearly made out. Its proof against officers individually was unwittingly aided by written statements produced by each at the trial setting out the daily progress of his group.

The Japanese defence was a combination of military necessity and superior orders. This was that a deterioration in the war situation required that the Japanese combat unit urgently move to Jesselton and that the prisoners be moved to Ranau; that Sandakan was cut off and the evacuation had to be overland through the jungle; that the unit commander and individual group leaders had been ordered to get to Jesselton quickly; that the POWs fell sick on the way and that the Japanese helped them to the next rest house, where they died and were buried. However, the prosecution did not seek to blame the accused officers for the decision to move the prisoners, or for the route selected. Responsibility lay elsewhere and possibly on General Baba, who was later tried at Rabaul. Yamamoto and his group leaders did not select the prisoners, did not equip them or arrange the food supply. They received the prisoners from Hoshijima on the road outside the compound. Another unit had the responsibility to provide food for the Japanese and prisoners at various points of the journey. The prosecution case simply was that each accused officer bore the responsibility for the manner in which the march of the group under his control was conducted and that the speed and conduct of it caused a succession of deaths spread over many days, the sick being forced to go on until they died. Group leaders could see quite clearly that their conduct of the march was killing prisoners and would kill more, but relentlessly continued the march without pause. In the end, the objective facts established this case beyond doubt. The case then turned to the need to march and to continue it in this way, which the Japanese claimed was ordered or was unavoidable.

In line with their defence on the grounds of military necessity and superior orders, the Japanese sought to lay responsibility for the speed of the march, and the subsequent deaths, on HQ for ordering the march and on Yamamoto and his orders to group commanders. However, assuming there were orders which required them to march and continue it at a speed obviously causing many deaths, the legal question would arise whether, at a war crime trial, superior orders could excuse a forced march obviously causing death, any more than they could justify shooting prisoners because they were delaying the unit getting to Jesselton urgently and in the time ordered. As prosecutor, I was anxious to avoid the case of guilt and any sentence having to rest on the legal question, particularly because the Japanese attitude to superior orders was more rigid than ours. In this and other trials, I sought to meet defences on the facts. It would be difficult to justify internationally any severe penalty based on a finding that a defence, based on superior orders or military necessity, was not open legally.

However, the legal question did not arise and the decision given by the court did not depend on it, because on no view of any of the evidence were there orders which required the unit or group commanders to march at the speed and manner which they all did, as already described. On no view of the evidence were there orders which deprived group commanders of a discretion to decide how far to march each day or whether to delay the march to save the sick from dying from its speed. The defence of urgency and orders concerning it failed on the facts. There was no real urgency and no order which required any officer to move at the speed he did. On their own claims, no order went that far and in any event, such claims concerning urgency as were made could not but fail to be rejected for a number of reasons.

Any supposed orders as to urgency would have been given in Yamamoto's general briefing of the officers of his unit before the march started as Yamamoto moved off in the first group. The original versions given by these officers as to what Yamamoto said varied, but it was clear there was no time fixed for arrival of the prisoners at Ranau or the unit at Jesselton. Of the versions given, the most likely version was that the unit briefing was to leave no prisoner behind and to get to Jesselton as soon as possible.

Yamamoto himself received no specific superior orders as to the speed of the march or the required time of arrival, and no Japanese claimed that he was given an order which required him to arrive at Ranau within a specified time. The most that was claimed was that there was some type of expectation that groups would take no longer than twenty-one days to get to Ranau. The problem for the Japanese was that the record showed, and they admitted, that all reached Ranau (or Paginatan just short of Ranau) in much shorter times, many in about fifteen days. Yamamoto conceded that although the march was supposed to be a quick one, each group leader had a discretion as to how far he marched each day and as to whether he delayed his march at any point, but that each was told to leave no prisoner behind.

However, it was the objective facts admitted by the Japanese, which showed there really was no urgency in the march and certainly none which could justify the admitted rates of marching, which in most groups was day after day eight, nine, ten, eleven and twelve miles a day over the mountain trails, while prisoners died every day.

These objective facts were many. Just under a week elapsed after the HQ order was received before the march began, and the march then set off in small groups, some a day apart, so some did not start for six days after the first. One group was able to pause for a day and the last four groups stopped at Paginatan (twenty-three miles short of Ranau) for some weeks. Many prisoners died there on arrival. There was no reference to or permission from HQ. Some of the Japanese remained with the prisoners while others in the unit continued the march without them to Ranau and then Jesselton. The claims of urgency were only for the Japanese unit to get to Jesselton and not for the prisoners to get to Ranau, yet it took Yamamoto eighteen days to go from Ranau to Jesselton, which is no more than half the distance of Sandakan to Ranau, while it took the first group (his) only fifteen days to get to Ranau with sick and dying prisoners, other groups taking from fifteen to seventeen days. The Japanese who stayed behind with the prisoners at Paginatan were able to go from Ranau to Jesselton in nine days—half the time taken by Yamamoto, although he claimed he was required urgently at Jesselton!

The claims concerning urgency and superior orders having failed on the facts, there remained the questions of proof of what occurred in each group and the proof of each individual officer's guilt in committing acts of inhumanity which could be considered as war crimes.

Such proof, based on the circumstances of the march of each group, was provided by nine charts, one made by each group leader and tendered in the course of his defence. Each chart set out particulars of each day's march, including the starting and finishing point, the number of miles travelled, the number of prisoners who died each day and the sicknesses causing particular deaths, and comments as to the food and medicines supplied on particular days. The uniform claim in their evidence, with support from the charts, now was that there was a sufficient ration issued to the prisoners.

In their interrogations, there were conflicting claims by some of food shortages. It seems the uniform claim at the trial, for some an about-turn, was that it was not "underfed" prisoners, as the charge alleged, who were compelled to go at the speeds which the Japanese had to admit. Of course, what the Japanese said at the trial removed any possibility of an argument that groups dare not delay unless all died for lack of food. Where there was survivor evidence, it was that the prisoners were starving due to the little food they were given and that they ate frogs, snails and other things from the jungle, while the Japanese had plenty to eat. It was a repeat of Sandakan. The ration for all was light and the Japanese took a share which left little for the prisoners.

By these charts, the Japanese unwittingly put the case against each leader individually beyond doubt. Typical of the charts was one which showed distances travelled on successive days, on the mountain section of the trail, as nine, eight, eleven, eleven, twelve, twelve miles and that on each of these days one, two or three prisoners died. The same chart said, "Rained cats and dogs every day without exception—road was very bad." The charts had been translated into English by the Japanese. The charts were a cross-examiner's dream. People do not die at an instant from beriberi, dysentery or malaria. Why no pause on a single day? Why go twelve miles in one day over this terrain with the dying? The answer which was uniform was that the Japanese were very kind to the prisoners, and when they fell sick they helped them along to the next stop where the prisoners unfortunately died and were buried. But why then go twelve miles the next day with other prisoners similarly sick? What appeared in the charts was put against many statements in earlier interrogations such as, "Each morning . . . I took POWs with me regardless of whether they were fit enough to travel or not" and "Any that did not die during the night-time had to go on next day regardless of the condition of the men." "All I required of them was that they should reach the night staging area . . . POWs had to travel regardless of how sick they were."

The Japanese approach to these and many other

admissions made in the interrogations was to dismiss them and, in effect, say, "I now want to tell what occurred." There was now an almost universal statement, not earlier mentioned, that before leaving they had been told there was a delicate international situation and that they were to be kind to the prisoners and when they fell sick they were to help them along to the next resting point. This was, as it were, the official version on an official occasion—the trial.

The uniform Japanese claim that concern and kindness were shown for the sick prisoners and that none of them was shot was in conflict with the evidence of the two survivors in respect of their groups and Japanese admissions in respect of the last group. There was no direct evidence to rebut what the Japanese said in respect of the other groups, but the evidence of what happened in three groups and the uniform evidence of the Japanese of what happened in nine groups, pointed to it being a concocted unit lie. Objective evidence supported this view. This was the evidence of bodies strewn along the trail instead of buried at rest houses. Further, there appeared to be no logic for the admitted order to shoot to have been confined to the last group, while each other group leader was ordered not to leave any of his prisoners behind.

Yamada and I then addressed. Yamada made a most able address, a great deal of it on generalities, while I was obliged to put together the detail of the evidence against each accused. Yamada referred to the charges as only of "suspected murder and ill-treatment" and referred to the alternative nature of the charges as "several nets ingeniously installed in order to fish them [the accused]." I recorded in my diary notes of 28 January 1946 the generalities he used that day to state the defence. He said:

> It is beyond reasonable doubt that 37 Japanese army H.Q. was necessitated at least from the point of view of war operation to remove forces from East Coast to West in order to meet with the sudden deterioration of war phase around North Borneo as a result of the U.S.A. landing forces at Leyte

> Island . . . Yamamoto received a telegram order . . . to take his unit as quickly as possible. Consequently it cannot be denied that from the beginning that move was doomed to become a quick march unlike ordinary marching . . . As it was impossible to separate POW, if he wished to accomplish his duty to escort POW, he had to come to the conclusion that the POW were also bound with the nature of the order from Army H.Q. . . . As there was no time to wait until the rainy season will be over and as there is no better route to choose in such a deep jungle land of Borneo, Captain Yamamoto was put from the beginning in a position to accomplish the most arduous march under very difficult conditions. Consequently there was no alternative for him but to make up his mind to accomplish his duty in spite of the great handicaps of season and natural conditions which influenced considerably upon his undertaking.

He concluded:

> I should like to say that it [the deaths] was a tragic product of this war which took place in the wild jungle land of Borneo. Nobody can be blamed for this inevitable disaster which was beyond the control of human beings. It is a filthy line of black pages of this great war, which we must never repeat over again. I do expect that this darkest adventure during this war will give the lesson to all human beings to check the war in the longest time to come. I pray the court would confer the fairest and most reasonable judgement on these 11 accused persons.

When the court adjourned and we waited for its decision, Yamada and I talked in a friendly fashion, much as counsel in Australia do when a jury is "out". I complimented Yamada on his able address, as indeed it was, and he returned the compliment saying, "You have a very methodical brain", no doubt referring to my analysis of the facts. As I noted in my diary for that day:

> Col. Yamada in the course of the case looked 8 or 10 years older—a deep worried furrow constantly on his brow in the

> last few days. I think he appreciated the case was going against him and from the Japanese reverence for the Japanese officer, this was the most vital case of all—9 officers as against 2 [not officers], the most in any case. He told me today he only had 1½ hours sleep the night before.

The reference in my diary to Japanese attitudes to officers as against the non-officer group was perhaps provoked by Yamada's question to me as to why a private, whom the evidence showed was involved in the killing incident in the last group, had not been charged. I put his question back to him, "Do you think he should be charged?" He laughed and said, "The others wonder why he isn't in it with them too. He was present when the POWs were killed and he did leave sick POWs behind without food." I said, "Maybe we will charge him yet—it is best not to try him with the officers." He replied, "I think you have been very humane to him."

Later in the same conversation, while also referring to the Hoshijima trial, he enlarged on his earlier compliment and said that all the records of the proceedings would go home to Japan and that "your name will go down in history forever." I said, "Do you mean I will be a war criminal next war?" He laughed and said, "Of course not and there must never be any more war."

We talked of political attitudes in Japan and Australia. He asked me many questions about the Labor Party then in government and about its social attitudes. I felt he was interested to know the Government's likely attitude to capital punishment in relation to war crimes, but was not prepared to ask me directly.

I asked him about militarism in Japan, as I was interested to know whether he was really against the military caste in Japan, as his remarks in his capacity of counsel suggested. I had heard that although he had military rank, his work in the legal field in Borneo during the war was rather that of a civilian, that he was wealthy and contemplated trying to enter parliament as a member for the Hiroshima district, where he had once lived. I asked whether the bulk of the ordinary

Japanese people and the businessmen had in fact wanted or accepted war as necessary for Japanese expansion, or were they talked into it by the militarists. He did not give me a direct answer, but said Japan made a terrible mistake in letting the militarists get control and that the militarists were responsible for Japan's position "today", that war was a terrible thing and benefits nobody, even the side which wins, and that Japan had grown up too quickly without educating the lower stratum of her people.

We talked about our own activities during the war. He told me that at one time he was the chief legal officer at Kuching. I gently raised the matter of the trial and execution of Captain Matthews there. I wondered why no report of his execution as required by international law was given. He said, "The position in Kuching was very unfortunate and very difficult to get the military to do anything." He seemed uneasy and changed the subject. I did not pursue it further, although I thought he knew a great deal about the "Sandakan Incident" and the trial.

He raised the question of the menace of Russia and expressed the opinion that the USA and Russia were likely to come to blows. I said I thought Russia was all right, but was misunderstood. His view was more perceptive and mature than mine, as the missile crisis in Cuba, the cold war confrontation in Europe, Berlin, Hungary, Afghanistan, the confrontations in Vietnam and Africa were to prove.

He told me how beautiful his country was and said I should visit Japan. On another occasion, when we talked, he suggested I should visit him and be his guest. We were on friendly enough terms for me to chide him about the case, as counsel in Australia sometimes do in an adjournment. Having in mind the Japanese evidence that all prisoners who died were buried usually at a rest house, I said, "There is one mystery for me—how did all those skeletons that Sticpewich saw get there?" He replied, "You put it best in your opening address when you referred to the 'wall of silence' and that what occurred will be hidden forever in the deep jungles of Borneo."

The court returned. It found four, including Yamamoto, guilty of murder and the other seven guilty on the alternate charge. Asked if they wished to say anything before sentence was passed, Yamamoto and six others made short statements.

Yamamoto spoke earnestly about the officers who had been under his command in a combat unit for many years, including a period in action in China. It must have been a tragic occasion for him being drawn into a situaion which he had not sought, when the war he had actively fought for some years went against his country. He had led his officers on a march and in consequence they were now all awaiting sentence, possibly of death. He used the occasion to refer to the differing personalities of his men, much as any officer might do in respect of those who had shared an officers' mess over years of association and combat. As he did, I felt sorry for these young officers. Most of them were university graduates thrown into the war. They were pleasant fresh faced men who stood in contrast with the evil faced Hoshijima. Yamamoto described each—one was quiet and reserved; another always took the initiative; another stammered (we had nicknamed him "Stuttering Sam") and was very reserved and would himself do what was ordered, rather than delegating it to his sergeants; another was like a "cut bamboo shoot"—very sharp and so on.

Each of the other six officers spoke on a pattern set by the first. Most said they "loved" and were sorry for the prisoners and each referred to some isolated incident indicative of his kindness to or friendship with a prisoner. The use of the word "love" may have been due to a translation problem due to different concepts concerning this emotion. Thus, one said that after the first day's march, he caught a fowl and dined on it with a POW and another Japanese, and the POW said he had never tasted anything so delicious. Then on the night they reached Ranau (with less than twenty POWs), the three again dined together and the POW said, "It's a funny thing, the first meal we had together was fowl and the last is tapioca." Another Japanese officer said he was sorry for the POWs so he decided one night to try to give them a "treat" and get them "a" fowl. He went all through the jungle, but came to a stream which he couldn't cross, so he had to come back without the fowl. As he put it, "My eyes were filled with tears." One officer, to demonstrate his friendship with one POW, a medical sergeant, related at length his talks with the sergeant. He said they often talked together in English and that one day talking about the English language, he asked the sergeant what was the longest word in the English language. The sergeant thought of long medical words, then the Japanese officer replied the longest word was "smiles", because there was a mile between the two s's.

The six who spoke made no statements about the march or concerning the POWs who died, or of the predicament of himself or about his family. I found the speeches puzzling, particularly that of the Japanese who told the story about "smiles" at great length, when he was obviously facing a possible death sentence.

It is not unlikely that there were some instances where the Japanese acted kindly to some prisoners, for I came to see that it was not uncharacteristic of individual Japanese to have changing, and by our standards, contradictory attitudes. However these acts of kindness or sympathy, sometimes genuine and sometimes not, invariably followed or were followed by utter brutality or inhuman disregard of the life or limb of prisoners. Then afterwards the token incident of kindness would be seen by the Japanese concerned or asserted by him to demonstrate his general kindness. The brutality or inhumanity would be ignored or treated as if it did not exist, or as irrelevant to his real attitude, because it had been done in the course of his duty or in accordance with what he saw as the policy of his superiors.

The court returned late in the evening and sentenced all accused to death, except one officer who was sentenced to life imprisonment. It was 28 January 1946. The decisions given on this and other trials were subject to the supervisory process which required confirmation of the verdicts and sentences by army HQ acting independently of the court martial and on army legal advice. The army confirming authority agreed that the murder convictions were supported by the evidence, but because of conflicting advices concerning whether the evidence supported the forced march convictions, the authority did not confirm any of the convictions or sentences, but directed a re-trial of all the accused to be held at Rabaul when the two surviving prisoners of war were well enough and could be brought there from Australia to give oral evidence in lieu of the written declaration given by them at the Labuan trial.

The new trial was heard at Rabaul in May 1946. A new defence based on a new Japanese version of the facts was introduced, possibly under the influence of the view expressed in one of the advices that he who ordered the march was the one responsible. As my analysis of the evidence showed, the forced march charges were clearly proved. Japanese HQ was now asserted, by this new claim, to have laid down an exact daily programme for the march which group officers were bound to obey. The new claim and new evidence was positively false and an invention, as the prosecution stated. What was now said in evidence, somewhat uniformly, had not been earlier said and was in the teeth of what had been said in answer to interrogations and at the first trial. The reply to the earlier versions was the now well worn response, such as "I now want to say what happened", or the variation, "At my interrogation I said—so and so—I want that deleted." The prosecution submitted that "the evidence showed, far from acting humanely within their orders, the group leaders deliberately drove POWs onward knowing they would die." What was said at the second trial was also inconsistent with the content of the daily progress of the march as set out in the sheets tendered by each group leader at the first trial. The individual differences in the progress of the march in different groups was quite inconsistent with some binding daily progress plan issued from HQ to all in the groups.

The seven group leader officers were again convicted of the forced march charge and on the advice of the Judge Advocate General, Colonel W. B. Simpson, that there was "ample" evidence to support the decision, these convictions were confirmed. The prosecution evidence at each trial in substance was the same.

Yamamoto and Abe were each again convicted of murder and these convictions were confirmed. The two other accused, the warrant officer and the sergeant, were acquitted. This was because it now appeared that the evidence was not sufficient to establish their guilt beyond reasonable doubt. At the first trial, Botterill, by his written statement, had identified warrant officer Gotanda only by his rank, as the one he saw shoot four prisoners. At the second trial, when he saw Gotanda, he did not identify him as the culprit, but said a corporal shot the prisoners. He also referred to an act of kindness by the man he identified. However, he did identify Gotanda, who disputed it, as the Japanese who went back to two straggling prisoners and returned with only one. This prisoner later died, but at the time told Botterill that Gotanda had shot the other sick prisoner. Although what Botterill had been told by the dead man was admissible under the War Crimes Act, it left a doubt and Gotanda was acquitted, correctly.

What happened at the first trial illustrates the great dangers which lawyers know lurk in the proof of disputed identity, such as when it depends on the office of the person charged. This same danger is likely to exist and indeed be extreme in any of the pending trials of war crimes in Australia, where an identity issue has to be determined after forty years. As a lawyer with minimal experience in 1946, I failed to advert to the weakness of endeavouring to establish the identity of Gotanda without Botterill seeing the accused man. My later experience as a judge in the criminal field tells me that the reviewing officers, the first court martial and I were all wrong, as became apparent when Botterill was called to give evidence personally at the second court martial and after seeing Gotanda. The case against the other Japanese, a sergeant, depended on the disputed but probably correct evidence of another Japanese, that the sergeant had ordered a shooting. He was also given the benefit of the doubt and acquitted.

At the second trial, Yamamoto and Abe were again sentenced to death by hanging. Each of the other seven officers, convicted on the forced march charge, were sentenced to imprisonment for ten years.

The confirmation process, appellate or supervisory in nature, resulting in the new trial, reached a decision which I believe was the proper one. Two errors and therefore injustices were corrected and sentences which, on a comparative basis were more just, were imposed on the seven. The officers were thrown into a situation not of their choosing, they were not found to be guilty of any shooting; they were found guilty of less criminal conduct than that of Hoshijima or the General who ordered the marches.

I have referred in some detail to what happened, because it illustrates two things which are important when I come to discuss war trials generally. The first is that even with courts trying to do their best, some errors will occur, particularly where, as in war trials, most of the witnesses are dead. The second is that there was an appellate, new trial process available to adjust errors and that these processes were exercised in relation to the court martial trials, with true judicial independence, conscientiously applying the standards of proof required to determine the guilt of Japanese, former enemies who had destroyed most of the witnesses.

There is a compelling inference but not proof to the criminal standard against individual Japanese, that in each of the nine groups the POWs who could not go on were shot, and that Yamamoto's order to all that no prisoners were to be left behind meant they were to be shot. Although only two were found guilty of shooting POWs, the verdict of history should be that it was truly a death march of all nine groups. The evidence in this trial and in many others, shows that there were many Japanese who committed atrocities, including killing prisoners, who were never tried or convicted and who were let go free because no witnesses to what occurred survived. Convictions for killing of prisoners on the first march and, as will be seen, on the second march and, at the end, at Ranau, depended on chance admissions by the Japanese.

The deliberate killing of the Sandakan prisoners, so that in the end there would be no witnesses, did not entirely succeed, but it did save many Japanese from prosecution or conviction and execution.

Yamamoto and Abe were executed by hanging at Rabaul on 19 October 1946.

7

THE TRIALS OF TWO CAPTAINS AND A GENERAL —THE SECOND DEATH MARCH

The trial of Captains Takakuwa Takuo and Watanabe Genzo, the officers in charge of the second march, did not present the same problems as those which confronted the trial of the nine officers involved in the first march. These two officers were prison officers who had charge of the prisoners before, during and after the march and as such, had knowledge and some responsibilities for them at all stages. During this march, in contrast with the first, each was responsible for and made decisions about all of the groups of prisoners on the march. A problem common to both trials was that there were only two survivors from each march, so direct prisoner evidence was most limited. As to the killing of the last prisoners at Ranau after the last survivor escaped, there was obviously no prisoner witness. However, at the trials concerning the second march and the events at Ranau, the absence of prisoner witnesses was not so critical, because there had been extensive revelations made to Allied interviewers by many Japanese and Formosan guards concerning the shooting of POWs. As a result, both before and at the trial, the systematic killing of POWs on the march and at Ranau was admitted by the two accused officers. In consequence, the trial was directed to the excuses of these two officers for the admitted killings. The excuses were that they acted on superior orders to take already sick POWs to Ranau, that they were constrained by some type of military necessity and that they humanely put sick POWs out of their misery. As to the Ranau killings, the excuse was once again a somewhat vague claim of military necessity.

The second march was important in the trial of Lieutenant General Baba Masuo, as it was the point at which his responsibility concerning Sandakan POW deaths could most clearly be proved.

There was some "buck passing" between Takakuwa and Baba at their separate trials, that of the former at Labuan and that of Baba, eighteen months later, at Rabaul. Although Baba and his HQ (the *37th Imperial Japanese Army*) at Jesselton, North Borneo, had issued the orders concerning the second march, he claimed at his trial that his order to move the POWs out of Sandakan was only provisional. He said that he was awaiting information and that the final order to Takakuwa was to move only the fit prisoners to Ranau, leaving the unfit at Sandakan. Takakuwa however, claimed that the order from HQ was to move all the POWs, to close down the Sandakan prison compound and for him to become the prison commandant of the new POW compound at Ranau. He asserted that he had given detailed advice to HQ to the effect that many POWs were not fit to march. As no further order arrived he commenced the march from Sandakan on 29 May, as he was required to do by the order which still stood. According to the evidence of his second in command, Watanabe, that message was sent as a priority wireless message on 26 May and was indeed to the effect that if the POWs (there were 824) were sent to Ranau, only one-fifth would survive. Inconsistently, Takakuwa, who claimed he had to obey the order, then disobeyed it in part. On his own evidence, only 536 POWs were taken on the march, while 288 sick were left behind, although the order was to move all. He admitted he disobeyed the HQ order by not taking all POWs, but said in evidence that he was justified in disobeying orders in this respect, on the grounds of practicability. He claimed those left behind were incapable of walking. Again inconsistently, he admitted that of the 824, there were not less than "400 stretcher cases", yet in disobeying orders, he left behind only 288. The figure of 400 "hospital cases" was confirmed by Sticpewich, who gave the further evidence that in his group of fifty (the second group), forty-two were hospital patients, six dropped out after three hours' march and about the same number the next day, and that none was seen again.

In separate trials of Takakuwa and Baba, each used defences which threw responsibility for the march on to the other. However, this was of no great consequence, because of the different nature of the charges and because in any event, there was a mixture of falsity and inadequacy in the claims and defences of each. For example, the gravamen of the case against Takakuwa was his orders to shoot POWs on the march and at Ranau, in respect of which he did not claim there was any superior local or HQ order.

THE TRIAL OF TAKAKUWA AND WATANABE

Takakuwa and Watanabe were tried at Labuan from 3 to 5 January 1946. There was, against each, a charge of the murder of an unknown number of POWs on the second march and three charges of massacres of the last POWs at Ranau, being thirty-three in all, in groups of five, seventeen and eleven, on the same day.

These charges could be clearly proved and the evidence was sufficient to establish guilt of serious war crimes. There was no need to include, as there had been in the first march trials, charges of causing death by the conduct of the march. Although Takakuwa admitted responsibility for the decision to burn down the Sandakan buildings and leave behind 288 POWs (events which were testified to by Sticpewich and by some Japanese) and although it was known that none of the POWs left behind survived, there was no evidence available at this trial as to how these men met their deaths or the extent to which Takakuwa and Watanabe were responsible. What was done to the compound and the 288 before the march left and the conduct of the march, including the brutalities inflicted on the POWs, were used toward rebutting the defences of humane killing, military necessity and obedience to superior orders.

Although the march was divided into ten groups, all stopped at the same location each night and moved off next morning in succession. Thus both Sticpewich and Short, the two survivors and the individual guards, were in a position to say a great deal about the march as a whole under the command of the two accused. The ten groups were arranged into three larger groups, each of which larger groups moved together in close succession. Each day a leap-frog scheme was used so leading groups changed. The killing of the POWs who could not go on took place at the rear of the march. At the end of each of the ten groups were four guards. These also were rotated. Under this scheme, the guards who did the killings changed, so most guards were put in a position where they were involved in shooting some POWs. The same rotation scheme was used in shooting the last POWs at Ranau.

Before the march started, Takakuwa announced to the guards the orders for the conduct of the march, including the killing of POWs in certain circumstances. These guards consisted of forty-eight Sandakan prison guards, assisted by one hundred older soldiers from a Sandakan unit. All were under the command of the two accused.

So many were aware of and were involved in the killing of the POWs on the orders of the two accused that inevitably much of what occurred was revealed by many guards during their questioning after the surrender. They had been compelled to participate, some unwillingly, in Takakuwa's murders in a scheme which sought to involve them all, including the Formosans. The Formosans were never very friendly with the Japanese, and when the war ended they blamed them for their predicament. During the Labuan trials, some resentful Formosans murdered a Japanese in the prison camp the night following his sentence to a few years' imprisonment, apparently because they considered the sentence too light. Near the end at Ranau and before the last shooting orders there, discipline broke down. One Japanese, who had been harshly beaten for a minor error, shot and killed an officer, and shot at and wounded Takakuwa before he committed suicide.

The second march differed greatly from the first in respect of group loyalty. There had been only one revelation of the shooting of POWs by the Japanese involved in the first march, and that was by an outside officer, who revealed Yamamoto's direction to do so. This no doubt led to Yamamoto admitting the order, taking responsibility for that shooting, and seeking otherwise to excuse it. The same pattern of revelation and admission occurred in respect of the second march and at Ranau, but in this case the revelations were by very many Japanese of very many acts of shooting. It is perhaps significant that most of the written statements of the guards referring to the shootings and the orders to shoot are dated two days earlier than that of Takakuwa, at a time when all were held in the one compound at Labuan.

In all the circumstances I have related, there was little that Takakuwa could do but admit the shootings and the orders he gave to kill, and to seek to minimise and excuse what had been revealed. This he did in his statement and later at his trial with some attempted improvements. The great volume of evidence from Japanese and Formosan sources, and some from Sticpewich, established the general nature of what occurred. Having given orders before the march started that POWs who could not go on were to be shot, Takakuwa moved off at the front of the march and Watanabe, moving at the rear, was in charge of the disposal of POWs. Watanabe arranged how it was to be done and gave the orders. He admitted he did not raise any argument about the proposal or protest to Takakuwa. He organised the shooting parties and the recording of the names of those shot and, at times, nominated POWs to be shot, but claimed he was not present at shootings and did not himself shoot any POWs. On his orders, two Japanese, one a sergeant-major, supervised the shooting. When the march commenced each morning, those who could not go on were left behind and their names recorded.

Those who fell out during the march were left behind with a guard until the march passed. They were all shot by the rear party. Later in the march, many who wanted to continue, but who were considered unfit, were made to stay behind and were shot after their names were recorded. Some, who were beaten to secure their possessions, in one case a diamond ring, were left behind unconscious and then disposed of. Takakuwa issued orders to shoot any POW who attempted to escape. Some attempting to escape were shot.

In the many statements admitting shootings, some said they only did so because they were so ordered. Matsuba Shokichi said that when ordered to shoot a POW at Ranau, he told the sergeant he did not want to and, when reprimanded and ordered a second time, he fired and missed, whereupon the sergeant himself shot the POW. Sticpewich added comments at the end of each of the written statements by those who admitted shooting POWs. In respect of many of the guards, including Matsuba, he said that at Sandakan they had only beaten POWs when ordered to do so, or in the presence of a sergeant or officer, and that on their own, they had never been cruel. Of some, who admitted killing when ordered, Sticpewich said that at Sandakan they had beaten POWs under orders, but had been fair on their own. Some had misappropriated food and given it to POWs. Of another, Shoiji Shinsuke, nicknamed "Sparkles", who admitted killing under the supervision of Watanabe, Sticpewich said that on occasions he lost his temper and beat POWs, but apologised later and gave his victims presents and had often secretly brought food to POWs sentenced without food to the cage. The same guard had also warned POWs when special orders had been given to increase the "discipline" by intensifying beatings on the least provocation. Others were habitually sadistic and cruel.

Whatever the purpose of Watanabe in making all the lower ranks killers of POWs, it ensured that there were many in a position later to reveal what had happened and so contribute to the conviction of the two officers who gave the orders which involved nearly all in the murders.

On Watanabe's figures, 536 POWs left Sandakan and only 183 (142 Australians and 41 British) arrived at Ranau. He said in his statement that 90 were shot and that to balance his figures he concluded 54 escaped. So far as Allied information could go, only 5 did, 2 of them surviving. According to Short, of his group of 50, only 8 or 9 reached Ranau. By Watanabe's calculations, presumably the difference—209—died from illness, but he said no record was kept of the causes of death of POWs. Later when questioned, he said about one-third of those who set out were shot. This would be about 180. As with the first march, it is impossible to say how many were shot, but it would be many more than the Japanese conceded.

The Japanese gave 1 August 1945 as the date on which the last of the POWs at Ranau were shot and killed. Takakuwa, then confined to his hut with malaria and a shot wound from the guard who attempted to kill him, called a conference of Watanabe and the NCOs, at which the decision to shoot the remaining POWs was announced. Seventeen too sick to walk were transported the few yards to the compound cemetery by ten Formosan guards and a sergeant. They were placed on the ground alongside two mass graves already dug. Watanabe was in charge and was present when the Formosans were ordered to shoot the POWs. Eleven were marched along the track with fifteen guards under a Japanese sergeant-major. According to one guard, when they arrived at a pre-arranged place, they stopped and the prisoners were told there were orders to shoot them. They were asked if they had anything to say. There was no reply. They were given a drink of water and cigarettes, which they smoked. They were taken away one at a time by the sergeant and one guard and shot, the guard being rotated. The five officers, including the senior officer, Captain Cook, and the two medical officers, were marched by a sergeant and ten Formosan guards along the Ranau-Tambunan trail a short distance on the pretext that the kempei-tai wished to interview them. They stopped at an arranged point and sat down to have a smoke. Without warning, all were shot and killed. They were buried in two graves. Except for those who had escaped, the last of the Sandakan POWs were dead.

In the face of these events and orders, the substance of which was admitted by the two accused officers in their signed statements and in evidence at the trial, it is difficult to see how there could be any defence to charges of murder and massacre. On any philosophy and under any system of law, it could not well be other than murder. However, the explanations of the two accused officers for what had admittedly occurred were advanced as defences to the charges in support of pleas of not guilty.

The explanations, defences or claims concerning the killings, were in substance that the POWs had to be moved on HQ orders; that prior to the start of the march, many were sick and would not survive the march; that Allied landings at Sandakan were imminent (elevated by Takakuwa, although there was no landing, to a belief that the Allied army was just behind him along the trail so there could be no delay); that military necessity required that no POWs escape to the advancing enemy or otherwise cause trouble for the Japanese with the natives; and that the POWs were an encumbrance to the Japanese military operations. It was also claimed that in any event they would soon die and that it was humane to kill them when they could not go on, and that they were humanely treated and humanely killed. Their bodies were thrown into the jungle because there was no time to bury them.

Apart from these claims not providing any legal defence to the deliberate killing of POWs in the admitted circumstances, most of the claims were contrary to the facts. For example, the circumstances of the march from start to finish and what occurred at Ranau made any defence based on humanity and killing as a last resort, quite ridiculous. At every stage of the march and of the imprisonment of POWs at Ranau, there was unimaginable barbarity, cruelty and acts of deprivation, well established, not only by the evidence of Sticpewich and Short, but also by that of some Japanese and Formosans. The lack of humanity, which treated the death of POWs as irrelevant, commenced as the march started, when the stretcher cases were brought out from the hospital and left in the open and all the buildings burned. Some Japanese, including Takakuwa, admitted that one of the buildings burned contained the medical equipment and supplies, which were destroyed and that the sick were left behind with a few guards, without medical supplies or attention. All the officers, including the medical officers, had been ordered to go on the march. Takakuwa made the extraordinary claim that he gave instructions that the 288 left in this way were to be brought on to Ranau "after they had been given time to recover their health" and they were fit to travel. It was admitted that some prisoners who proved unable to commence the march from the road outside the compound were shot.

Then as to humanity on the march, it was admitted that the Japanese had medical supplies, but the POWs had none. There were medical aid posts at points on the march at which the Japanese could be treated, but on Takakuwa's orders these posts were not available to POWs. It was also admitted that at the later stages of the march, the POWs, for some days, had no food and attempted to survive on roots and shrubs, while the Japanese had issues of food. On the evidence of Sticpewich, when the prisoners had no food the Japanese had ample rice to eat and frequent issues of fish. Takakuwa claimed that there was some food issued later to POWs, but conceded the Japanese were better off because a reserve rice ration was carried for them from Sandakan. The evidence of Sticpewich was that fourteen days' rice ration on a very light scale was issued to POWs when the march started, that some was later taken back and that, contrary to what Takakuwa claimed, there was no further issue, although the march took twenty-eight days. Just prior to the march, the vast accumulation of rice at the compound (Sticpewich estimated fifty tons) was moved by truck on to the road and so was not destroyed in the fire. Nearly all of it was left behind.

The prisoners, unlike the guards, were given no reserve ration. Despite their condition, instead, they were used to carry ammunition and other stores. Individual guards often compelled prisoners to give back items of food, so Sticpewich had the issues of food for his group distributed and hidden and the prisoners pretended they had eaten it. When a POW died or was shot, according to Sticpewich, the Japanese took his rice ration, but later men, about to die or likely to be shot, handed their ration to other POWs who concealed the food. Then they shook hands. The claim that men were only shot after everything had been done for them, was quite false.

In the same way, any claim made by the defence that the killing of the thirty-three POWs at Ranau was a humane act of last resort was ridiculous on the admitted facts. It will suffice to quote several things said by Takakuwa, either in his statement or at his trial. They reveal some of his motives and those of other Japanese. As to his orders to kill the last POWs, he said in evidence:

> . . . there were . . . attempts to escape. As the position became worse and many sick were dying and others were attempting to escape, we did not have any more fit POW to carry rice and arms belonging to the Kanno unit, I decided it was best to dispose of them as they became very encumbersome.

and to the following question,

> Was not the reason for the killing the 33 POW because they were weak and too ill to be of use to the Japanese?

he replied,

> Those were not the only reasons. The biggest reason was because the POW might attempt to escape and also there was a shortage of food and they could not transport rice or convey weapons for the Kanno unit.

There could have been no risk of escape by the prisoners who were shot. None had been fit enough to escape with Sticpewich. What Takakuwa said could not apply on any view to the seventeen carried to the cemetery and shot. The real fear was that the POWs would fall into the hands of the advancing Allies on or after the surrender. One guard earlier had said that all the prisoners would be killed if the Americans landed and attacked them. In his earlier statement, Takakuwa had said of the officer in charge of the Ranau army garrison:

> . . . on my arrival at Ranau [when] he learned that the POW would be of no value for working parties, he expressed the opinion it would be better if the POW at Ranau were to die off quickly, implying they might be assisted to die. I told him they were receiving 100 g of rice per day at the moment and this was not enough for them to work on. I suggested increasing the ration to 300 g per day, but he said that they had already tried that before on the Ranau POW and they were still unable to work on it. He therefore refused my request to increase the rations.

Significantly he had said in his statement concerning the march:

> In the course of conversation with Colonel Otsuka [Sandakan Garrison Commander] on 27th May 1945 before I left Sandakan, he mentioned that under the present conditions it would be advisable to leave POW behind while marching to Ranau. Far better that they should be disposed of as they would be in the way of any fighting that took place along the trail. On many occasions prior to this, Colonel Ostuka had expressed the opinion that it would be better if all POW were dead.

The common excuses and defences of Takakuwa and Watanabe failed on the facts, and the case against each on the charges of murder and massacres were made out beyond argument, irrespective of whether the Takakuwa or the Baba version of the orders for the march was correct.

The further defence of Watanabe of obedience to the superior orders of Takakuwa, failed on the facts, apart from the question whether it was legally open in the admitted circumstances. There was abundant evidence that in respect of what on their face were general orders of Takakuwa, Watanabe, as the second in command, acted on his own discretion in many respects and did so enthusiastically, and that he efficiently planned schemes to dispose of the maximum number of prisoners. He actively supervised from day to day the making of decisions as to when a POW could not go on and later who should be stopped from going on, and himself at times made the decisions and gave the orders to others to shoot on a rotating basis. At Ranau, when Takakuwa was sick, he actively implemented his decisions and supervised one of the three massacres.

The court found each guilty of the crimes charged. Takakuwa was sentenced to death by hanging and Watanabe to death by shooting. These decisions were confirmed and petitions by each man dismissed.

Watanabe was executed at Morotai on 16 March 1946. Takakuwa was executed at Rabaul on 6 April 1946 on the same day as Hoshijima. It was perhaps fitting that the two men who, as commandants, covered the entire period of imprisonment of the Sandakan POWs, 2400 of whom died in captivity, went to the gallows together.

THE TRIAL OF COMMANDER BORNEO FORCE—GENERAL BABA

Lieutenant General Baba Masuo was tried before an Australian court martial at Rabaul between 28 May and 2 June 1947. The court of six officers was presided over by Major-General Whitelaw and the accused was defended by Major-General Yajima, assisted by a Japanese civilian lawyer. Baba was the only general to be tried by an Australian court. This occurred, it seems, because of the special position of Australia in relation to Borneo, the Labuan trials and the Sandakan POWs. In a similar situation, General Yamashita, who was in command in the Philippines, where many atrocities against US prisoners had occurred, was tried by a US military court. The trial of other Japanese generals was by the Tokyo Tribunal.

General Baba had been the GOC, *37th Imperial Japanese Army*, the army of occupation of Borneo during 1945 until the surrender, and covering the time of both death marches. The first march had been planned before his arrival in Borneo, but he implemented the plan and gave the movement orders for that march. He was charged with committing a war crime in violation of the laws and usages of war by unlawfully disregarding and failing to discharge his duty as commander of the Armed Forces of Japan "to control the conduct of members of his command, whereby they committed brutal atrocities and other high crimes against the people of Australia and its Allies."

A charge so framed is directed to a failure to control those under command, rather than of directly ordering the doing of some act, itself a war crime. Thus such a charge could be made out in respect of the second march, if the accused failed to ascertain what occurred on the first march, the condition of the POWs and the condition of the route they were to take. Furthermore, such a charge could be made out if the accused failed to ensure there was adequate provision made to enable prisoners in their condition to undertake the march, and hence failed to prevent sick POWs being taken on the march without sufficient food, medical supplies, attention and without footwear and thus fail to prevent a repetition of the deaths and atrocities of the first march. The omissions would have to be shown to involve a wilful disregard of or a reckless indifference to the safety and lives of the POWs. Charges so laid have been referred to as "negative criminality" and as such criticised by some writers (eg Minear). A charge in the same terms earlier had been laid and found against General Yamashita. The US Supreme Court had upheld the charge to be of a crime under international law. That Court in so doing said:

> It is evident that the conduct of military operations by troops whose excesses are unrestrained by the orders or efforts of their commander would almost certainly result in violations which it is the purpose of the law of war to prevent. Its purpose to protect civilian populations and prisoners of war from brutality would largely be defeated if the commander of an invading army could with impunity neglect to take reasonable measures for their protection . . .

After referring to various treaties and in particular the 1907 Hague Convention, it continued:

> These provisions plainly imposed on [Yamashita] who at the

time specified was military governor of the Philippines, as well as the commander of the Japanese forces, an affirmative duty to take such measures as were within his power and appropriate in the circumstances to protect prisoners of war and the civilian population. This duty of a commanding officer has heretofore been recognised and its breach penalised by our own military tribunals.

These quotations were included in the directions of the Judge Advocate to the Baba court martial.

Later the legality of such a charge was upheld by the Tokyo Tribunal by a majority of eight judges to one, Judge Pal of India dissenting. The same eight judges found the same charge proved against ten defendants as well as other charges. Two were found guilty only on this charge. They included the general in charge of the army responsible for the notorious massacres and rapes at Nanking.

However, at the trial of Baba, evidence was presented which proved "positive" criminality based on Baba's direct orders, particularly those for the second march. He gave the order which he knew full well would cause the death of most of the prisoners. This was within the charge laid, although less would have sufficed to establish the charge. It was notified in advance to the defence which raised no objection. There was no evidence, nor was it alleged he was responsible for the shooting of prisoners on the marches or at Ranau.

The prosecution put before the court evidence, including statements by Hoshijima, Yamamoto and Takakuwa concerning the respective marches and events at Ranau admissible under the War Crimes Act, to prove that war crimes were committed by persons under Baba's command and that there were orders given by HQ concerning the marches. Baba, in his evidence, volunteered that numerous and serious war crimes had been committed under his command on the two marches and at Ranau, and made repeated apologies for them.

It was shown that Baba was directly involved in the orders of HQ and the planning of the two death marches. It was beyond question that anything alleged to have been done by him or his HQ to prevent or minimise what occurred to the prisoners over a period of eight months, was totally ineffective. Even if he did not know what was happening to the prisoners, and the evidence and some of his admissions suggested the contrary, he did nothing effective to find out. The strong inference was that he was aware of or anticipated, at least in a general way, what was occurring to the prisoners on the marches, and that at least he was indifferent to their fate and regarded them as an encumbrance to his difficult problems of defence. There was an historical as against a criminal inference that he and higher command in Japan were more directly involved in the elimination of prisoners, but from a criminal proof point of view, the evidence at the trial clearly established at least that Baba was recklessly indifferent to the safety and lives of the prisoners at the hands of persons under his command.

Although a case of "negative criminality" was established in respect of both marches and Ranau, the strongest case was in relation to the second march, where "positive criminality" was clearly proved. In relation to this march, the evidence in its simplest terms established that on 20 May, Baba issued the order that all POWs, regardless of their condition, be moved to Ranau and that the Sandakan prison compound be closed; that Baba on his own admission then knew what had occurred on the first march, including that a large number of POWs had died; that when he ordered the march he knew of the condition of the POWs still at Sandakan and that if sent to Ranau most would die on the march; that his order was acted on and the camp was closed, and that 288 unable to walk were left there and died, and of 536 who went on the march only 183 reached Ranau.

There were many claims, explanations and apologies by and on behalf of Baba, but these central objective facts and the inescapable inference of the direct responsibility and guilt of Baba were never dislodged.

The sick and starved condition of the POWs at Sandakan, with hundreds of bed patients before the march, was proved. A staff colonel of Baba's HQ had visited the camp in April and learned of their unfitness and that many could not survive a march. After this evidence and other evidence as to the appalling conditions the prisoners had to endure had been given to the court, Baba simply said in his evidence that he knew the condition of the POWs and that he had seen the report of his staff colonel on his return from the visit to Sandakan. He did not claim he was unaware that the POWs were as bad as the evidence disclosed. He also admitted he knew of the "unexpected" results and the number of deaths of the first march, and that he had Yamamoto tell him what had occurred. He claimed, by way of excuse for what had happened on the first march, that he had given orders concerning food and medicines for the prisoners on that march. He must have known that any such orders were not carried out or he had not organised any means of doing so. He admitted he knew the condition of the route and had a reconnaissance made of it, and said after the first march he had issued instructions to have some steep parts of it improved. He claimed, without any corroboration, that he issued instructions for an improvement in the supply of food and medicines for the second march, but the evidence disclosed that the supply of medicines and medical assistance for POWs was non-existent and that there was little food for the POWs except for the ten days' ration at the start.

One of Baba's staff officers confirmed that the order was to move all POWs whatever their condition. Baba did not claim otherwise, but said that as no date was stated in the movement order, this meant that no final decision had been made. However, unfortunately, a general on his staff, junior to him, had said that the order did not fix a date and that meant, as obviously it did, that the order was to be implemented as soon as possible. The defence lawyer suggested that Takakuwa, in a panic when the bombardment of Sandakan occurred on 27 May, started the move before final orders were given. Baba claimed he was considering other alternatives. This is not what his order said and not what Takakuwa had understood it to be. Baba said that the order was only provisional because it provided Takakuwa with a list of units he should consult. As all of these were in the Sandakan area, such as the Sandakan garrison and the nearby supply units, and because he was not required to report back, Takakuwa understood, obviously correctly, that he was to consult these local units only as to the method of carrying out the order.

It was admitted that Takakuwa's message of 26 May, warning that only one-fifth would survive the march, was received the same day and seen by Baba at midday. It was claimed by Baba and supported by the oral statement of one staff officer that the same day a message was sent to Takakuwa to move only fit POWs. No such message was received by Takakuwa before he left on the night of 29 May, nor was any such message sent on to him. If he had received such an order, he, who had delayed fulfilling the order while he reported four out of five would not survive the march, would hardly have acted as he did, including destroying the camp, if he had received a second and different order. As the original order was to move all POWs regardless of their condition at a time when their condition was already admittedly well known to HQ and Baba, including that most would not survive a march to Ranau, why would the order be changed when HQ was told what it already knew? Takakuwa said he carried out his orders when he did not hear further from HQ, because he was aware that HQ knew of the condition of the prisoners when they issued the order nine days earlier. It can be added that if only one-fifth would survive the march, as stated in the message admittedly seen by Baba, then there would have been little point in evacuating so few and leaving almost all at Sandakan; why not rather make some arrangements concerning the sick and starving POWs there, whose rice ration had been cancelled by the HQ order the month before? If there was some concern for the four-fifths sick claimed to have prompted a second HQ order, why not put some red cross markings on the compound, as Sticpewich said had been suggested when the Allied bombing intensified in May? His evidence was that Captain Cook, when his request was refused, had waved red cross material when the planes came over and had been beaten for doing so. It is clear, as the prosecutor argued, that the supposed variation of the order was an invention. It was a desperate attempt to save Baba from the truth that he had given the order which he clearly knew would send nearly all of the last of the 800 or so prisoners to their deaths.

Whether some last minute variation of the order was received or not, the criminal responsibility of Baba concerning the second march was clear. The overall plan from January onward had been to move all the prisoners to Ranau, in two marches. He had plenty of time before the Allied landings, which did not commence until the end of April, to plan the move. He claimed that after learning of the disasters of the first march he ordered "more scrupulous research" into what was to be done on the later projected march. He claimed his orders were for the delivery of food stuffs to the Sandakan POW camp for preparation for those to go on the march. However, it was his HQ which had issued the order only weeks before the march cutting out the POW but not the Japanese rice ration. The cut still applied when the march began.

Then, in respect of each march, Baba made a bald statement that he sent an officer, Captain Nakayama to Ranau to find out how the prisoners were after arrival and to make special arrangements for their speedy recovery to health. He said that on 10 June, he learned from Sandakan what had occurred. The march would by then have been about halfway. He said he thereupon sent Nakayama to ensure the end of the march was properly conducted. He said, somewhat conveniently, that he had not heard from Nakayama by the time he, Baba, surrendered three months later. Baba had said that the same officer had also been sent to Ranau after the first march with similar orders. Despite the alleged missions, the very opposite happened to the prisoners at Ranau after each march, as described earlier. The exhausted prisoners were given arduous carrying over long distances, which repeated the death march conditions. Some of the carrying was on HQ orders, one of which after the second march was that prisoners at Ranau were to be used to carry ammunition for the Kanno machine gun unit then being moved on HQ orders through Ranau. According to Takakuwa, the order added that it did not matter if POWs died in doing so.

At least Baba must have known through Nakayama what was occurring at Ranau to the 250 survivors of the first march. The carrying by them over twenty miles and back had started on their arrival. Nakayama must have found out. He obviously did nothing. He was sent by Baba with the orders claimed, Baba must have also known before he ordered the second march and before he sent Nakayama on the alleged second mission. The carrying duties of the survivors of the first march was the principal cause of the 250 prisoners being reduced to six by the time of Nakayama's alleged second visit.

Baba's unsubstantiated general claims had to mean that many Japanese officers at different locations, by their individual decisions, had deliberately disregarded or disobeyed the orders of the general commanding officer, and that everybody had concealed from him what had happened, except Yamamoto, and presumably he did not say that many prisoners had been shot. It would mean that the general's envoy carrying his orders had done likewise. It became obvious that Baba's claims amounted to a desperate attempt on the part of a general in an impossible position to conceal the fact that he was well aware of what was occurring and that he gave the orders well knowing that at the hands of his subordinates he was sending very many sick and underfed prisoners to their certain death. In truth, he was the one principally responsible for the consequences of the death marches. I believe this was clearly proved at his trial.

Military necessity on account of the war situation was raised by and on behalf of Baba, but not strictly as a separate legal defence. Thus it was not argued that putting sick POWs on a forced march likely to cause most to die could be justified, because they would be an encumbrance to the Japanese defences or might escape or be rescued by an advancing enemy. The defence was essentially a denial of responsibility for what occurred, which were admitted to be war crimes. Baba simply relied on the war situation as the context in which he had to make and have carried out difficult decisions. The defence complained of the poor quality of the Japanese in Borneo under Baba's command, of the difficulty of defending Borneo with poor communications and with little air or sea support, and being unable to determine whether the Allied attacks would come in the east or the north. He claimed the Allied bombing and shelling of Sandakan on 27 May caused confusion, resulting in Takakuwa's impetuous decisions. He referred also to the Allied landings at Labuan and Brunei on 9 June and at Miri on 20 June and the attacks on Weston and Beaufort on 24 June. The bombardment of Sandakan, although there was no landing, probably did act as a spur to Takakuwa (possibly under the influence of Otsuka) to burn down the Sandakan compound buildings and leave the 288 POWs in the open to their certain death.

Those war problems and stresses did not meet the case against Baba or excuse him. His conduct in relation to the second march, the decision for the move and the occasion to provide for its proper conduct was well before the war operations to which he referred. Baba knew what occurred on the first march not long after its completion, and on his own evidence the second march was the second step taken to implement a plan made early in 1945. It became clear that a deliberate decision was calmly made with reckless disregard for the POWs and that in ordering the second march, nothing was done when it was open to be done, to prevent a repetition of the known disasters of the earlier march.

Baba was found guilty. Accepting in full the criminal standards of proof, the decision, with respect, was clearly correct. He was sentenced to death by hanging. A detailed petition on the same lines as his defence was rejected and his conviction and sentences confirmed. The sentence was carried out at Rabaul by the Australian Army on 7 August 1947.

8

WHY DID ALL THE SANDAKAN POWs DIE?

2400 Sandakan prisoners of war, many under twenty-one, lost their lives and five times or more that number of relatives and friends in Australia and Britain mourned their loss and wondered why these things happened and were allowed to happen.

Two questions concerning these North Borneo prisoners have long been asked. The first is why did the Japanese, by a sustained course of action, apparently deliberate in purpose, starting at Sandakan and extending to the death marches and Ranau, kill all these prisoners, principally in 1945? The second to be dealt with in the final chapter is why there was no attempt to rescue them? Neither question has really been answered and little attempt has been made to do so.

The almost complete destruction of so large a group long held in captivity occurred only to the Sandakan prisoners. It was not a mass killing in the heat of battle, but a drawn out affair of killing by starvation, forced marches and shootings. What were the Japanese motives? Was the death of all but a few something which just flowed on from the ruthless pattern of conduct which the Sandakan commandant, Hoshijima, set in train resulting in the deaths of about half the prisoners while at Sandakan and leaving the rest candidates for death when they had to be moved out of Sandakan? Were they disposed of because their presence no longer served the Japanese war effort and because they then became part of what had become a Japanese front line?

These two factors, namely Hoshijima and the war situation, each played an important part in what occurred. However, other factors were operative, particularly during 1945.

There can be little doubt that it was Hoshijima's inhuman attitude to the prisoners, typified by his announcement in 1943 that they would be driven under the tropical sun until their bones rotted, that was the direct cause of the brutality and death at Sandakan.

Some commandants and some guards were more sadistic than others. Thus in Ambon, brutality became extreme with the coming of a new Chief of the Guard Section, Navy Lieutenant Ando, as was revealed during the Ambon war trials.[1] Undoubtedly, Hoshijima was in the most brutal class of commandants. Most Japanese guards sensed and followed the policies and attitudes of their superiors, quite apart from any orders.

What occurred at Sandakan until late 1944 was simply the result of an efficient but sadistic commandant getting the most out of his unco-operative and unwilling slave labourers in aid of an arduous and urgent engineering project of military importance. Consistent with this was his utter disregard for the sick, whom he treated as unworthy of feeding, because they did no work. There could not have been any intention, plan or conspiracy to get rid of prisoners prior to work on the airstrip having to be abandoned.

It is unlikely also that the decision of HQ to order 500 of the fittest POWs to be moved out of Sandakan in January 1945 was made only in order to kill them. The fittest were probably chosen because ammunition and stores had to be moved for the evacuating unit and in order to lessen any threat from the prisoners, should a large number of still fit men have been left there. However, those who gave the movement orders and those who carried them out were not in the least concerned whether prisoners died during the march. The orders for the first march that none were to be left behind were in accordance with Japanese policy that, at all costs, none should escape to make damaging revelations of Japanese conduct.

These orders were interpreted in the Japanese way so that considerations of humanity and shootings and the death of prisoners otherwise, were set aside in order to fulfil the orders and policy referred to.

By 1945 changes in the war situation caused difficulties for the Japanese at Sandakan. After the US victory in nearby Leyte, Allied air and naval power threatened to cut Sandakan off. General Baba, Japanese Borneo HQ, Colonel Otsuka, the Japanese garrison commander at Sandakan and Hoshijima himself no doubt were concerned by the threat offered by the large number of prisoners and the dwindling size of the Japanese garrison force there, as units were moved elsewhere.

All of them, and Hoshijima in particular, would have remembered with concern the 1943 underground movement, masterminded by Australians with Matthews at its head. They would have regarded the Australians as a troublesome and resourceful group. At his trial, Hoshijima referred to the events of 1943 as the "Sandakan Incident", which he obviously regarded as very serious. He connected it, wrongly I believe, with the Chinese uprising at Jesselton at about the same time. While the trial of Hoshijima was in progress, I discussed the "Sandakan Incident" with Sticpewich, who had some role in the underground organisation. He told me that there had been some communications with US submarines and US guerillas by radio transmitter and that the Matthews group was considering the possibility of a plan, contingent on US help, for the prisoners to seize control of the compound and a nearby ridge before the Japanese forces some miles away could intervene. The ultimate plan would be to link up with the US guerillas. The prisoners had a few weapons, including one hand grenade. Although Sticpewich did not mention it to me, it seems that some miles beyond the compound a large number of rifles, ammunition and grenades had been buried by the North Borneo constabulary. According to Sticpewich, the hope was to get some weapons from US sources and storm the guard house. The prisoners worked outside the wire and civilians in the underground had sea communications with the US guerillas on Tawi Tawi. When the underground was uncovered, the planning was only in the primitive stages. There were differences of view amongst the officers as to a possible future breakout because of the many who were sick.

The point now to be made is that after the underground had been discovered and many civilians had been tortured, the Japanese probably knew or guessed that plans of this type had been made. They would have known that some prisoners who escaped in 1943 had joined the US guerillas, particularly as the Japanese in the Philippines published pictures of Blow and Gillon and put a price on their heads. The US and Filipino guerillas had been able to operate in nearby Tawi Tawi right through to 1945. What the Japanese knew and believed concerning the "Sandakan Incident" will never be known. What was disclosed by the tortures and the later trials held by the Japanese in Kuching has never been revealed. I felt that Colonel Yamada, who was a legal officer in Kuching at the time of the trials there in 1944, knew a great deal about the "Sandakan Incident", but I did not feel I should ask him or that he would tell me, if I did. It is likely that the "Sandakan Incident" coloured the Japanese attitude to all the prisoners thereafter. It will be recalled they went on a vindictive punitive and indiscriminate witch-hunt for a year following the Jesselton incident.

The decision to starve the prisoners once the airfield work had ceased could have been that of Hoshijima alone, simply due to his complete lack of humanity and his professed policy dating back to 1942 that POWs were only fed to enable them to work. Although unofficial, it is quite likely, however, that it was done in concert with HQ. On its order, the fittest were moved out of Sandakan on the first march. At the very same time the starvation of those left behind was commenced. These two steps would ensure there would be no threat from prisoners at Sandakan.

Although it was clear at his trial that Hoshijima was responsible for the deaths of the Sandakan prisoners, I believe that higher authority behind the scene, both in Borneo and in Japan, was also responsible for all that occurred in 1945. HQ must have known what was happening to the prisoners in 1944–45, because some of it flowed from its orders. Colonel Suga, who was in charge of all prison camps in Borneo, and members of General Baba's HQ staff visited the compound. No one intervened. They must have acquiesced in all that occurred. High command in Japan had given directions which established official policy concerning prisoners. In the Japanese way the directions were neither precise nor detailed, but they conveyed policy, leaving those on the spot a discretion to achieve that policy in whatever extreme way they chose. Sometimes a word or two was added for the appearance of propriety, but directions read as a whole were meant to convey and were understood by the recipients to convey the message. Prison commanders had no difficulty in reading between the lines. The policy was clear enough and there would be no interference with the sternest implementation of it. Exactly that happened.

HQ in Borneo and prison authorities such as Suga and Hoshijima would well have understood the two relevant policies of higher command. One was that inhumanity and the death of prisoners was acceptable, where the person on the spot considered it necessary. Prisoners were to be despised, worthy of no consideration and lacked all rights. The attitude of Hoshijima of no work no food, extended right up to Tojo himself. The other policy was that there should be a suppression of what was happening to prisoners, lest publication be used for "propaganda" or to damage the interests of Japanese in some other way. No prisoner of war must escape. There was to be a totalitarian-like secrecy as to what was happening to people behind the Japanese "curtain". By 1945, the prevention of escapes and the suppression of information of atrocities had become more urgent because of the fear of reprisals and because of publicity given in the Western press to Allied expressions of concern about war crimes and the proposals to prosecute them. Throughout 1944 there had been fairly open discussions between the Allies about punishing war criminals at the end of the war. The likelihood of retaliation or some such action in respect of atrocities would almost have certainly been known to Japanese leaders. Although would have been suppressed in Japan, it would probably have seeped down to intermediate command. Samples of higher directions indicative of the policies referred to are as follows:

An early instruction by Tojo to commanders of prisoners of war and civilian camps read:

> Prisoners of war must be placed under strict discipline, so far as it does not contravene the law of humanity. It is necessary to take care not to be obsessed with the mistaken idea of humanitarianism or swayed by personal feelings toward those prisoners of war, which may grow in the long time of their imprisonment.[2]

The opening words and the last sentence conveyed the intended message.

A regulation issued by the Japanese War Ministry in 1943 provided:

> In case a prisoner of war is guilty of an act of insubordination, he shall be subject to imprisonment or arrest, and any other measures deemed necessary for the purpose of discipline may be added.[3]

The provision concerning "any other measures" gave to prison commanders and those under them an unlimited discretion to do what they wanted. They did and there was no interference.

Bergamini, in his book *Japan's Imperial Conspiracy*, summed up the Japanese policy concerning the killing of prisoners and the method of conveying it:

> The first discretionary hints to kill prisoners rather than let them fall into the propaganda-making hands of the enemy had been issued in stages by Imperial General Headquarters during the latter half of 1944.[4]

On 17 March 1945, a secret telegram was sent by the War Ministry to prison camp commanders as follows:

> Prisoners of war must be prevented by all means available

> from falling into enemy hands. They should be either relocated away from the front or collected at suitable points and times with an eye to enemy air raids, shore bombardments, etc. They should be kept alive to the last whenever their labour is needed.
>
> In desperate circumstances, when there is no time to move them, they may, as a last resort, be set free. Then emergency measures should be carried out against those with an antagonistic attitude and utmost precautions should be taken so that no harm is done to the public.
>
> In executing emergency measures, care should be had not to provoke enemy propaganda or retaliation. Prisoners should be fed at the end.[5]

This secret direction, discovered after the war, is of great significance not only in relation to what happened to the Sandakan prisoners, but also to what might have been its application to prisoners generally had the war not been terminated in the way it was. Apart from its operation in the last five months of the war, it evidences much of what earlier had been Japanese policy.

There is infinite scope in this direction to read between the lines. It is a supreme example of Japanese methods of making pronouncements and giving directions, at least those in relation to prisoners, military and civilian. Prison commandants and others on the spot were given discretions in indefinite terms to do their worst in situations stated in general terms. At the same time, to use the word of Bergamini, "hints" are given as to what is expected. In Japanese terms "by all means available" and "emergency measures" mean and would be understood to mean, that even inhumanity and death were not to stand in the way of achieving an objective. The Japanese applied to themselves standards in which death was irrelevant. This was so with kamikaze pilots and the holding of a position to the death. The death of despised enemy prisoners was even more irrelevant. Each prison commandant was left, according to local circumstance and his own disposition, to determine which prisoners had an "antagonistic attitude" requiring that "emergency measures" be taken against them. Any or all the prisoners at a compound who knew of past Japanese atrocities there could be considered by the commandant to be "antagonistic" if they fell into enemy hands. All of Hoshijima's prisoners could be so regarded. The Australian POWs particularly could be classified as "antagonistic" on the basis of their involvement in the 1943 "Sandakan Incident".

This direction therefore applied precisely to the situation concerning the prisoners at Sandakan at the time and to what happened to them in the ensuing months. It was not long after the direction was given that a colonel on Baba's HQ staff visited Sandakan compound and HQ issued the order for the second march to "relocate" the prisoners and the compound away from Sandakan, a likely Allied landing point and front. The direction would apply to Takakuwa who took over as prison commandant just two months after it was issued. His admissions and the evidence at his trial showed that on the march and at Ranau, he was obsessed with the need to use "all means", principally shooting prisoners, to prevent their escape. Sick prisoners who could not keep up with the march were shot, as he put it, because if left to escape to the natives, they "might cause trouble for the Japanese." They might fall into the hands of the enemy who had or were about to land. At Ranau, he had the last of them shot, admittedly because a few had escaped and shooting the remainder was a way of preventing the remainder escaping. Takakuwa did not refer to the direction, but as a defence to the admitted shootings, he claimed that shooting the prisoners to prevent their escape to the enemy was a military necessity.

The direction that prisoners should be kept alive was ominously limited to "whenever their labour is necessary." The unstated corollary was that when their labour was no longer needed (or they were incapable), there was no reason to keep them alive—the no work no food policy. This of course confirmed the policy already adopted by Hoshijima of starving the prisoners to death when the work at the airstrips ended. The same policy was implicit in the HQ order to cut out the rice given two weeks after the direction. It was also the admitted policy of Takakuwa and the Ranau garrison commander which led first to the starving and then the shooting of the prisoners at Ranau when they could no longer carry rice and ammunition for the Japanese.

The direction was not strictly an order to kill or starve or march prisoners to death. It could not provide a defence of superior orders, if that had been otherwise available. Those responsible for this and other directions gave themselves, consciously or unconsciously, a let out by only hinting and by some token face-saving additions. These additions in their context would never be considered relevant by the recipients, who would understand the obvious thrust of what they were told to be otherwise. The reference to the possibility of setting prisoners free was so hedged in by the primary injunction that no prisoner should fall into enemy hands and as to how the "antagonistic" were to be dealt with, that the occasion to release prisoners would never be considered to arise. With one exception, no prison commander ever set a prisoner free while the war continued, whatever the emergency. The exception was at Rangoon in Burma. When the Japanese retreated from Rangoon, they left some prisoners of war behind in Rangoon gaol. However, the Japanese general who made the decision to leave Rangoon, did so in defiance of orders from Tokyo and took with him, probably as hostages, 400 prisoners, who were considered capable of walking.[6]

The use of the face-saving formula asserting humanity and kindness while pursuing inhumanity and disregarding life and limb was common in Japanese directions and in statements about themselves. Such a formula appears in the instruction of Tojo concerning the discipline of prisoners. The real message was of strict discipline and not being carried away by humanitarian misconceptions. Similar tokenism and lip service to consideration for prisoners mixed in with the utmost barbarity have been earlier referred to. The formula "The Japanese soldiers are very kind people" and isolated minor acts were advanced as proof of humanity in the face of overwhelming evidence of inhumanity and killing.

The decision, when the war front approached, to kill all the prisoners to prevent their rescue which would allow them to tell what they knew for "propaganda", was not confined to Borneo. There were at least two other similar decisions taken, one carried out and the other frustrated. One was at Palawan, a Philippine island and the other was at Manila. In December 1944, 150 US prisoners of war at Palawan were deliberately incinerated in slit trenches on the approach of a US convoy. In February 1945, when by an unexpected dash by General MacArthur's flying armoured columns, the prison camp on the outskirts of Manila was taken and 5000 emaciated US and European prisoners of war and civilian internees were rescued, it was found the commandant held orders from Tokyo to kill the prisoners. The two events preceded the quoted March directions, but as Bergamini,[7] who relates the events stated, there had been in 1944 "hints" from Tokyo to kill prisoners rather than let them fall into enemy hands and Manila had a direct order from Tokyo. Tokyo had overruled General Yamashita in his decision not to defend Manila. A special suicide squad of 15,000 sailors and marines were sent from Japan. They were expected to die. The prisoners would die too. It was just after this order failed that the secret March direction was sent directly to all prison commandants.

Properly understood, this decision to kill POWs when a war front approached a prison area is a chilling one, if one now looks back to it in relation to the thousands of prisoners who were alive when the war abruptly ended. 14,526 Australian prisoners of war were recovered from Japanese prison camps.[8] If the war front had approached prison areas or those areas had been cut off, as occurred at Sandakan, the discretions most likely would have been exercised in the kind of ways it was against those prisoners. But for the sudden end of the war, there would have been a drawn out no-surrender war which required Allied attacks on many areas where prisoners were held. Whatever else may be said about dropping the atomic bombs, it undoubtedly saved the lives of Allied prisoners in Japanese hands. They were saved, as were the Manila prisoners, by a sudden and unexpected event, in the one case the atomic bombs and a quick end to the war, and in the other a quick rescue action by MacArthur.

The prisoners in some areas were still in danger, despite the general surrender. Those in the many compounds at Kuching, the capital of Sarawak, were in great danger between the general surrender in Japan and the surrender in Borneo, delayed for twenty-six days, during which time General Baba and many Japanese in Borneo had determined to fight on. It took envoys from the Emperor to persuade Baba to surrender on 11 September, and it took envoys from Baba and some fighting to persuade the Japanese who had retreated into the interior to surrender, some almost three months later.

Commanders of certain areas of North Borneo and of Sarawak did not surrender until even after Baba's surrender. Miri in Sarawak fell to the Australian Army on 23 June, but the Japanese only retired a short distance away. A week before Miri fell, over one hundred Indian POWs were massacred at nearby Kuala Belait. After the general surrender, the twenty-eight civilian hostages held outside Miri were shot and the Japanese retreated further inland refusing to surrender. There was no attack on Kuching, but if there had been, either before or just after the general surrender, prisoners, not only those who had earlier been at Sandakan, but also other military and civilian prisoners, may have suffered the same fate as those at Ranau. The Japanese surrendered and handed over the prisoners at Kuching on 6 September. The Sandakan officers and NCOs at Kuching had sensed that they were in peril when the Japanese there did not immediately recognise the general surrender. After their release, they were appalled to learn that they had lost all their troops, but realised that they were lucky not to have suffered in the same way. Apart from Sticpewich, about forty of them were to provide the substantial body of evidence by sworn declarations concerning events at the Sandakan compound at the trial of Hoshijima. The Japanese did not know until after the Borneo surrender that Sticpewich had survived.

The March direction needs to be seen in the context of the state of the war at the time. It would have been by then abundantly clear to Japanese leaders and to many other Japanese officers that Japan had lost the war, but intended to fight on to the death. These same officers knew or expected that there would be retribution or other action in respect of atrocities revealed. By March, the German Army had collapsed and the Allies were at the doors of Berlin, and German atrocities in concentration camps were already world news. In the Pacific war, most of the Philippines had come under Allied control, and the Japanese had been thrown back or defeated in other areas. Iwo Jima had been seized and the capture of Okinawa was almost complete. US had air superiority and a week earlier Tokyo had been bombed, with the loss of 80,000 lives. Many Japanese units in areas where prisoners were held had been more or less cut off.

The direction appears to contemplate the end of the war with a Japanese defeat, as the words "to the last" and "at the end" indicate. At the end, prisoners, if they had not been dealt with as "antagonistic", were to be given a farewell meal to make things look better. In the meantime, while the war continued, all measures, including getting rid of them, were to be taken to prevent their escape or to their otherwise falling into enemy hands. Local commanders conscious of atrocities under their command, would conveniently interpret the "antagonistic attitude" and "emergency measures" phrases as applicable to any or all prisoners who knew of or might tell of these atrocities. At whim, a commander might extend this to all his prisoners to prevent their falling into Allied hands. Towards the end, a Japanese officer in jeopardy of "retaliation" would not be concerned about precise words, but more by the policy conveyed. The direction gave him an open cheque.

What happened to the Sandakan POWs can now be summed up. The deaths were knowingly and deliberately caused, first by starvation and then by other means, because their labour was no longer required. In 1945, they became an encumbrance in an inconvenient location, thought by the Japanese to be a likely Allied landing spot. They were considered to be a threat to the Japanese at Sandakan by reason of the "Sandakan Incident" and independently because, with Allied air and sea superiority, their presence made Sandakan itself, including the compound, a target for their rescue. The earlier inhumanity and death of prisoners dating back to 1943 and escalating up to and into 1945 made it imperative that no prisoner should escape, who could provide evidence of these atrocities.

Higher command in Japan had considerable responsibility for what occurred at Sandakan, on the marches and at Ranau. They avoided giving direct orders as to what was to be done to carry out their general policies, but this could not absolve them from legal or moral responsibility for what occurred. Those at an intermediate level in the chain of command, such as General Baba and his Borneo HQ and Colonel Suga in charge of all Borneo prison camps, were similarly legally and morally responsible. Finally, officers on the spot bore the same responsibility. Even if superior orders would have been a defence, there were no superior direct orders which required them to kill POWs by starvation or shooting.

The moral responsibility of Hoshijima, Takakuwa and Baba stood out above the rest. The conduct of others, although brutal, criminal and avoidable, was less premeditated, such as that of the officers of the regular fighting unit, who were thrown into the task of escorting the POWs on the first march. The same could well have occurred if another unit had been assigned the same task.

The Japanese methods of dealing with and eliminating the POWs changed. Initially, Hoshijima starved them and this was known to HQ and supported by its orders. The forced march was employed to dispose of prisoners, at least on the second march. Indirect means were used to achieve objects, and actions were taken, unofficially but deliberately, to attempt to conceal the Japanese responsibility for the deaths.

The Japanese were expert in "buck passing", in relation to the treatment of POWs. In 1945 this intensified as Higher Command and Borneo HQ avoided giving direct orders. Later they both disclaimed responsibility for inhumanities and POW deaths on the basis that they had not been the result of their orders.

Some at the lower level tried to "pass the buck" back. One was the astute Hoshijima. As Japanese defeat was imminent and talk of war crimes trials was current, he ensured that the cutting out of the POWs' rice ration should appear to be a result of an official order so that responsibility could be passed from him to Borneo HQ. After the war, when the interrogators arrived, he had his excuse ready. HQ had ordered that rice be cut off because of shortages and consequently he did his best to obtain substitutes.

The war crime trials held at Labuan, the later trials held at Tokyo, and elsewhere, certainly served to reveal what had happened in various areas and who were responsible. But they also served to reveal Japanese attitudes, policies and motivations and, when these are analysed, they provide a basis for an attempt to understand why the members of the Japanese armed forces, almost universally, were so inhuman and caused so many deaths. The story of Sandakan provides a tragic, but spectacular example of how higher command, intermediate levels and officers on the spot were each responsible, in different ways, for this outrageous act of inhumanity.

9

JAPANESE ATROCITIES EVERYWHERE – WHY?

There are deeper and more general questions to be asked which lead to what, in fact, lay behind the particular reasons and motives of the Japanese responsible for the Borneo atrocities. These questions go to the character of Japanese culture, to their national attitudes and to the international environment in which Japan found itself at the time.

One question often pondered, but seldom answered, is why were the Japanese in the Second World War, at all levels of what was an efficient and well-disciplined force, so inhumane almost universally to both military and civilian prisoners? Unlike the Germans, the Japanese had no specific policy and set up no organisation or apparatus for the mass extermination of selected classes of persons. However, in contrast with what occurred in the Japanese prisoner of war compounds, the Germans in their camps where British, Dominion, European and American prisoners were held, mostly observed the prisoner of war rules and there was a high survival rate of prisoners. The percentage of POWs of all Allied nations who died in Japanese custody was 27 per cent—that of Australians was 35 per cent. The equivalent figure in Europe was 4 per cent.[1] Why then, in the absence of the systematic and selective extermination policy of the Germans, were so many prisoners of the Japanese, contrary to the laws of war and often with little apparent reason, brutalised, mutilated, beheaded, shot, starved or otherwise killed by what appeared to be a series of individual acts of many different Japanese in widely different areas? To what extent does the answer lie in the character of the Japanese people and its armed forces and in some of their more enduring traditions? To what extent was the brutality due to rising Japanese nationalism, fired by resentment of Europeans and Americans and made more violent by some kind of inferiority complex? To what extent did it depend on the activities and influences of the militarist group which seized control of the Japanese nation in the years leading up to 1931 and then in 1941?

None of the questions posed can be answered with confidence, but the events of the war years, analysed now with some detachment against the background of Japan's prior history, do reveal some of the Japanese dispositions and characteristics which made these things possible.

To assess the causes of atrocities in particular or in general requires some awareness of the circumstances in which they occurred and the relationship which higher command had to them. In earlier chapters, I have surveyed the scene in Borneo in some detail to provide some sample of a wider pattern of Japanese conduct.

In other places as well as Borneo the level of ferocity, brutality and death reached extremes and no occupied area escaped brutality and death. The overall scale of their atrocities is indicated by the total number of Japanese tried and convicted by trials in very many different locations. As will appear later, just under 6000 were tried, thousands sentenced to imprisonment and about 900 were sentenced to death and executed. Those tried were the few responsible who could be positively identified, and a case proved to the criminal standard. At the Tokyo trials, there was some general evidence that over a million died as a result of Japanese atrocities. 302,000 cases of atrocities leading to death were specified.

The death marches at Bataan, the Burma Railway project and the Nanking and Chekiang massacres were such extremes.

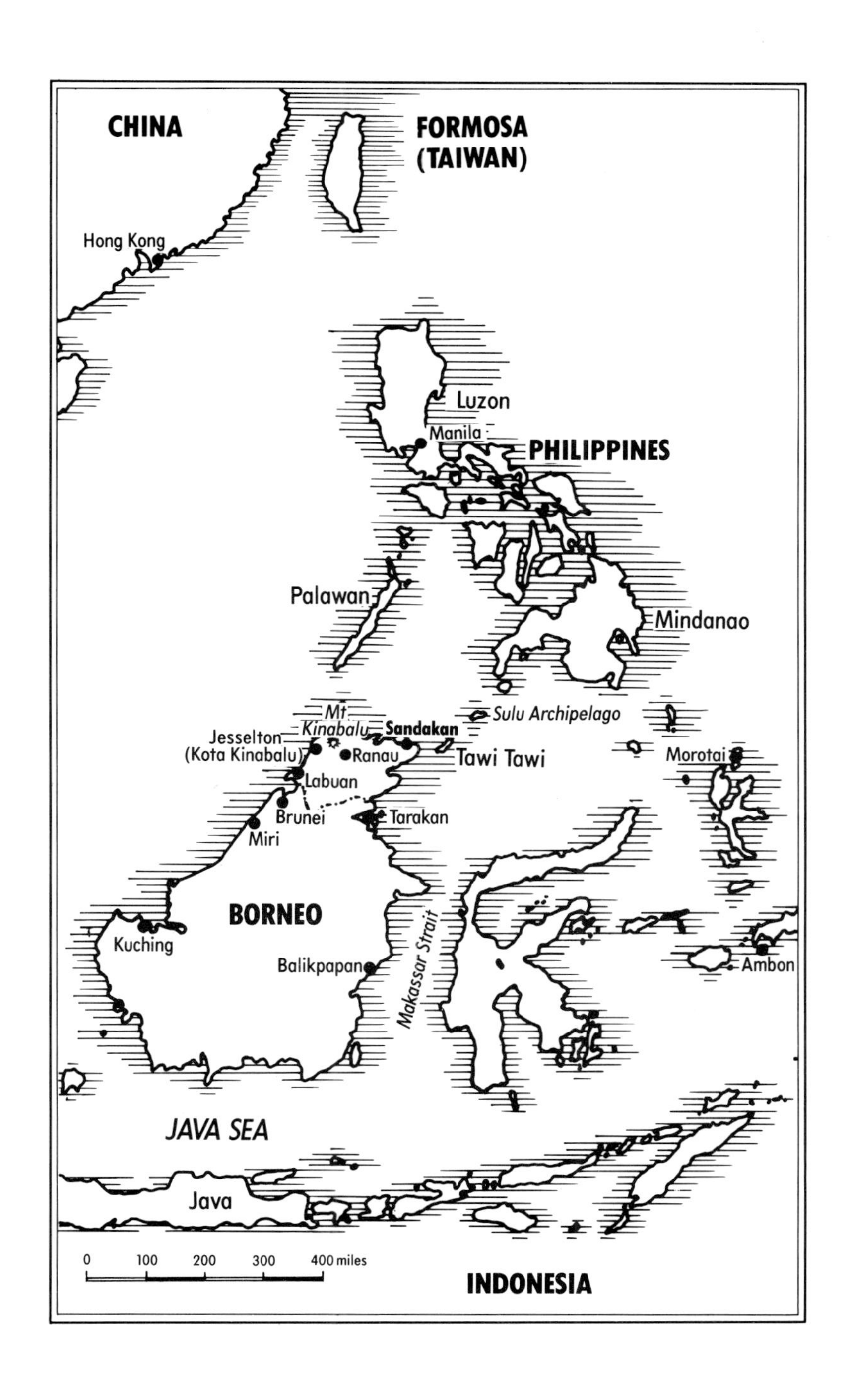

CHINA
FORMOSA
(TAIWAN)
Hong Kong
Luzon
Manila
PHILIPPINES
Palawan
Mindanao
Sulu Archipelago
Mt
Kinabalu
Sandakan
Jesselton
(Kota Kinabalu)
Ranau
Tawi Tawi
Morotai
Labuan
Brunei
Tarakan
Miri
BORNEO
Kuching
Balikpapan
Makassar Strait
Ambon
JAVA SEA
Java
0
100
200
300
400 miles
INDONESIA

The author (right) with Captain Toole, a British medical officer, and Dyak (Iban) girls in front of a long-house, Kampong Mankassin, Lubai River, Sarawak, 16 October 1945.

Setting out in a perahu down the Lubai River with Captain Toole and two Dyaks, en route for the next Dyak kampong, October 1945. (see pp. 39–40).

With Dyaks (Ibans) at Marudi, Baram River, Sarawak, November 1945 (see p. 40). Marudi was a Z Force (SEMUT) base in 1944–45.

The author (as Captain Moffitt, prosecutor) leaving his tent for the trial of Captain Hoshijima, Labuan, January 1946 (see pp. 50–1).

Japanese defending officers talking to Hoshijima (facing, in white shirt) during an adjournment in his trial (see Chapter 5). The "war room" was the tent used for the war trials court.

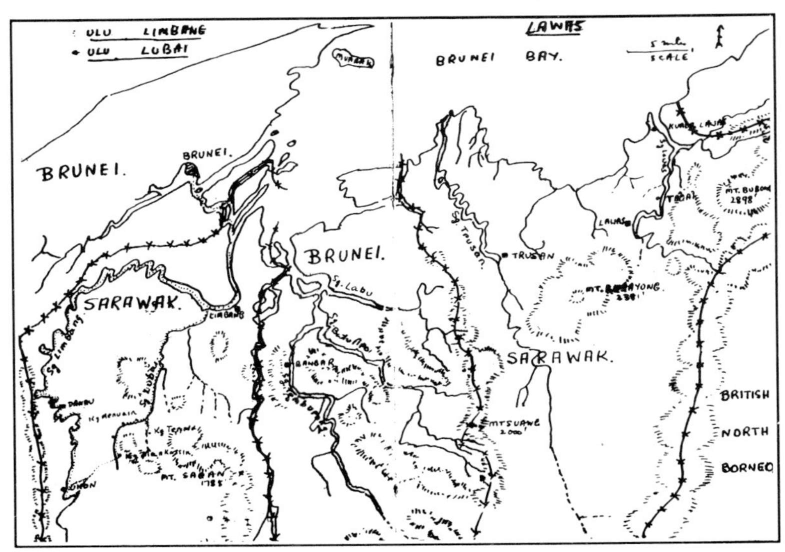

Sketch from author's diary, showing his journeys from Brunei along the Limbang, Lubai and Lawas rivers in 1945 (see Chapter 3).

NOTES

in all the units — about 10% in each. This
is the best piece of evidence in support
of our contention that when the food
& medicine were short the Jap in the
compound [illegible] the PW's share of food
& medicines.

16 Jan '46 (Wed).

The next witness was the civilian
(Jap) governor of Sandakan —
KUMABE Tamuki — an old bald
man with a long white beard.
He bowed from the hips 3 times
as he entered the Court. He
was the ex-Ambassador to Baghdad.*
Like most of the witnesses the
Japs call [illegible] put H further into
the mire for he said the natives
toward the end were mostly anti-
Jap & pro British & wouldn't bring the
food in or use their prows; that if
PW were released some of the natives
would have helped feed them [illegible]
them their prows.

Just at this stage H had a sudden
bout of Malaria — the Court adjourned, — surely
wondering whether this is the man who denied

* Afterwards learnt he was also Ambassador to Iran, Persia
& during the critical stages ambassador to Spain.

The author's diary entry for 16 January 1946 referring to the Japanese Governor's evidence and Hoshijima's attack of malaria during the trial (see pp. 89–90).

NOTES

medicine to POWs dying of malaria of 5-67 a day. I am sure the way the Court referred to the adjournment must have hit something in the Jap defending officers.

HOSHIJIMA AS SKETCHED WHILE GIVING EVIDENCE.

H was examined by a doctor & the case is off till Friday. I did a few

Captain Hoshijima, Sandakan POW Commandant, sketched during the trial. He was sentenced to death and hanged at Rabaul on 6 April 1946.

Kumabe Taneki, the civilian Governor of British North Borneo, stationed at Sandakan, sketched during the trial.

NOTES

ONE OF THE 3 DEFENDING OFFICERS. – CAN'T SPEAK ENGLISH SO DOESN'T TALK MUCH – PREPARES BULLETS FOR OTHERS TO FIRE – EX JUDGE IN JAPAN.

11 Jan (Thur).
No case today but they [illegible] the same preparing the next case – it will be a very difficult one because of lack of evidence.

One of the Japanese defending officers, a pre-war judge, sketched during the trial (see pp. 73–4).

SKETCH PLAN FROM MEMORY
SANDAKAN 8 MILE
PW COMPOUNDS

Plan of the Sandakan POW compound, drawn from memory by Sticpewich for use at the war trials. It corresponds closely with the aerial photograph overleaf.

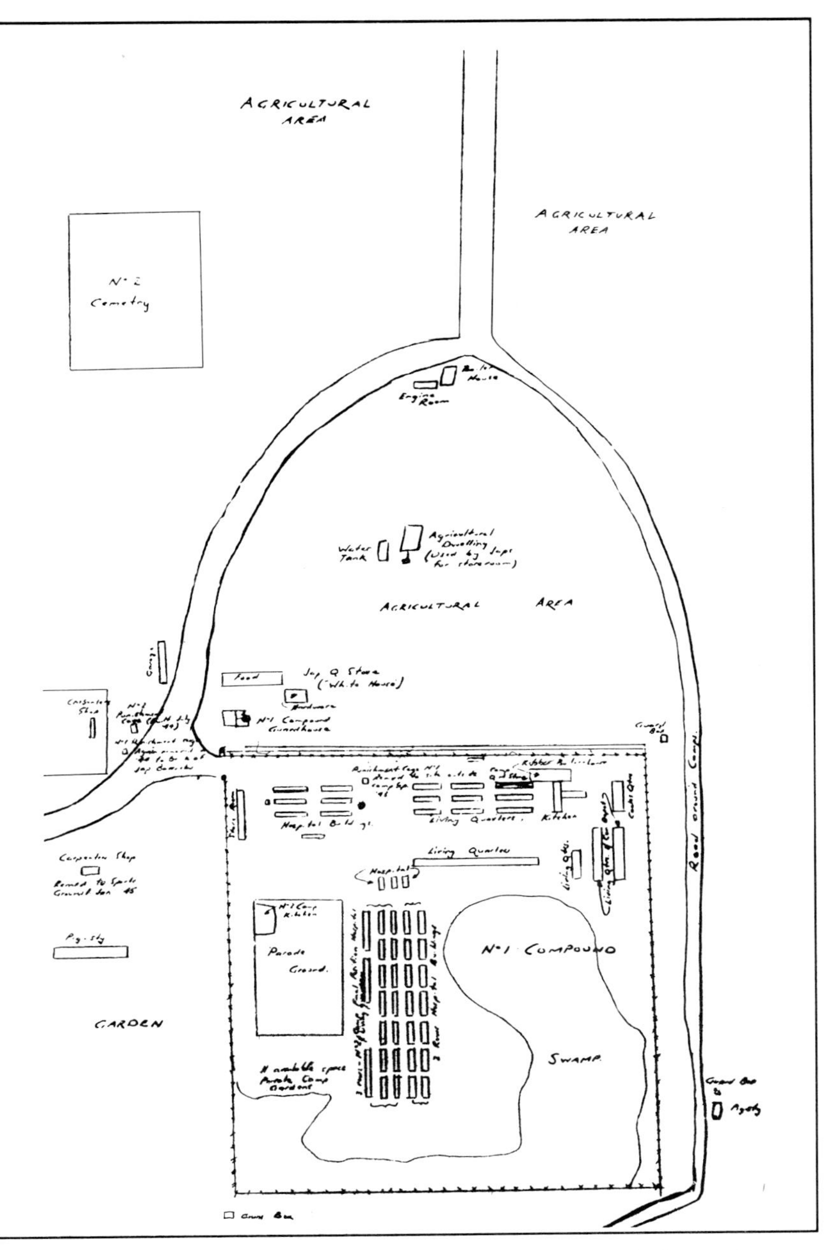

Note the position of two of the punishment cages, outside the wire but in view of the POWs, and of Hoshijima's house, where 1000 bags of rice were stored while 300 prisoners died of starvation in one month.

Allied reconnaissance photograph of the Sandakan POW compound taken on 6 March 1945, apparently in aid of the paratroop rescue project. The following key appeared at the side:

1. POW Camp administrative area.
2. Buildings probably part of administration.
3. Parade ground.
4. Drainage canals.
5. Guard towers.
6. Guard shacks.
7. Probable mess hall.
8. Probable automatic weapons pit.
9. Slit trench.
10. Small bridge.
11. Prison gates.

NOTE: Photo received too late for placement on Index Map.

(For clarification of indistinct labels, see p. 248.)

These three photographs are discussed in more detail on pp. 247–8.

This photograph of Sandakan airfield, taken on 31 May 1945, bears the following markings: "No. 1 strip unserviceable" (both strips were heavily bombed) and "PW Camp destroyed 31 May 45" (it was, in fact, burned down on 29 May).

The burned-out Sandakan POW compound, photographed after the war. Note the open terrain.

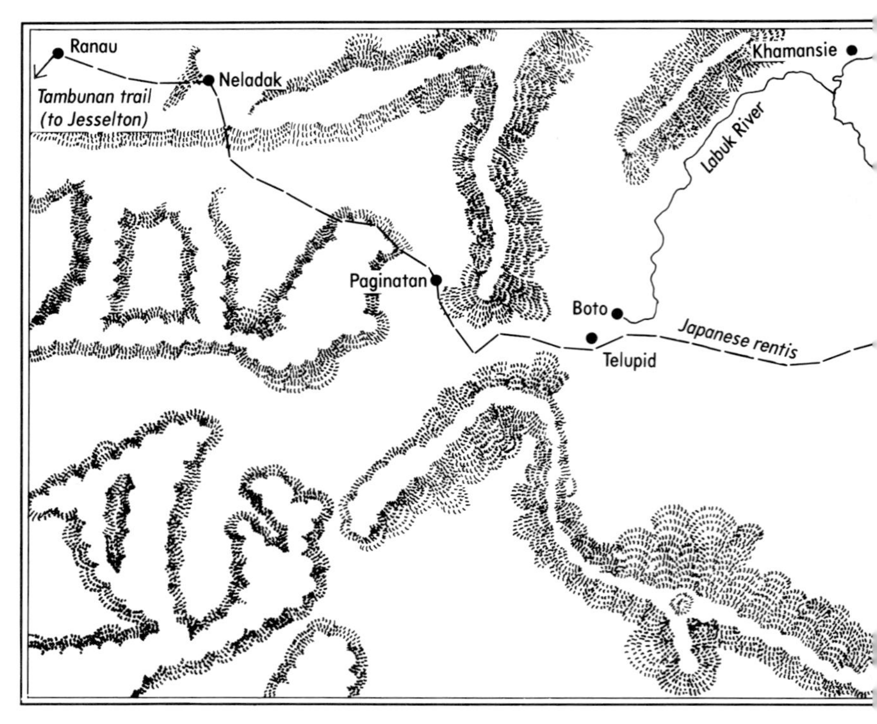

Nelson Short, Bill Sticpewich and Keith Botterill (centre) leaving Labuan hospital late in 1945. The others include pilots of the Auster rescue planes. The kit bag belonged to Andy Anderson, who escaped with Short's party but died in the jungle, and the Japanese rifle was given to Sticpewich by a native, who was meant to kill him with it (see Chapter 1).

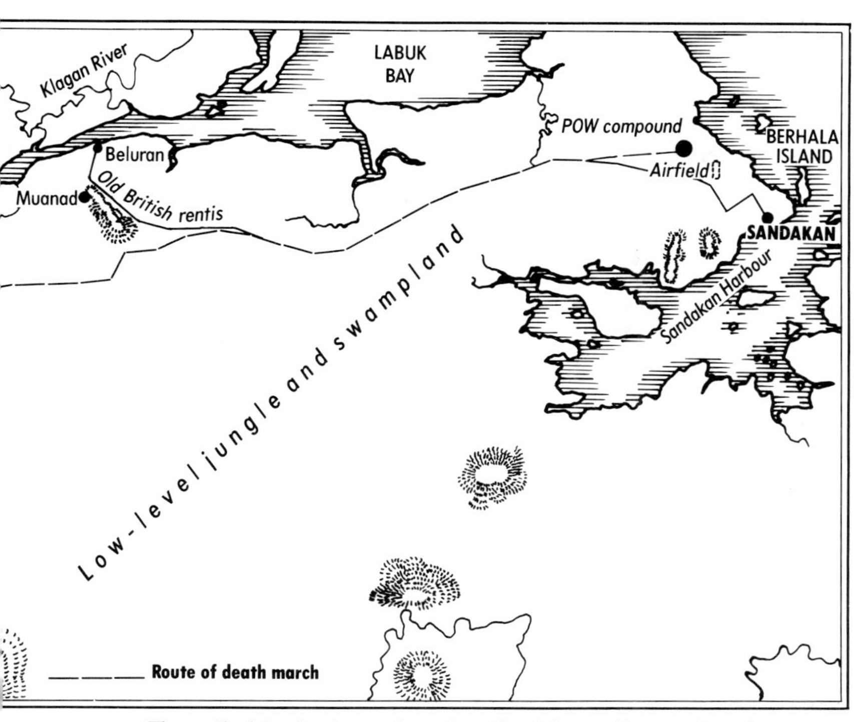

The trail of the death marches, from Sandakan to Ranau—based on a map drawn by an Allied investigation party in late 1945 (see Chapters 4, 6 and 7).

The Malay rescuers who hid and fed the POWs who escaped from Ranau (see pp. 3–4, 8–9), photographed in July 1985 wearing medals for bravery: Barega Katus (Keith Botterill, Bill Moxham and Nelson Short) and Dihil bin Ambilid, nicknamed Godihil (Bill Sticpewich).

Lieutenant (later Major) Rex Blow (left) and Lieutenant Miles Gillon, photographed in Malaya in 1941 before the fall of Singapore. In June 1943 they escaped from Berhala Island (just outside Sandakan harbour) to Tawi Tawi in the Philippines and served with the US and Filipino guerillas (see pp. 59–61, 278–80).

General Douglas MacArthur, Commander-in-Chief Allied Forces SWPA, wading ashore to return to the Philippines on 25 October 1944, accompanied by his Chief-of-Staff, Lieutenant General Sutherland, and high-ranking officers (see p. 255). Philippines President Sergio Osmena is on the extreme left. (Australian War Memorial 17738)

Lieutenant Colonel John Overall, MC *and Bar (Tobruk and Alamein), Commanding Officer of the 1st Australian Paratroop Batallion, which trained for PROJECT KINGFISHER (see pp. 237–41). Now Sir John Overall,* KT, CBE.

Lieutenant General Sir Thomas Blamey, CB, CMG, DSO, GOC AIF, GOC *Allied Land Forces SWPA (see Chapter 12). (Australian War Memorial 20399)*

On the Burma Railway about one-third of the 46,000 POWs of different nations and imported coolie labourers died. A project which should have taken years was attempted to be completed in a very short time, with utter disregard for life and the dictates of humanity.

At Bataan, following the surrender of the sick and starving survivors of the besieged Corregidor garrison, they, as POWs, were put on forced marches for seventy-five miles through villages and denied food and water, resulting in some 8000 US and Filipino deaths. One motive, in this case, seems to have been to openly humiliate the Americans and to demonstrate their inferiority. The same motive was apparent behind the parade in Korea of the British POWs brought from Singapore, and one on a lesser scale in Burma. Another motive at Bataan, it seems, was to warn others against future resistance to the "invincible" Japanese. The same motive was responsible in other areas, for the execution of prisoners after the surrender of the opposing force had been accepted. It was not a refusal to take prisoners during battle, but a reprisal against those accepted as prisoners, who had dared to resist earlier.

Such events occurred after surrender at Ambon, New Guinea and New Britain. The Mansfield and the Webb reports in respect of the latter reveal widespread diabolic tortures, mutilations, mass bayoneting, some for practice, and the shooting of Australian soldiers taken prisoner and later found with their hands tied. Also revealed were the rape, murder and mutilation of native women, some with breasts cut off, and the murder of native men. In most areas all Australians captured were killed. Much of what happened was beyond any military purpose, even that of terrorist example. Here and elsewhere, whole units ran riot, descending to mass primitive savagery, fuelled by the Japanese fascination with violence and death. There was no real motive, only sadistic satisfaction in doing what was done. The same kind of savagery was meted out to some of the native people in Borneo. The same primitive conduct occurred at Nanking.

The notorious 1937 Nanking massacres and mass rapes of the Chinese there, occurred after the surrender of the city.

In rampages over six weeks, thousands of women, including young girls, were raped, subjected to degrading tortures and murdered by soldiers, including officers. There were orders to kill all males in captivity, and accordingly tens of thousands of men and boys were machine-gunned in groups or otherwise killed.

It is difficult to assign precise motives for what occurred at Nanking, except to say that there was no attempt to restrain the long-standing Japanese racial hatred for the Chinese, fuelled this century by this large, but weak neighbour, having tried to restrain Japanese advances into mainland Asia. The same hatred of the Chinese led to Japanese atrocities against them in all occupied areas, including Borneo.

The same hatred spurred by vengeance was expressed in the massacres in April to August 1942 in Chekiang and its neighbouring districts. These massacres were ostensibly in revenge for the assistance of some Chinese to sixty-four of the airmen of the Doolittle air raid on Tokyo on 18 April who, unable to return, had crashed their aircraft and parachuted into China near Chekiang. The massacres of the Chinese followed an order by Emperor Hirohito himself[2] of a reprisal expedition against Chekiang, then capital of unoccupied China, issued only days after the Doolittle raid. The orders of the Emperor to the Japanese commander included an order that he should "concentrate on the annihilation of the enemy and the destruction of her enemy air bases in the Chekiang area." The expedition commenced two weeks after the Doolittle raid. Bergamini described what occurred:

> When they finally withdrew in mid-August 1942, they had killed 250,000 Chinese, most of them civilians. The villages at which the American fliers had been entertained were reduced to cinder heaps, every man, woman and babe in them being put to the sword.[3]

Later writings assert that biological warfare and poisoning of water was used against civilians in these areas.[4]

There were many other instances of mass killings, but of less magnitude. One such was of the survivors of a bombed ship found by the Japanese on Banka Island. All men were marched off and shot. Twenty-two army nurses were ordered to march into the sea, where they were machine-gunned. One, Sister Bullwinkle, although wounded, survived to tell the story.[5]

I relate finally one further account, in addition to that of mine concerning the Labuan trials, to support my assertion that each of the thousands of convictions at the trials themselves provide testimony to the widespread proven atrocities. This example comes from parts of the description of the evidence before the Ambon trials, as recorded by the pen of Shinji, the Japanese defence lawyer and writer, whose comments on the fairness of the war trial system will be quoted later. These trials resulted in four being executed, thirty-nine sentenced to imprisonment and fifty-five discharged. In one of his references to the evidence (according to the English translation by another Japanese), he said:

> After . . . 300 Australians and Dutches . . . had surrendered to the Japanese landing troops [they] were pierced on the chest to death or got their heads cut off. After the end of WWII, this incident was much described as the "Raba Incident".[6]

Of others captured at Ambon, he said:

> . . . being 528 Australians, 14 Americans and 7 Dutches, in which later 13 ran away out of the prison camp, 17 were killed and 379 died of various diseases. Those handed to the Allied Powers at the end of the war were only 139 in number, most of whom, moreover, were suffering from serious diseases and some of them died immediately after being released to their homes. Of the 17 POW who were killed, 11 got their heads cut off for running out of the prison camp to talk with the natives in the island, 4 for being guilty of food theft, 1 for attempted flight out of the camp and 1 for food stealing and prison breaking.[7]

He referred to the evidence concerning the death of the eleven of twenty-five who were taken out of the camp, starved and subjected to systematic beating and torture extending over eleven days. His reference to the evidence concluded with:

> the cries of agony and sounds of lashes were heard even at the foot of the hill. After the torture of beating and bashing, all except 11 (who had already breathed their last with agonies and been sent to heaven) were allowed to return to the camp.[8]

He also detailed the evidence concerning a number of systematic methods of inflicting torture.

The discipline of the Japanese armed forces depended not so much on military training, as in the West, but upon the deeply held beliefs of the Japanese soldier as to his honourable duty. Fundamental to the performance of his duty to do what he was ordered or expected to do, extending to his duty when in charge of POWs or civilians in custody, was a total disregard of all private considerations. On private occasions, the Japanese soldier felt or exhibited all the qualities of a human being such as kindness, compassion, a love of family and of children generally, and some sense of justice and truth. However, on official occasions in the performance of his duty as a soldier, he had no difficulty in putting all these matters aside. It was a matter of priorities, in which his duty stood to the exclusion of all else in a quite different way to the priority of the demands of duty of the best disciplined soldier in the West.

Considerations of humanity, the preservation of life, and respect for truth and justice had no independent existence. He did not think about them in the performance of his duty and whether they could be reconciled with his duty or how his duty could be performed in a way to accommodate them, or how a compromise could be made. He applied the same standards to himself. The irrelevance of death produced the kamikaze pilot and led to Japanese, told to hold a position, to fight to the death in their foxholes beyond the point when resistance could serve any purpose, other than their own death. Death, or in the end suicide, was what service as a soldier honourably required. Those who committed suicide by ceremonial hara-kiri and those who ordered, permitted or assisted others to do so, believed without question that in so doing they honoured their family, and were incapable of thinking of the consequence to their children, whom they loved, being left without a father or supporter. The same inability or unwillingness to think about the matter existed in relation to causing death or to acts of brutality in the performance of their duty to others, such as those in captivity.

Thus the nine Japanese officers given the task of escorting the 470 Sandakan POWs on the first march, who were told to get to their destination, merely "as soon as possible", saw their duty only to get there with all speed, to achieve which sick POWs were beaten or shot. The death of a large number of POWs by the speed of the march was irrelevant as well. In this and other cases, only the end was important, the means of achieving it being of no consequence.

These attitudes to death, violence and the irrelevance of ordinary human virtues in the performance of the duty of the soldier, a basic factor in the atrocities against persons in custody, predated the rise to power of the militarist group, which took Japan to war in the 1930s and 1940s. The leaders undoubtedly exploited these inclinations or did nothing to curb them, but they did not create them. They were the long existing characteristics of the Japanese soldier. National character evolves slowly and the past is reflected in later generations. The origins of these characteristics which are open to some debate, have a long history, but both the traditions of the warrior, including the Samurai and the Japanese fascination with violence, played their parts. Storry in *A History of Modern Japan*[9] points out that the *bushido* or the way of the *bushi* (warrior), popularised as a term in the late nineteenth century, acquired a sinister connotation which it did not originally have. In fact, contrary to claims of the West during the Pacific war, it existed in varying forms centuries earlier as an ideal of Spartan devotion by a warrior class to the arts of war, of readiness for self-sacrifice and loyalty to a martial superior. It existed in the twelfth century. These ideals, however, changed over time. In later periods some of the ideals and practices acquired a semi-religious status directed to the Tokugawa Shogunate and in about the middle of last century, on the restoration of the monarchy, it became directed to the Emperor. Late last century, these ideals were incorporated into the growing nationalism of the Japanese people.

In the context of a nation emerging late and slowly from feudalism, the elements of a feudal hierarchical society persisted, as it seems they still do, in relation to rank, courtesies, loyalty, respect and "face". Violence and death alongside beauty, each in its own way ritualised, played a dominant role in Japanese culture, including its arts. The writer Fosco Maraini in his book *Meeting with Japan* said throughout Japanese literature and drama "there runs a constant thread of sublime sacrifice and horrid bloodshed."[10] Martial arts involving violence were a matter of ceremony. There were ceremonies which paid homage to beauty and human softness. Hara-kiri, by any standards a gruesome and painful method of suicide, was a matter of great ceremony with religious aspects, in which another participated to administer the *coup de grâce*. It could be by the order or permission of higher authority to commit honourable suicide in this way. Somehow the Japanese were able to reconcile violence, death and beauty, as it were, almost in a single glance, as if the two former were aspects of the latter.

It was in this feudal society that a special class existed, those who by birth were the Samurai and, as such, the only ones entitled or fit to be warriors. Their strict code of conduct, particularly that of loyalty, was based on honour. With the coming of conscription to Japan in the second half of last century, which was opposed by the Samurai, any Japanese, regardless of his birth, could become a member of the warrior class. The citizen warriors proved their ability by the defeat in 1877 of the Samurai, during a civil uprising in one of the Japanese islands in which 30,000 died. Thenceforth and in the Second World War, the Japanese soldier in reality had neither training in nor a true understanding of the traditions of the Samurai, which he sought to emulate. To Fosco Maraini, a significant factor in the Second World War atrocities was that the Japanese were an "army of conscripts" not brought up from birth as were the Samurai, but entrusted with the "terrible power" associated with the Samurai rites concerning death.[11]

What Maraini said is undoubtedly true of many of the atrocities, such as those earlier referred to in New Guinea, Rabaul and Nanking and which occurred in many other places, where groups of Japanese ran amok, committing brutalities, murders, rapes and mutilations in order to achieve a kind of sadistic satisfaction. There was no warrior bravery, warrior discipline or, except on a few occasions, ceremonial Samurai "respectful" executions. Civilian soldiers, including conscripts, professing to follow the traditions of the Samurai, which they did not understand, but drunk with their uncontrolled and undisciplined power as warriors, let loose en masse the sadism which is inherent in the Japanese fascination with violence and death. It was this which gave *bushido*, formerly a term implying honour, its sinister meaning during this century. It was this sadism for its own sake, not part of the former warrior tradition, which explains many of the cruelties of individual Japanese, in excess of and far beyond what was necessary in order to carry out orders or policies of their superiors.

The characteristic group automatism of the ordinary soldiers and the unthinking application of what were regarded as warrior precepts and loyalties, and the fact that officers physically beat their troops and generally disregarded their well being are attributable to the conscript and citizen nature of the non-officer class. The point I seek to make is that, whatever their precise origin, the characteristics of the Japanese soldier which produced the atrocities predated the rise of the twentieth-century militarists and were not created by them.

To complete the reference to characteristics of the Japanese soldier observable at that time, it is appropriate to provide some detail and to illustrate. A Japanese soldier was capable of emotions, regarded as normal by Westerners, such as a display of friendship or love of family and children. On private occasions there were instances of soldiers having a friendly talk with POWs, or looking at photographs of one another's family and children. Even on a death march, there were occasionally friendly exchanges, perhaps some joke or meal shared with a POW. The same Japanese later, on an official occasion, might beat the same prisoner or even cause his death, acting as if the earlier relationship had never existed. This is well illustrated by the account of the behaviour of Colonel Suga by the American authoress Agnes Keith in her book *Three Came Back*.[12] While she was interned in Kuching, Suga frequently played with the children, including her child, brought them presents, showed consideration and kindness to her and facilitated her writing while in custody. And yet, he stood by when one junior to him subjected her to considerable ill-treatment because she had dared to complain of an attempt by another Japanese to molest her sexually. Suga had a British decoration from the First World War and had had a US university education. It will be recalled he was the senior officer in charge of all military and civilian prison camps in Borneo, including that at Sandakan which he frequently visited. Undoubtedly he knew and condoned what was occurring there over a long period. All communications to Sandakan from Borneo army HQ had to come through him. His HQ was in Kuching. He must have been directly aware of, and therefore have had some responsibility for, the many atrocities and deaths in the civilian and military prisons there. Although privately a lovable man, his actions on official duty were such that, but for his suicide in captivity at Labuan the day before his proposed interrogation about the Borneo prison camps, he would have shared the judgment and fate of Hoshijima and Baba.

The dilemma for the West in judging and understanding the Japanese was that, contrary to Western concepts, kindness and a love of beauty, for the Japanese, could co-exist with the acceptance of brutality and the destruction of human life. Not all Japanese soldiers in the Second World War displayed the dual nature of the humane citizen and the cruel soldier. Hoshijima, from the great volume of material seen by me, never revealed the former.

Some of the accounts of Sticpewich showed that some guards had the dual personality, while others never displayed a kinder side. Of significance are nicknames such as Ball Kicker, Ball Kicker No 2, Junior Ball Kicker, Big Pig, Little Pig, Ming the Merciless, King Kong, Nagabash, Hospital Pig, Makan Basher and Joe Louis. Other nicknames were more neutral and a product of POW humour or inventiveness such as Myrna Loy, Clark Gable, Churchill, Little Gentleman, Intercourse, Doll, Warthog, The Ghost, Big Annie, Goldfish, The General, Halitose Harry, Village Idiot, Dopey, Moon Rat, Maggots, Bull Frog, Suzy, Mad Harry, Mr Middleton Junior and Methodist. (The nicknames were used as aids to identification at the trials.) The Japanese, like any people, varied greatly individually. Some were prepared to break minor rules, such as giving POWs food, but this was probably seen by the particular Japanese as a private act, quite distinct from an official duty such as where he may later be directly ordered to shoot a sick POW, which he would do.

The different attitudes, on private as against official occasions, also applied to respect for the truth. On what he saw as an unofficial occasion, such as when talking more or less privately across a desk to an Allied interviewer, a Japanese would be inclined to tell the truth as to what occurred. Then on an official occasion, such as at a trial, he would say the opposite, if he perceived it to be in accordance with official policy. Except in the case of a more intelligent person, such as Hoshijima, there would be no attempt to reconcile the two accounts and, if asked, he would just as likely say both were true. The Japanese were great at making general statements of what was the general line, such as that Japanese soldier is "very humane" or "very truthful", or "Japanese soldier very kind and helped sick POW."

Although aware that according to a slogan, such as that the Japanese are humane people, they were supposed to be humane, a Japanese would accept that it did not matter if in fact he ill-treated a POW, when duty or the end so required. Then later, contrary to the facts, he would recite the slogan and perhaps by way of explanation add the further generality that POWs (or Australians) were "very bad people and had to be disciplined" or were "very lazy" and must be made to work hard. At the same time, Japanese often indulged in tokenism which helped them to reconcile their supposed humanity with what happened. On some occasion, perhaps as a reward or inducement, or in a moment of warmth, there would be some gesture of help, kindness or friendship; then looking back, the gesture, usually by then embellished as was the story of Hoshijima's horse, many times referred to at his trial, would be seen by the Japanese as proof of the generality that "Japanese soldiers [always] very humane." In this way, he appeared to be able to compartmentalise his mind to accommodate the cruelties in the performance of what was expected of him and the image of the Japanese soldier sought to be propounded. So far as I could discern, many Japanese came to believe the generalities they asserted when the facts were to the contrary.

What appeared from the Labuan trials was, I believe, general and not confined to Borneo. Much the same Japanese attitudes were observed at the trials of a British war crimes court martial in Malaya by the prosecutor Sleeman and later detailed in his book *Trial of Gozawa Sadaichi and Nine Others.*[13] He found "very little individualism" in the "mental makeup" of the Japanese witness. As he put it, the Japanese "lacking an individual personality is able to meet the exigencies of life . . . by having recourse to a body of ideas, collectively established and expressed usually in a single word, a maxim or a slogan." A Japanese would recite that Japanese officers were "kind and generous", the soldier "kind, honest and chivalrous" and the Japanese army "just and benevolent". Sleeman found that a Japanese asserted these things, although he knew the contrary from his own experience, but regarded the detail of these subjects to be "taboo". Sleeman added:

> . . . where a Japanese can bring himself to reflect on the inconsistencies between theory and practice, he will refuse to see that their number affect the overall picture. On the other hand, one or two "gestures" viewed against a background of high-sounding slogans, are taken as proving how beautiful the picture really is.

This exactly applies to the evidence of the officers in charge of the groups in the first death march from Sandakan, but particularly their speeches as to some single act of kindness before sentence, earlier referred to. Sleeman also observed the exclusion of personal considerations by Japanese in the fulfilment of orders which had to be carried out so "it does not matter how it is carried out."

Until the middle of last century, Japan had sought to lead an exclusive feudal life with its own customs and ceremonial ways shut off from the rest of the world. Intruders, even those shipwrecked, were disposed of or expelled. Then, as a puny nation, it had to succumb to the forced intrusions of European nations and the US into both its territory and sovereign rights, following intimidations by the US Navy under Commodore Perry. Japan then began the process of catching up with the Industrial Revolution, which had passed it by. This was achieved by a remarkable ability to copy, which attained avalanche proportions this century, as Japan overtook the world in the industrial and technological fields to advance from a minor island nation to a leading world power. The same change and imitation of the West did not occur in Japanese customs, ways and outlooks, at least up to the Second World War, and even now change has been gradual and in limited ways.

The interests of an expanding Japan in nearby mainland Asia, but in particular Korea, brought Japan into conflict with Russia. Puny Japan with its quaint ways surprised the world by its victories against Russia and in sinking the Russian fleet as this century commenced. Japan had discovered and proved its nationhood. With a rising sense of nationalism, Japan looked back, with a justified feeling of resentment, that it had been bullied and humiliated by the US, British and Dutch in their past intrusions, and their long sustained insistence on their territorial rights within Japan. As Japan rose to power with ambitions in Asia, which it regarded as its region, it resented past and continuing European and US control of Asian affairs through their colonies, dependencies and spheres of influence. The relationship of Britain and Japan as Allies in the First

World War, was a temporary marriage of convenience. It gave a free hand to Japan in Asia in return for a Japanese fleet in the Far East for Britain.

Resentment of the Europeans obviously played a part and was exploited by leaders for propaganda purposes amongst the Asians, as shown by the parading of POWs. However, it is too simple an explanation to attribute the atrocities against Allied prisoners and European internees totally to this resentment. Many Asians, as we have seen, were not exempted from Japanese savagery.

There is another factor in the question of the resentment of Europeans. This was an inferiority complex, with its typical accompanying and compensating aggression and demonstrations of superiority. The inferiority complex, found in individuals, may extend to nations, and peoples. When power or authority changes, there can be a lingering sense of inferiority despite the change, carrying with it a need to establish and demonstrate superiority. Many Japanese, by their actions in the Second World War, demonstrated this. The clearest example was the universal demand for respect and bowing often enforced by savage punishment. "Face" and the recognition of position in a hierarchy was all important, as it still is. Importantly this encouraged cruelty, particularly when authority was disregarded as by breach of some rule, no matter how minor.

Whether the explosive potential for atrocities in the Japanese soldiers became an actuality, depended greatly on superiors. The potential could be fanned or curbed. It was undoubtedly fanned and manipulated in the Second World War by higher command.

That the potential for violence against civilians and prisoners of war could be curbed was demonstrated during the war between Japan and Russia. The well-recorded gentlemanly and human treatment of at least some of the Russian POWs in that war, in particular the Russian sailors rescued after their fleet was sunk by the Japanese in 1904, is often cited as an enigma or as against cruelty being a characteristic of the Japanese soldier. What happened at Port

Arthur was due to the chivalrous character of General Nogi, who ruled his troops with an iron discipline which extended to severe punishment for the slightest misdemeanour against civilians or their property.[14] At the surrender, the Russian General made a gift to Nogi of his white horse and there were friendly exchanges between the victors and the captured prisoners.

The lack of atrocities against POWs at Port Arthur and the atrocities in the Second World War could well have been reversed if the policies of discipline and of non-intervention had been interchanged. It should be added that at the same period (1904), the same chivalrous attitude did not extend to orientals, such as the Chinese elsewhere on the mainland. Then and later, there was mutual savagery.

A claim which at times has been made, but which ought to be put in perspective, is that the brutalities and killings can be accounted for as the consequence of the Japanese belief that a defeated soldier has no justification for living and is dishonourable allowing himself to become a prisoner. While Japanese attitudes to being a prisoner no doubt made it easier for a Japanese soldier to act as he did to POWs, the real reason for the inhuman conduct was that to cause the death of or act inhumanely to anyone was irrelevant to the Japanese soldier in meeting any situation involving the discharge of his duty as a soldier. POWs were usually not killed out of hand on capture or surrender, but later when there was some apparent reason to do so. This was particularly so with the large group, including the 8th Australian Division, which surrendered at Singapore and was used as a labour force. On the Bataan march, some of the prisoners were deliberately or indirectly killed, while others were retained and incarcerated. The same inhumanities and killings, as the Borneo and other examples show, extended to civilians. The army nursing sisters, who escaped to Banka Island from a bombed ship, were not machine-gunned because the Japanese considered them dishonourable because of their capture. Thousands of Japanese in Borneo and elsewhere accepted capture without much difficulty. These included Baba,

Hoshijima, Takakuwa and Watanabe, the principal Japanese who had ultimate responsibility for the atrocities against POWs there. At his trial, Hoshijima said he did not subscribe to hara-kiri. Suga committed suicide not on capture, but only when he was about to be questioned.

The part played by Japanese leaders in the commission of atrocities in the early stages was mostly by inaction, in contrast with the stern action of General Nogi in 1904, to restrain the potential for savagery of the Japanese soldier. Even in the later stages, such as 1944–45, direct orders were not given from Japan to commit atrocities such as to shoot prisoners. An exception was the order from Tokyo to shoot prisoners at Manila. In the 1942–43 period, many atrocities resulted from top level orders for the use of prisoners in projects required to be completed rapidly, such as the Burma Railway, or the Sandakan airstrips. There were no restrictions on the means by which these goals were to be achieved, even when it must have been known what was happening to the forced labourers. Lack of consideration for and cruelty to prisoners was encouraged by policies such as that of "Asia for the Asians" and prohibitions such as those against the use of the British and Dutch languages and currencies.

The responsibility of Japanese leaders for atrocities committed by others, by both non-intervention or positive aiding and abetting, is recognised by the two classes of charge brought against Japanese leaders at the Tokyo trials. The former has been referred to as negative criminality and the latter positive criminality. These charges recognise what was the truth. The atrocities arose directly from the characteristics of savagery of the Japanese soldier arising in the way already described, but Japanese leaders also had some responsibility for them because, first, they did not seek to prevent them (negative criminality) as General Nogi did, and second, because they positively encouraged some of them, and in 1944–45 gave directions and orders which would lead to them (positive criminality).

The issue of orders at higher and intermediate levels and the pronouncement by Higher Command of policies were usually in general terms, without specifying how they were to be carried out. This facilitated the commission of atrocities and at the same time enabled superiors to disclaim responsibility. The subordinate would obey the order, treating the suffering or death of others or even himself as irrelevant. In this way, prison commanders and guards were given a discretion and a free hand. If the end was achieved, there would be no inquiry as to how it was achieved. There would be no punishment or reprimand if a prisoner was killed or ill-treated. This the subordinate well knew. Superiors could later disclaim responsibility on the basis that they did not order the brutality or killing and were unaware of it.

Many instances of these devices appear in respect of events earlier referred to. Hoshijima had orders to construct the aerodrome using POW labour. Otherwise he had a free hand. Neither Suga or others inquired or interfered with how he used the prisoners. He left the guards to make the POWs work hard and did not interfere with how they treated them. Orders that POWs were to get to Ranau as soon as possible or that none were to be left behind or policy directions that no prisoners should escape, meant and were construed to mean that POWs could be killed or ill-treated to achieve the object. Superiors would not and did not inquire into what happened to the POWs. At their trials Baba and the Tokyo defendants said they did not order the killings and brutality and were unaware of what occurred.

Giving a discretion provides an informal method of dealing with a situation. If a guard beat or killed a POW for some misdemeanour, the matter had been dealt with on the spot. This was the end of the matter. It avoided the need for it to be dealt with more formally by some inquiry. Now there was no need for any inquiry. It was as if the punishment or killing had not occurred. The Doolittle airmen captured in Japan were dealt with formally by trial as criminals. Thereafter captured airmen were informally beheaded on the spot as war criminals.

The discretion device, the informal method and the lack of inquiry or reprimand thereafter, taken with the policies of Higher Command, the general Japanese attitude to the irrelevance of death and the sadism of some, were the basic factors which led to Japanese atrocities being so widespread.

Although responsibility for the widespread atrocities clearly rested firmly on both the Japanese soldiers in the field and on the Japanese leaders, some Japanese after the war have sought to put the entire blame on the leaders and in this way explain what happened as an unfortunate incident in Japanese history, in which a few, by violence, forced themselves on the Japanese people. On this view, the Japanese soldiers who committed the crimes and the Japanese people with them, are absolved from responsibility and hence blame.

This approach is inherent in the earnest writing of Shinji Munemija, earlier referred to. He, as a Japanese civilian defending lawyer at Ambon, wrote on the subject of responsibility for war crimes in his book written for a Japanese audience and published in Japan in March 1946. Included is a chapter entitled "War Crimes and Responsibility of Government".[15] Although some parts of this chapter are not supported by the facts or at least those concerning the commission of war crimes generally, and although some of it is from our point of view illogical, it provides a sample of serious Japanese thinking on the responsibilities for war crimes. It is undoubtedly what Shinji believed and was not written for some propaganda purpose. Some of it is undoubtedly correct.

The substance of what Shinji has written is that the "Government", meaning the Japanese leaders, "incited" the armed services to disregard international law and treaties in order to serve its policies and that those, who committed the war crimes charged, did so because the Government sent them to places and put them in circumstances where they had no choice but to commit "crimes". Anybody else in the same position might have done the same thing. He argued then that the Government (meaning the Government after the war) must regard these soldiers (ie the ones convicted of war crimes) with as much respect and regret as they do those who "died glorious death" for their country or received injuries in the battlefield. Implicit in this is the contention that Japanese who were later executed as war criminals should be honoured in the same way as those who were killed in action in the service of their country. This must have been the attitude which led in later years to the erection of a monument at Nagoya in honour of the Japanese executed as war criminals.

Shinji regarded the Japanese leaders before and during the war as "inciting the people, including military and naval personnel" to suppose that the international law and international agreements had no sanctity and might be nullified unilaterally, solely on the grounds of expediency when "they impeded the aspirations, desires or views of one of the parties." Shinji is speaking as a Japanese lawyer with knowledge of international law. I believe that what he courageously said in this respect was abundantly correct.

He said the charges laid (at the area courts martial) were of two kinds. There were those of crimes by soldiers (or sailors) committed of their "own will" and those of crimes committed in observing their senior officers' orders. Of the former, being "those where there was no express orders," he said some were for "maltreatments" of POWs and of these he said "they did not, we are sure commit such action, thinking they were mistreating POWs, because in the Japanese army or navy, some kinds of autonomical [automatic] punishments were permitted." It is true that discipline is administered differently by the Japanese, such as the practice of slapping soldiers' faces by officers. War crimes trials were really not concerned with "on the spot" punishments of these kinds inflicted on prisoners by Japanese soldiers. Trials dealt with the serious excesses, such as sadistic and brutal beatings, often of sick men, the gouging out of an eye or the breaking of an arm. Of course, the "on the spot" punishment system gives the sadistic individual a blank cheque for brutality and other excesses, but this is conduct for which the individual is responsible on any basis, morally or otherwise. Similarly responsible is the superior officer who takes no action to restrain such excesses, committed in his presence.

Shinji, in respect of this class of crime (committed by

the soldier of his own will), refers also to the "maltreatment" testified to by islanders and seeks to excuse them by saying the Japanese responsible were "on the scene, not for their own will, but as their posts or duties of [as] guards forced them to do. This is quite inevitable; anyone else might have done as those guards did." There is no logic in this contention. If a guard of his own will sets upon a disobedient or lazy prisoner and beats and kicks him, breaking his arms and ribs or killing him in the process, he is not exculpated because the Government sent him to Ambon or Sandakan as a guard, or because another sent in his place to do that duty might have done the same.

It is the existence of these views on the part of a conscientious thinking Japanese with legal training and his publication of them in Japan in 1946, which is the matter both of interest and concern.

In calling on the Government, in the terms already quoted, to do something by way of recognition of the sacrifices of the soldiers which led to their being charged as war criminals, he warns that such steps should not be made an incentive for the revival of militarists. Shinji as a defending lawyer, was one who by his writing blamed the militarists entirely for the war crimes and the predicament of those tried and punished for those crimes. He concluded this chapter with:

> When the government is guilty, how would the morality of its people be maintained on high-level? When the government is indifferent to these sacrifices, it is quite impossible to see the establishment of a new Japan.

The conscientious view of Shinji, which appears to have become a more general view in Japan, conveniently shifts all responsibility for what occurred on to a few who were executed or have passed otherwise into history, leaving free of responsibility or blame the Japanese soldier and with him the Japanese people. However, it is a false view, which any proper review of the nature and circumstances of the many thousands of atrocities show. It is dangerous for the future for a nation or a section of its people to blame a few and exculpate the nation and the people otherwise.

Much of what Shinji says about the responsibility of the leaders is correct, as I think appears earlier in this book and as the evidence at the Tokyo trials showed. They were not only responsible for a violent ascent to power in Japan, for starting wars of aggression, but also in encouraging and permitting the same violence and individual brutality to be perpetrated on all, on prisoners of war and on civilians, regardless of sex or age or nationality or race.

In the end, an examination of the facts forces the conclusion that the cruelties, brutalities and war crimes of the Japanese were the crimes of a partnership in which both the leaders and the Japanese officers, and soldiers and sailors, were each personally responsible and guilty morally as well as legally. The wide spread of atrocities could not have occurred except for the conduct and attitudes of individuals in the ways explained, nor without the deliberate encouragement of the leaders. They had come to power by terrorism and terrorism is a powerful weapon in the hands of an army in an aggressive war of expansion and conquest. Then when conquest turned to defence and retreat, the Japanese leaders and many prison commandants and officers in the field acted as gangsters do, who having murdered, have to murder again to conceal earlier killings and misdeeds.

Then all this ended when the atomic bombs dropped on Japan and brought a sudden end to the war. But for this, the killing of persons in captivity on the Sandakan example would have continued and escalated. Many times the number of Japanese civilians killed by the two bombs would have died, some by military operations and some by starvation. Overall deaths of US, British, Australian, Japanese and other soldiers and sailors and of civilians, Japanese and those in occupied territories, no doubt would have reached, even passed, the million mark. This was how in August 1945 the people of Australia, who had stood under the threat of invasion, saw with relief the dropping of the bombs.

It was afterwards that the world looked back with horror to learn of the destruction wrought at Hiroshima and Nagasaki and, what overrode all else, realised the awesome precedent which had been created for the nations of the world. By chance, the precedent had another side. It demonstrated to the world in a forceful way, which no mere warning of scientists or private national tests could do, what the use of these weapons (which in any event were to come to be held in national arsenals ready for use) really meant. The actual use of the bombs in 1945 not only ended the war, but saved the world until now from conflict between the super powers in the days of the Cold War and inspired them and other nations to prevent, as best they could, the proliferation of the bomb to other nations.

10

WAR CRIMES —LEGAL, MORAL AND PRACTICAL QUESTIONS

The war crimes of the Second World War and their trial were matters of intense debate from 1944 until about 1950, from the time when the proposals for trials were first debated at the London Conference until the trials at Nuremberg and Tokyo and by various regional military courts were complete. In later years, some writers have challenged the legal bases of war crime trials and the fairness and morality of the victors trying the vanquished, particularly the defeated leaders of Germany and Japan. In current years the pursuit and trial of war criminals of the Second World War has been revived in various countries such as the US, Canada and Australia, and with it have arisen questions of the fairness of and legal basis for doing so now.

There has been concern that the trial of war criminals of the Second World War does not appear to have deterred others and prevented war crimes in later wars, such as the Vietnam, Afghanistan and the Iran–Iraq wars. There has been and still is concern as to the application against ourselves now and in the future of the precedents created by war trials past and present.

Through all these debates and criticisms, some well informed, some not, I find there are many misconceptions, and that even the interested public is little aware of what basically is involved in "war crimes" and their trial.

One important consequence of the trials has been that it has provided a vast store of basic and mainly accurate information concerning what Germany and Japan did behind closed doors. Without this information, the world and history would not have had a reliable version of what occurred and of the motives of those involved. But for the trials, much of what occurred in the prisons and concentration camps would not have been revealed as a complete and convincing picture. This is particularly so in relation to the Sandakan prisoners. My direct part in the Labuan trials has been a principal source of what I have been able to write concerning the Sandakan prisoners and of the Japanese involved in their deaths. I have sought to show, using Borneo as an example, that the trials were conducted fairly and were directed to revealing faithfully and objectively what really happened, and in a way which contributes to our history.

In the context of this work and the larger picture beyond Borneo which it seeks to project, it is important that I, a lawyer and participant in the trials, should make some reference to the legal bases of war crimes and the moral and practical implications involved in embarking upon them.

War crimes dealt with after the Second World War fall into two broad classes. The first consists of crimes against humanity committed principally against POWs and civilians in occupied countries. The other class consists of crimes in connection with waging an unjust war.

The humane treatment of people during war was the subject of two peacetime international treaties—the Hague Convention of 1907 and the Geneva Prisoner of War Convention of 1929. The former provided in general terms for the humane treatment of prisoners of war and civilians who came into the custody of a combatant nation during war. The latter, following atrocities in the First World War, made express provisions for the treatment of prisoners of war. Japan was a party to the first treaty, as was Germany, and each signed the second treaty, but when war started in the Pacific in 1941, Japan had not ratified it, as had Germany and the

Allied nations. When the war with Japan started, Britain, its Dominion allies and the US notified Japan of their unilateral intentions to observe the 1929 Convention in relation to Japanese prisoners of war. Tojo, then as Japanese Foreign Minister, formally stated that, although not bound by the 1929 Convention, Japan would apply it to all American, British, Canadian, New Zealand and Indian prisoners of war. In addition, there are numerous specific treaties, such as the Geneva Red Cross Conventions, some made last century, dealing with the treatment of the wounded, hospital ships and so on.

The argument of those who have claimed that there is no war crime on the part of an individual in relation to the inhumane treatment of prisoners, is that the treaties in question were made between states, so as to impose obligations on the party states and not on any individual. Therefore a breach of the terms of a treaty, so this argument goes, cannot be a crime of an individual. Some also assert that the treaties confer no authority on a party nation to constitute a tribunal and empower it or prosecute, as crimes, breaches of its provisions. Finally, it has been said that for a victor nation, by force of its post-war legislation or executive act, to constitute tribunals to try defined war crimes of individuals of a defeated nation, is to create crimes and courts retrospectively, so that war crime trials are not judicial proceedings, but are an executive exercise of power by a victor nation.

Similar arguments have been advanced in respect of the war crime of waging an unjust war. It has been contended that war is an instrument of national policy, that leaders cannot be made responsible for the acts of their country in going to or prosecuting a war and that whether a nation went to war unjustly was not susceptible of judicial determination. Further, it is said that there is no relevant treaty on which such a war crime can be founded. At the Tokyo trials, essentially all these arguments were raised on behalf of the Japanese accused and in particular the one that assents there is no such crime as waging an aggressive or unjust war. The Tribunal, however, in its decision, rejected the argument. In a dissenting judgment, Judge Pal of India concluded that there was no such crime on the part of a national leader under international law. In later years, some writers, principally American, have challenged the view that waging an unjust war is a crime under international law. The fundamentals, as a whole, on which the Tokyo decisions rested have been challenged by some writers who have argued that in consequence, the trial of the leaders of a defeated nation (Germany in the Nuremburg trials and Japan in the Tokyo trials) was a naked exercise of power of victorious nations against the leaders of a defeated nation and, as Tojo himself put it at his trial, "victor's justice", a term adopted for the title of the leading work of Minear which challenges the principal bases of the Tokyo decisions.[1]

The Japanese leaders charged at the Tokyo trials in connection with the waging of a war of aggression were also charged with responsibility for war crimes against humanity committed by others. Submissions that there were no such war crimes of an individual and that leaders could not be made responsible for the crimes of others were each rejected. In one of the early court martial trials of Japanese in Singapore, perhaps the first, being by the British Army in relation to Indian prisoners of war, a challenge was mounted by the defence that there was no war crime by Japanese officers in relation to the ill-treatment of prisoners of war, because Japan was not a party to the 1929 Convention. The submission was rejected, on the basis that, so far as a specific treaty need be relied upon, the Hague Convention of 1907 was sufficient.[2] As earlier stated, no such challenge was raised at the Labuan trials. Charges were framed as inhuman treatment of prisoners. In any address, the only treaty relied on was that of 1907.

There has been an avalanche of books and articles written concerning particular trials, particular charges and sentences.[3] There have been claims of unfairness concerning particular procedures and the constitution of tribunals. Much of what has been written is in conflict. There are opinions for and against the decision not to charge the Emperor and concerning the significance of this to the course of the Tokyo trials. The French judge dissented from the decision of the majority to convict leaders because the Emperor had not been charged. Some Russian writers said the Tribunal was too lenient, while some US writers have said the opposite. Some Russian writers have accused the US of conspiracy with Japan not to charge some Japanese leaders, while some US writers have said it was unfair to have held in custody a second group of Japanese leaders while an earlier group were on trial thereby delaying their release for at least two years. There have been opposing views as to the responsibility of Tojo and whether he should have been found guilty. There were also violently opposed views concerning the guilt of General Yamashita, the Japanese Commander in the Philippines, in respect of the atrocities committed there. The US lawyer defender of Yamashita criticised both the trial and the refusal of the US Supreme Court to intervene. All these particular issues and differences of opinion, important as they are, are outside the scope of this book in which I am attempting to provide some lay understanding of war crime trials in the context of what occurred particularly in Borneo and more generally in other territories occupied by the Japanese.

There were two systems employed to try the Japanese, as was done in Europe to try the German accused. One was by military courts using court martial structures to try Japanese in areas where atrocities had occurred. Those conducted by Australian courts martial were pursuant to the *War Crimes Act* 1945 which followed the pattern of Regulations for the Trial of War Criminals (UK 18 June 1945).

As he wrote soon afterwards, Rear Admiral Earl Mountbatten, Supreme Commander, South East Asia Command, had immediately on the cessation of hostilities, laid down his policy, to which he referred in these terms:

> I . . . laid down that the Japanese should be tried on criminal charges only, that is to say brutality, etc. . . . It was . . . essential, from the very beginning of this process, that no one should be charged unless there was very strong prima facie

> evidence that he would be convicted on evidence [both of criminal conduct and his identity] which could clearly be seen as irrefutable . . . If these two requisites could be met, he would be brought to trial; if they could not, he would not be charged—for I considered nothing would diminish our prestige more than if we appeared to be instigating vindictive trials against individuals of a beaten enemy nation.[4]

There were Australian military courts in Singapore, Morotai, Labuan, Wewak, Rabaul, Darwin, Hong Kong, Ambon and Manus. 924 were charged, 644 convicted, 280 acquitted and 148 sentenced to death and executed. The trials at Rabaul included some senior officers, including Lieutenant-General Baba, earlier referred to. Other Japanese were tried by similar British and US courts. In all about 5700 Japanese were tried for crimes against humanity and 920 were executed. Minear[5] asserts these to be the figures but they are uncertain. Bergamini[6] says US, British, Australian and Chinese military courts tried 4000, acquitted 800, sentenced 2400 to imprisonment for three years or more, and executed 809. In addition, several thousand Japanese captured by the Russians in Manchuria died in Siberian labour camps. He added that the Chinese had war crimes trials, but that complete figures were not available.

The other system of trial similar to that at Nuremberg, was by the International Military Tribunal of eleven judges of eleven Allied nations which sat at Tokyo from 1946 to 1948. Its chairman was Sir William Webb, then Chief Justice of Queensland and later an Australian High Court judge. It tried the major war criminals, nearly all of whom held high government or military office. They included four prime ministers, one of whom was Tojo. In all, trials against twenty-five heard together, proceeded to judgment. All were convicted, seven were sentenced to death and the others were sentenced to terms of imprisonment. Some charges were dismissed. These decisions were made by eight, in the majority. Two dissented and one dissented in part. He considered some of the charges should not have been dismissed. Charges included the planning, preparation, initiation and waging a war of aggression in violation of international law, treaties, agreements and assurances, and participation in a common conspiracy "to do so".

The Japanese Emperor was not charged. This was a political decision, and as such probably a wise one, aimed at the peaceful rehabilitation of the Japanese people and was no doubt aided by the critical part played by the Emperor, after the atomic bombs had been dropped, in bringing the war to an end by the great force of his pronouncements at a time when there was still considerable militant opposition and when assassinations and suicides were rife. In consequence, the Tokyo trials did not directly deal with the Emperor's involvement in the matters for which Japanese leaders were tried. Charging the leaders while omitting the Emperor, led to criticisms at the time of the trials and some difficulties on the matter of consistency of justice at the trials. It provided one of the two grounds of dissent by the French judge. In later years, the well researched work of Bergamini[7] has revealed the active role the Emperor played in actions found by the Tribunal to be war crimes. The foreword by Sir William Webb refers to his misgivings on the consistency question at the time of the trials.[8]

At the Tokyo trials, most were also charged with what later has been called "positive criminality", namely perpetrating, abetting or permitting crimes against humanity. There were charges later termed "negative criminality" laid against some. For example, General Matsui, the officer in charge of the Nankin operation where the notorious rampages of mass murder and rape occurred, was convicted of deliberately and recklessly disregarding his legal duty to take the adequate steps which would have stopped these events. He was sentenced to death. To support the charges, Australia produced evidence of inhumanity to Australian POWs in various areas.

The Potsdam Declaration of 26 July 1945 had declared that "stern justice shall be meted out to all war criminals, including those who have visited cruelties on our prisoners". At the London Conference two weeks later, the Allies set the charter for the Nuremberg and Tokyo trials. In earlier discussions, consideration had been given to disposing of war criminals by executive action. Napoleon had been imprisoned for life on St Helena without trial and by executive decision. However, the London Conference chose the judicial process with the use of special tribunals for leaders and the use of military courts otherwise. The attitudes and policies of the Allies was summed up by Robert Jackson, the former US Attorney-General and the prosecutor, in his opening address to the Nuremberg Tribunal:

> The privilege of opening the first trial in history for crimes against the peace of the world imposes a grave responsibility. The wrongs which we seek to condemn and punish have been so calculated, so malignant and devastating, that civilization cannot tolerate their being ignored because it cannot survive their being repeated. That four great nations, flushed with victory and stung with injury, stay the hand of vengeance and voluntarily submit their captive enemies to the judgment of the law is one of the most significant tributes that power ever has paid to reason.
>
> This Tribunal, while it is novel and experimental, is not the product of abstract speculations nor is it created to vindicate legalistic theories. This inquest represents the practical effort of four of the most mighty of nations, with the support of fifty more, to utilize International Law to meet the greatest menace of our times—aggressive war. The common sense of mankind demands that law shall not stop with the punishment of petty crimes by little people. It must also reach men who possess themselves of great power and make deliberate and concerted use of it to set in motion evils which leave no home in the world untouched. It is a cause of this magnitude that the United Nations will lay before your honours.

A principal misconception concerning war crimes and their prosecution arises from a failure to appreciate the fundamental differences between public international law and municipal law (the domestic law, civil and criminal of a country). With municipal law there is a sovereign legislature to enact law, there is a standing court system to expound and apply the law and an executive to enforce the judgments of the courts. None of these permanent constitutional bodies exists, at least at present, in relation to enacting, expounding and enforcing international law. Despite this, international law exists and places obligations on individuals, and recognises that there are acceptable means of constituting tribunals to deal with breaches of international law. Scholars may argue about its content and about acceptable means of enforcing it, but no scholar of law or of history, particularly in relation to war, would argue against its existence and enforceability. The subject is dealt with by numerous authors of different nationalities in their books on (public) international law and the laws of war, many written last century and some even earlier. One such is the leading English text, the monumental Hall's *International Law* with nine editions written by a succession of authors back to 1880, which students, such as I, studied before the Second World War.

The absence of any legislative source of international law means that it has to be found elsewhere from what is perceived to have been accepted by the civilised international community of nations. As Hall states in his 1924 edition:

> [As] the rules by which nations are governed are unexpressed, the evidence of their existence and of their contents must therefore be sought in national acts—in other words, in such international usage as can be looked on as authoritative.

The preamble to the Hague Convention 1907, to which all leading nations, including all those who became combatants in the Second World War, were parties, acknowledges the source of international law. It referred to "the inhabitants and belligerents" being "under the protection of the law of nations, derived from the usages established among civilized people from the laws of humanity and from the dictates of the public conscience."

International law has an existence which is distinct from the contractual obligations of states which are signatories to treaties. However, treaties may provide important evidence of what is accepted by leading nations to be rules governing the conduct of war. It is the general usage of these rules or their general acceptance by states which establish the international rule, as then perceived by leading writers or as pronounced, by tribunals regarded as internationally authoritative. An accumulation of treaties or a course of decisions may reveal general principles of international law.

International law applies to individuals as well as states. Law, whether municipal or international, which prohibits conduct, so as to make it unlawful, does so for all. A machine gunner who opens fire on an ambulance with Red Cross markings, contrary to the rules of international law, is guilty of a crime under international law and is liable to punishment by the opposing army, if he falls into its hands. The rule and the law is not dry and ineffective, as it would be if only the enemy state were liable and the machine gunner simply were to be given a nice breakfast when made a POW. The fallacy, which still persists, is that individuals are not liable for war crimes because states alone have the contractual obligation which flows from the relevant treaty. The fallacy arises from a failure to understand the true nature of international law.

It is beyond question that international law applies to individuals and recognises that military tribunals of a combatant nation have the right to punish individuals for breach of it. This has been recognised and accepted long before the Second World War and indeed prior to this century. In 1942, the Chief Justice of the US Supreme Court said:

> From the very beginning of its history this court has applied the laws of war including that part of the law of nations which prescribe for the conduct of war, the status, rights and *duties* of enemy nations *as well as enemy individuals.* [The emphasis is mine.][9]

As that decision also points out, it has long been accepted that military courts have jurisdiction to try and punish persons for breach of international law. The jurisdiction of such a court of a State to do so depends on the person charged with a breach of international law falling into the custody of that state.

This decision of the US Supreme Court, of high international standing, that individuals may be guilty of a breach of international law triable by military courts of their enemy, is in accordance with and confirms well recognised principles of law long applied. This is exactly what was done by the Allies in putting individual members of the German and Japanese armed forces in their custody on trial before military courts for breaches of the rules of war, such as inhumane treatment of prisoners of war. In its judgment, the Tokyo Tribunal accepted the US Quirin decision as authoritative on international law that individuals, including national leaders, could be responsible for conduct which was illegal under international law.

Some critics, wrongly, have treated the trial of war crimes, after enemy surrender in the Second World War, as novel and for this reason vindictive on the part of the victorious Allies. After the First World War, there were lengthy discussions at the Versailles Conference concerning German war crimes and the trial of German officers for alleged breaches of the laws of war. Germany accepted that such breaches were susceptible of trial, but persuaded the Allies to permit German military courts to undertake the trials. Despite the extensive atrocities, particularly in Belgium, the Germans only put a few of their nationals on trial (the Leipzig trials), convicted a few, imposed light sentences on them and acquitted the rest. Some of the convicted managed to escape from custody. The commander of the U-boat which torpedoed and sank the hospital ship *Dover Castle* was acquitted on the view that superior orders were, without qualification, a defence.

The defence of superior orders in relation to a war crime is a vexed question, but if applied absolutely can be used to exonerate almost all war crimes, even those concerning the gas chambers of the Second World War, and do so in respect of all short of Hitler. The preferred view, I believe, is that, although relevant in a proper case on the degree of punishment, it is no defence where there is no direct order or where what is ordered is a crime which is or ought to be manifest as such to the subordinate. Where there is no direct order, but what is done is under the influence of pronounced policy of Higher Command, which was often the Japanese method, the Japanese who commits the crime has no defence and Higher Command may be found to be a party to the crime of instigating, authorising or permitting the crime. Lord Wright gave examples published in 1946[10].

> . . . an order, such as to burn women and children of a village in the village church or to machine gun a crowd of innocent hostages, or to murder a number of airmen who attempted to escape but were recaptured, or to inflict hideous tortures to extract information are all instances of manifest criminality.

The German Leipzig trials, and hence trial by a country of its own war criminals, proved to be a futility. It was understandable that, after the Second World War, the trial of alleged war criminals was not handed over to the Germans and the Japanese, but they were tried, as international law had long accepted, by courts constituted by the nations into whose custody the alleged war criminals came.

Again, to quote Lord Wright:

> Nor is it an answer to the law that it is being enforced by the victorious belligerents against the vanquished. Someone must act as policeman if law is violated. The policeman must belong to the stronger side. So it is in ordinary national life. The policeman represents the force of law and order; his action involves an exercise of power; so does the action of the victorious belligerent which seeks to punish violators of the laws of war, but it also seeks to vindicate the law for the benefit of humanity. That the stronger may sometimes in fact be substituting power for justice is no doubt a calamity when it happens, but this possibility is not relevant to the argument when what is being sought is justice, not revenge . . .
>
> Not only is the practice of trials of war offences by military courts of the other belligerents established by international law, but it is obviously the only practical course,

certainly in such circumstances as those now existing.[11]

Lord Wright, long a House of Lords law lord, was one of the great jurists of this century. He was the Australian adviser and delegate on war crimes in the critical year 1945. In January 1946, in a penetrating and illuminating exposition, he outlined the principles and considerations involved in the prosecution of war criminals, including national leaders. His views,[12] which should be read and which, with respect, in principle are correct, answer some of the criticism levelled at the Tokyo trials. It leaves open questions whether the conduct of the trials were fair and the conclusions justified by the evidence, but these are separate questions. As stated, the Tokyo court was constituted by leading judges of eleven countries, presided over by a judge who held high judicial office in Australia. The conclusions of the court were supported by the unanimous opinions of eight of its members. The decision of the Tribunal is the decision of these eight judges. The limited dissents, although important, are not part of the international precedent created. That decision, was that each of the crimes found to have been committed were war crimes of individuals at the time they were committed. That decision is now authoritative for the future and was formally and expressly accepted by Japan by the ultimate peace treaty.

The bases for the conclusion that commencing and waging an unjust and aggressive war was already a crime under international law prior to the commencement of the Second World War on the part of national leaders, cannot be better stated than by Lord Wright in the article already referred to. A critical part of his analysis was this:

> . . . between [the First World War] and the commencement of the war just ended, civilized nations, appalled by reviewing the destruction and suffering caused by the first great war and appalled by the thought of the immeasurable calamities which would flow from a second world war, gave much thought to the possibility of preventing the second war. The Covenant of the League of Nations did contain certain machinery for that end. Certain conventions were summoned

to declare that unjust and aggressive war was to be prohibited; one of these actually declared that it was a crime.

In 1928 the Pact of Paris or the Kellogg-Briand Pact was signed or adhered to by over sixty nations. It was a solemn treaty. Its central operative clause was brief . . . but its terms were plain, clear and categorical. The nations who signed it or adhered to it unconditionally renounced war for the future as an instrument of policy.[13]

The question was extensively debated at the Tokyo trials, when the Japanese advocates argued there was no crime as charged. The judges formulated reasons for holding the charges to be in accordance with international law. They relied on the Nuremberg Judgment which said:

> The question is what was the legal effect of the pact [that of Paris]. The nations who signed the pact or adhered to it unconditionally condemned recourse to war for the future as an instrument of policy and expressly renounced it. After the signing of the pact any nation resorting to war as an instrument of national policy necessarily involves the proposition that such a war is illegal in international law; and that those who plan and wage such a war, with its inevitable and terrible consequences, are committing a crime in so doing.

Sir William Webb, later in 1971, commented:

> Until the twentieth century the right to wage war was a sovereign right exercised by all nations without check except the fear of defeat. Losers paid indemnities in money or territory, and rough rules of chivalry were applied in judging international right and wrong. After WWI, however, all the major powers made efforts to agree upon standards of war conduct and upon principles of international law which might be used in judging those who initiated war. Finally in 1928, sixty-six nations signed the Pact of Paris condemning recourse to war as an instrument of national policy except in self-defence. Japan was one of those nations . . .

> The Pact of Paris did not explicitly state that the war leaders of a signatory nation could be held individually responsible if that nation broke the pact. Some international jurists of standing have taken the view that the pact did not impose individual liability. However, I cannot attribute to 66 nations—some of whom signed the pact only after years of deep consideration of their national interests—such futility as to subscribe to an international law for breach of which no individual human being could be punished.

Referring to the seven cases where the Tribunal imposed capital punishment, he added that this had been done on the basis of the evidence that "the accused were not only responsible for aggressive war, but also for leadership which had allowed otherwise well disciplined Japanese troops to commit pillage, rape and murder in areas outside the forward field of battle."[14]

One of the main criticisms of war trials often still made is that they acted retrospectively. What is meant by retrospectivity in relation to crime and why it is objectionable should be understood. Retrospectivity which is abhorrent to all fair-minded people, is making or deeming conduct criminal which was not criminal under any applicable law when the conduct occurred. To punish a person for a crime retrospectively created is not an exercise of justice, but of executive power, in the case of a war crime an exercise of power by a victor nation. For reasons earlier stated, war crimes of various types were crimes when the conduct charged occurred. As to the war crimes of inhumanity, for example the shooting of POWs or the causing of their death otherwise, as by deliberate starvation, it is beyond argument that this was a crime under international law on the part of the individual well before the Second World War. There were precedents for it dating at least back to the First World War.

As to the war crimes on the part of individuals of commencing and waging an aggressive war, as already stated, the reasoned judgments at Nuremberg and Tokyo relying on accepted indicia of international law, and the opinions of jurists such as Lord Wright, establish that before the commencement of the Second World War, these crimes had been crimes on the part of individuals under international law. The German and Japanese leaders were not convicted of crimes retrospectively created. It is true that no individual had earlier been charged with such a crime, so that there was no earlier decision providing a precedent. This, however, does not stand against that being the international law or the conduct being a war crime when it occurred. The pronouncement after the Second World War ended, as to what the law was before and during that war, did not create crimes retrospectively, any more than when a municipal court first pronounces what the law is on some topic. It is basic to any legal system that ignorance of the law does not excuse. It is no excuse for a commandant who massacred his prisoners or gassed Jews to say that he did not know in so doing that he was committing a crime punishable under international law.

It may be argued that it is unfair or immoral to punish national leaders for a breach of international law as individuals in relation to the launching of a war of aggression, when there has been no precedent for such a charge in any earlier war. This is one aspect of the Tokyo trials which concerned Judge Pal. However, if at the relevant time, that was the international law, it can be asked, was it unfair to apply it to a leader who, seeking to have his country dominate Europe and advance his own power, was responsible for it aggressively invading one minor nation after another in breach of solemn treaties entered into by his country, being treaties which outlawed and made illegal such aggressive acts? Was it unfair in respect of the Japanese leaders who did likewise, for example in relation to the countries such as Thailand or the Philippines, which on any possible argument had never threatened Japan in any way?

Some have been confused by the circumstance that it was after the war was ended that by national legislation such as by the *War Crimes Act (Aust)* 1945, or by the Allied making of an international agreement (as by the London Conference of 1945), tribunals were set up and procedures provided to try charges of war crimes. It has been argued that doing so is tainted by the evils of retrospectivity. Properly understood, there is no retrospectivity and no unfairness in setting up such tribunals after the war. If what a person did was (under international law) then a crime, there is no unfairness, if he did so thinking that there was no court available to enforce the law or that his country would win the war and not take action to discipline him. He is in no different a position than that of the person who commits a crime in peace time believing those in power will not enforce the law, or that he is in or will get to a haven where action will not or cannot be taken to extradite him and the extradition law or the authority in power is later changed.

Lawyers, rightly, do not apply the term "retrospective" to the constituting of courts or providing procedures to try crime which has been committed in the past. The constitution of courts by a nation or nations having in its custody the person to be tried was in accordance with international law. This was so in respect of the Nuremberg and Tokyo Tribunals, as well as the many military courts. Constituting them after the war did not give retrospective operation to the pre-existing law.

It should be accepted as the correct view that courts properly constituted in accordance with international law tried what when committed were under international law crimes against humanity, or of prosecuting aggressive war on the part of the individuals charged. These were the decisions given by many lawyers of many nations in the course of the many trials. These views have been strongly supported by lawyers of eminence such as Lord Wright. These decisions were accepted as valid by Axis nations in the final peace treaties which legally ended the state of war. For the future, international law has been determined.

Those who have criticised the war trials, in particular the Tokyo trials, have made little attempt to meet the fundamentals or arguments on which these conclusions are based. Attacks of legal aspects of the trials have been rather directed to collateral matters. In some books, the judgment of one judge at the Tokyo trials, Judge Pal of India, who found almost every issue differently to every other judge, has been elevated to the level of gospel, not by Japanese writers, but writers in Allied countries, particularly America, some of them disenchanted by the Vietnam war. The decision of Judge Pal, and some commentaries on it, such as those of Minear, raise a number of questions of great importance, such as how "aggressive" war and self-defence in war are to be defined and determined. What has been said in this field and others point to the difficulties in these and other concepts, particularly in a different setting and perhaps in a different war, such as the Vietnam war. However, I think the judgment of history will be that Hitler and his Nazi leaders and the Japanese militarist leaders, embarked on aggressive wars of expansion, which did not invoke the problems which some saw in somewhat academic analyses of concepts of aggressive war and self-defence. Whether it is "night" may be difficult to determine or define when it is twilight, but it is no problem when it's midnight. Important as are the dissenting views and conflicting opinions when applied in different situations or to future wars, they are outside the scope of this chapter.

There are, however, two further and important questions which arise in relation to the war trials of 1945–48. The first is how fair were the trials in their general structures and how fair were they in particular cases. Involved is the moral question whether the victors could fairly try their enemies. The second is a perhaps frightening question, namely what precedent has been created for the future? This raises the practical question as to how wise were the Allied nations in their decision at the London Conference in 1945 in making the executive decision to invoke the judicial process of international law to deal with the war crimes of the Second World War.

In the years following the trials, there were claims and counter-claims concerning the fairness of the procedures used, and that some decisions were wrong. The open trial system made it possible to debate these questions. Justice administered in the open with reasons published is the best guarantee of truth and fairness. It puts a stamp on the war trials systems as an attempt to administer justice fairly.

A major matter of continuing criticism by some has been that the trials were unfair because they were the trial by the victors of their enemies. However, as already indicated, this had long been the method prescribed by international law. The jurisdiction to try breaches of the rules of law is exercisable by a belligerent during a war until its termination legally by the peace treaty, and rests with the nation having the custody of the alleged offender. Without such trials during war, people would have been executed without trial for suspected war crimes. Even so, many were. When the leaders of Germany and Japan came to be tried, it may have been possible to assemble judges from neutral countries, but there was no international structure or jurisdiction to do so. In any event, the determination of what countries were really neutral in the world conflict, and who could supply judges of accepted international standing and competence would have raised its own problems and controversies. The best that could be done was, as with the Tokyo Tribunal, to select leading judges from eleven different Allied countries and have the trials held openly. It may be that in the future the United Nations could do what it has not yet attempted and set up some permanent structure using neutral countries to try war crimes. This could raise problems which might frustrate its effective functioning.

Some offered criticisms based on the procedures used in their own country in respect of the trial of local crimes. Some of these criticisms were not soundly based because the trial of war crimes encounters quite different problems which require some different solutions. What is fair has ultimately to be judged as a matter of logic. In the end, the real question is, was the clear truth arrived at as a matter of logic on the whole of the evidence produced? The circumstances in which war crimes were committed were usually quite different to those concerning domestic crime. There were problems by reason of the death of some witnesses and the scattering of others, and because the events had occurred some years previously in territory under the control of Germany or Japan, each of which had pursued policies of concealment. Special procedures concerning the receipt of evidence were necessary.

There can be no valid criticism, if, in the end, findings of guilt were in fact based on clear evidence found logically probative by honest judges.

Ultimately, the most important question concerning the war trials held in the period 1946–48 is, was in fact a just and true decision given based on the evidence? That is a question always difficult to answer in respect of any trial domestic or international, except where one is thoroughly familiar with the trial, the evidence given and all its implications. It cannot be done by the sniping approach of one with a bias to condemn, who seizes on one aspect of the evidence or the procedures and ignores the totality. It is almost an impossible task to say a particular decision at the Tokyo trials was wrong where the evidence against all took nearly two years to give and where there are just under 40,000 pages of transcript of evidence and some 4000 documents. As with any judicial system, the best that can be done is to constitute a court with honest men expert in the judicial method, who come to a decision after hearing open debate on either side. In the case of the Tokyo trials, a cross-section of such men from eleven nations sitting in open session and giving in the end reasoned judgments was the best that could be done.

At the court martial trials, as well as at Tokyo, the Japanese were permitted to provide their own defending officers and usually did so. They were usually lawyers. Some, such as Colonel Yamada, at Labuan, had high qualifications in British law. Lieutenant-General Baba was represented by a Japanese major-general assisted by a Japanese civilian lawyer. In some areas, on request, the Japanese were given the assistance of Allied army lawyers, who in some instances directly appeared for the Japanese, presumably with that independence which is ingrained into the Western lawyer. Many Australian lawyers of distinction acted as prosecutors, judge advocates or court martial members. All Australian decisions had to be confirmed by senior legal officers in the Australian army. Convicted Japanese were at liberty to, and did present petitions concerning convictions and sentences and these were dealt with by senior lawyers unconnected with the trials. That this was a real and not a formal process is shown by their variation of some verdicts and sentences.

The trials were held very soon after the war ended when memories were fresh and the identity and location of defence witnesses would be known or readily ascertainable. As at Labuan, trials were usually held close to where the relevant Japanese were then held in custody. Indeed, the Japanese defence usually had the advantage, as they had at hand an abundance of witnesses to what had occurred, while the prosecution usually laboured under the handicap that critical witnesses were dead. At the Tokyo trials, the defence had ready access to an unlimited store of documents and witnesses. They had prior knowledge of the available evidence.

For the reasons I have given, it is difficult, although not impossible, to say that the trial of any individual resulted in an unfair decision or wrong punishment. Having regard to the great number of trials and some difficulties encountered, it is likely that some errors were made. It is fortunate that a serious injustice to one accused, the warrant officer in the first death march trials, was avoided. Some aspects of the trial of Yamashita and possibly his conviction are open to serious question.[15] Some of the evidence presented related to conduct over which he could not possibly have had control. This included what happened in Manila after Japan overruled him and sent Rear-Admiral Iwabuchi with 15,000 men to take over the defence of Manila. Yamashita had acted in an exceptionally ethical way in Manila. In contrast, in the trial of General Baba, extreme care was taken only to put against him crimes committed in circumstances where he could have prevented them.

In later years, further information has come to light relevant to past trials. For example, the researches of Bergamini into Japanese documents not earlier produced, throw light on the policies of Higher Command in relation to POWs. Local inhabitants have revealed matters concerning the Sandakan prisoners who were left behind when the second march left and concerning some occurrences on the marches.

Sir William Webb, some twenty odd years after the Tokyo trials, considered that the new material not presented at the trials indicated that the Tokyo findings "could have been based on evidence of guilt even more convincing than that tendered at the trials" and that, with the possible exception of one sentence, there was no miscarriage of justice.[16]

I have been at some pains to describe the Labuan trials in some detail. Looking back at those trials with a memory refreshed by re-reading the transcripts and a contemporary diary, and with some knowledge of later revelations and the intervening experience as NSW Supreme Court judge for twenty-five years, I can say with confidence that the decisions reached, taken with the confirmations and variations resulting from the intervention of the supervisory authority, were just decisions fairly arrived at on convincing evidence. The Labuan trials are an example of fairness being able to be achieved in perhaps the most difficult of all trials, because of the paucity of witnesses and an earlier deliberate attempt by the Japanese to destroy all evidence, which almost succeeded. Despite the Japanese attempt in the closing stages of the war to dispose of evidence, those principally responsible were tried and convicted, using proper means and relying on convincing evidence.

Going to the views of those who directly participated in the trials, I quote some opinions of a Japanese civilian lawyer, Shinji Munemija, LLD, who was one of the Japanese defending counsel at the Ambon war trials where there were many convictions and some death sentences. He set out these opinions in his book *The Account of the Legal Proceedings of the Court for War Criminal Suspects*, written in early 1946 in Japanese for a Japanese audience. Under the heading "Adoption of Anglo-American way of legal proceedings", he said amongst other things:

> It is considered that the war criminal trial conducted in accordance with British and American legal formula has given a suggestion of great significance of the drastic reformation of Japanese judicial system. Under the Anglo-

American legal proceedings, the accused can enjoy their human rights and freedoms entirely, and the prosecution and the defence, and the accuser and the accused charge and rebut against each other on an equal footing, with the justice of judges. Contrary to this, however, the conventional Japanese criminal trial, although drawn up in imitation of the judicial system of Europe, may be called to have made little progress from a fuedalistic torture-first trial. The judges and prosecutors have inherited the dominant bureaucratic sense, hard to eradicate, that they have, as representatives of the State, full reasons to control the right and freedom of the accused only to prove their guilt.

> It is, however, as sure as fate that it is not long before Japan will be, no matter whether it may want or not, restrained to adopt the Anglo-American way of legal proceedings.[17]

Having referred to the problems of Japan following the Anglo-American pattern involving "a high level of people's common sense about legal proceedings", he added:

> Nevertheless, this Anglo-American way of legal proceedings is not all perfection. It has still room to be studied and improved. The defence technique of the accused has too much power in it, "which permits even the accused to rebut and object . . ."
>
> In conclusion, the writer may be allowed to point out that the prosecutor's execution of their desperate effort to incriminate the accused at any cost in the Japanese court, thereby maintaining their credit and face, a never-to-be-seen phenomenon in a British or American court is very detrimental to fair trial and justice.[18]

It should be added that Sir William Webb, referring back to the 1946–48 period, said the Tokyo trial "was commended for its fairness even by the Japanese vernacular press."

It can be inferred that the Japanese defending lawyer and author, Shinji, considered the Ambon trials to be fair. As he said, "The Allied trials stood in contrast with Japanese trials."

They stood in contrast with the Japanese trial of Captain Matthews, professing to exercise jurisdiction under international law, which relied for evidence on that procured by extreme tortures resulting in the death of many people to support conclusions in proceedings then and since closed from world scrutiny. The Allied war trials stand in contrast with the summary execution without trial of Allied airmen classified, whatever the circumstances, as war criminals. They stand in contrast with the execution without trial of those suspected of involvement in the Jesselton uprising.

A further question concerns the wisdom overall of the executive decisions of the Allied leaders in 1945 in setting in train what was to provide a precedent for the unpredictable future. The Allies had three alternatives: to do nothing and set free the leaders and others; to execute without trial the leaders and others such as camp commandants; and/or to use the judicial method of trial of those persons apparently responsible. These questions were debated at the London Conference of 1945. Despite the treaties and promises after the First World War to outlaw war and so prevent a repetition of the tragedy of the First World War which had achieved nothing, the world had again been engulfed in a war which caused the death of millions of people and the untold suffering or hardship in most families of the world. Those who became leaders of Germany and Japan had each in their different ways seized control in their own country by assassinations, terrorism and intimidations. They then launched Germany and Japan into what most of the rest of the world saw as a war of aggression, seeking respectively domination of Europe and the Asian Pacific regions, making unprovoked attacks on neighbouring countries, many of them small and incapable of effective defence. In the process, they used the same tactics of terrorism and intimidation as they had used to come to power. In addition, despite the many earlier treaties making inhumanities in war illegal, refined by further treaties following the atrocities of the First World War, there had, in breach of them, been brutalities and killings, including mass exterminations in the concentration camps of Europe and the prison camps in the Pacific and Asia, beyond any modern experience. As was to appear, leaders were actively engaged in these happenings.

Whatever was done, a precedent for the future would be created by its leading nations. If trial was to be the course taken, then, after a war of utter lawlessness, the principles of humanity and justice would be re-asserted and international law would be re-affirmed, in particular that which had made aggressive war and inhumanity in war unlawful. That, of course, was the ideal and hoped for deterrent for the future, but the precedent would result in the execution of many, so there would be a real risk that in future wars that, if misapplied, the precedent intended to prevent future inhumanity, would itself be the instrument and excuse for inhumanity.

Whatever the difficulties, and there were many, the only practical alternative was the third. If this alternative was adopted, should leaders as well as those who directly committed atrocities, be tried? If leaders were tried, the dangerous and unpredictable use of the precedent created would arise for the future, with the blessing of the leading nations. To let go free those who were really responsible for creating situations in which endless inhumanities had occurred, would make it utterly unjust to execute their subordinates. This was the dilemma of the French judge at Tokyo when the Emperor was excluded from those tried.

In 1945, there was no practical alternative than to do exactly as was decided at the London Conference. The future would have to look after itself. No doubt some domestic and international political propaganda and some elements of retribution were involved in the setting up and conduct of the Nuremberg and Tokyo trials, but overall, they and the military courts were a genuine attempt to deal judicially and fairly with and reveal the truth about what had occurred.

Just under half a century later one may ask whether the attempt in the period 1945–48 on behalf of the people of the world to demand compliance with formerly agreed standards of humanity and by punishment of atrocities to deter them in the future, have succeeded. To seek some answer, one must look to later wars, such as Vietnam, Afghanistan and Iran–Iraq, but there has been no judicial or real examination, as there was after the Second World War, which has revealed the true level of atrocities in these later wars.

In a world which has moved closer to atomic war and in which one country sends its armies into and imposes its rule or philosophy on another country on the pretext of some kind of invitation of its puppet government or some insurgent group, or where one country makes some attack or bombs another as a reprisal for terrorism or because that other is engaged in some hostile action against a third country, which nation and which leaders are the aggressors in a criminal sense? If some are war criminals, what means are there to bring them before some tribunal and try them?

For example, which nations were the aggressors in the Vietnam war? Could any national leader be said to be criminally responsible for the waging of a war of aggression? Different people would give different answers. How would these questions be answered in respect of the Afghanistan, Central American or Iran–Iraq wars? What of different types of inhumanities than those dealt with at the war crime trials? What of the bombing of civilian areas and other acts of terrorism against civilians to exact surrender or diminish the will of a nation to resist? Going back to the Second World War, what of those who ordered the dropping of the atomic bombs on Hiroshima and Nagasaki, or the bombing of London, Berlin, Dresden or Tokyo, and those who did the bombing?

One may ask in respect of future wars, in which any of the Allied nations of the Second World War are participants, what assurance is there that war crimes, now accepted on their precedent as requiring punishment, including execution, will be dealt with by fair trials requiring the strict proof of criminality which generally marked the Second World War trials? How will the precedents be used in the hands of many different nations, some with their own, perhaps primitive, ideas of justice? That there may be primitive ideas of justice and the misuse of precedents in relation to war crimes is powerfully demonstrated by the concepts of justice and the punishments for war crimes by Japanese trials and executions during the Second World War. The few trials held by the Japanese were by military courts using the torture first methods referred to by Shinji Munemija. One such was the Matthews trial in Kuching in 1944. Another was the trial of the airmen from the Doolittle raid who crashed in Japan. This trial set the precedent that airmen were war criminals who deserved execution. Thereafter, many airmen were punished, sometimes by death, without trial or inquiry as to their mission or their part in it. Many in many different regions were beheaded on the spot when captured. All airmen taken to Rangoon gaol in the period 1944–45 were classified, without inquiry, as war criminals, segregated, punished and imprisoned under extremely harsh conditions, leading to many deaths.[19]

The criminal responsibility of those who plan bombing raids and those who pilot aeroplanes or who aim bombs, such as at areas marked by the pathfinder, present factual and legal questions concerning criminality of great difficulty, which are quite different to those which arose in trials concerning the treatment of persons in custody, the principal subjects of the Second World War war trials in Europe and the Pacific.

The precedents will be apt to give rise to almost insuperable problems and some danger when they come to be applied to later treaties aimed at regulating the conduct of military operations in future wars. This could arise acutely in respect of many of the provisions of the 1977 protocols to the Geneva Convention of 1929. The protocols have been agreed to by a number of nations, including Australia, but many have not yet ratified them. The Prime Minister in 1986 indicated that it was proposed to ratify the protocols, but this has not yet occurred. The protocols have been inspired by worthy ideals to make future wars more humane and to avoid "total war". Despite the commendable motives, the protocols incorporate unrealistic attempts to introduce detailed rules of war intended to isolate civilians and civilian activities from military, including bombing operations. Some require value judgments or are ambiguous to the extent that opposing sides will apply or construe them differently. Despite the good intent, the experiences of all wars this century shows that when war comes using weapons from the sky or from a distance, countries at war will not be deterred from their objectives, whether civilians are affected or not, and that reprisals against each other and the destruction of sources of supply, communications, manufacture and power will continue. Under the protocols, the dambusters airmen of the Second World War would be found liable to be war criminals because of the consequences to civilians downstream.

On the pattern of the Japanese treatment of airmen, some of the provisions of the protocols will be a recipe for reprisals and executions of any as war criminals, who fall into enemy hands when civilians have been killed or civilian establishments have been damaged, whatever the circumstances or the involvement of the person captured.

Another consequence of the precedents created, but involving, I believe, some misunderstanding of them, has been the continuing pursuit in later years of suspected Second World War criminals in various countries, including Australia, which is about to commence trials for war crimes some forty years after the war legally ended. Trials held at so late a time and at places so remote from where the alleged crimes occurred disregard concepts of fairness, which were regarded as critical at the 1945–48 trials. The essence of what was done concerning war crimes in that period was to select the serious cases where guilt appeared clear and promptly dispose of them at locations where accused persons had ready access to documents and to witnesses with fresh memories. The subordinates were tried first and in the end the leaders. It was implicit in what was done that having selected and tried cases on this basis, the trials would be brought to an end. This in effect was the view and policy pronounced by Earl Mountbatten as has been noted. It was the view apparently accepted by the Dominions in 1948. On 13 July 1948, the Secretary of State for Commonwealth Nations sent a cable to the Dominions, which included:

> In general no fresh trials should be started after 31 August 1948. . . . In our view punishment of war criminals is more a

> matter of discouraging future generations than of meting out retribution to every guilty individual . . .[20]

The cable related to trials in relation to the war in Europe. Australia did not dissent[21] and brought the Japanese trials to completion by about 1951.

There were many who committed war crimes, but were not charged. These included, for example, the many Japanese soldiers who shot prisoners on orders, some of them cheerfully. There were some shootings which were subject of no charge, because the direct evidence then available was not sufficient to prove guilt to the criminal standard. Decisions having been made as to who should be tried, a halt was called. All this was in accordance with the procedures and jurisdictions recognised by international law. All these trials were held by belligerents during the state of war, which continued until the formal peace treaties. By these treaties, the defeated belligerents accepted the war trial decisions. That was to be the end of this aspect of the war. The former belligerents and their respective peoples were then at peace.

The trials in later years, such as now proposed in Australia, are not the trials of war crimes in the way contemplated by international law. Trials can no longer be by the military court of a belligerent. Australia is conducting domestic trials of Australian citizens not formerly so and who were not necessarily members of a nation with which we were at war.

For reasons already stated, there is no retrospectivity in what is being done, as there was none in the trial by Israel of Eichmann. In each case, the crimes to be charged or found were crimes when committed. This was so, although the courts to conduct the trials were not then in existence and Israel as a nation did not then exist. The proposed Australian trials are not war trials, but trials by domestic courts under Australian law into which the relevant international law has been incorporated by legislation. Although international law is to be applied in this way, the concept of war crimes as incidents of war dealt with by belligerents while a state of war still legally exists and then getting on with the peace, has been ignored.

Although trials of Australians by Australian domestic jury courts are our own affair, what is being done is of international significance. It ignores international considerations in which international law draws a distinct and legal line between war and peace. Although no doubt there are Germans and Japanese who were party to atrocities, but were not charged because of the lack of sufficient evidence or some policy reason, it is in accordance with international law and accepted international relations that we as a nation and a people are at peace with Germany and Japan and all their people. This is so even although, so far as Australia is concerned, there may be and most likely are some Japanese businessmen with whom we deal who were involved in atrocities. Since the Japanese Emperor, Hirohito, for whatever reason was not charged, or found to be a war criminal, and since the formal peace treaty was signed and the Allies accepted him as head of State, it is clear that on an official occasion, such as his funeral service, he should have been respected as head of State and that heads of State of Allied nations should have attended the service in accordance with international protocol.

All this does not mean that some blanket should fall on history, on the truth or on discussion of all that happened in the past. It does not mean that the attitude of individuals should be constrained. It does mean, I believe, however that nations should call a halt to the legal pursuit of alleged war criminals of a war now ended for nearly half a century. An exception might be made, however, in an isolated case of a leader in the planning and execution of extreme atrocities such as Eichmann, but even only then, if there was some special reason why the case was not fully investigated and brought to trial years before.

Quite apart from the anomalous character of these impending trials, there is the serious overriding question as to how fair they can be, accepted at the London Conference as a particular essential in the trial of war crimes.

Delay, particularly gross delay, as any judge or litigation lawyer well knows, is the thief of justice. This is particularly so in criminal cases in the reliability of proof, in the ability to defend, in decision making and in the imposition of punishment. Courts in Australia under the influence of a Privy Council, High Court and US decisions, have permanently stayed some prosecutions on the ground of a delay for but a fraction of forty years, in cases which could have been investigated or brought to trial in earlier years. The proposal in Australia is not just to try one or two exceptional cases, such as the Eichmann or Klaus trials. Some hundreds of cases of war crimes in northern Europe are under investigation for trial here, and as the Menzies report shows, general and particular allegations and investigations, some by the Australian Federal Police and some by ASIO, had been made many years ago but were not then pursued to trial. It is a new mass investigation of what could have been done years ago. The renewed activity has inspired some 200 fresh allegations made locally or from Russia.

The problem of unfairness is posed by rhetorical questions, to which I believe no satisfactory reply can be given. How can certainty of guilt and irrefutable proof of identity be fairly determined now? It is no answer to state the obvious that the crimes were serious and that murder is murder, whenever it happened. How can events so long ago on the other side of the world in a political climate of which those who have to decide guilt are unaware, be adjudicated upon here now? How reliable can witnesses be to such long past events? Prejudice from the horrors of those times will be apt to colour dim memories. How reliable can documents be without the support of reliable witnesses to events and surrounding circumstances? If an accused by way of defence of guilt or in mitigation of punishment wishes to argue that what he did was minor, in difficult war circumstances or part of some military or resistance operation, how can he, a resident of Australia for many years and now an old man, remember, locate and produce witnesses, some of whom may be dead? How can he search for, locate and produce documents, as he might have done, if he had been accused in earlier years and had been tried near the place of his alleged crimes? The USSR has now indicated a willingness to allow prosecution witnesses to the commission of these alleged crimes to come to Australia to give evidence. It is in its interest to have shown to the world that the Western democracies have hidden these war criminals over the years. Its interest is in convictions, not acquittals. On the totalitarian approach to trials, it is not in its interest to allow outside its curtain those who would give evidence to the contrary of its interests and who might then defect. There are many ways, other than a blunt refusal of a passport, to frustrate efforts of accused persons to locate witnesses, ascertain what they are willing to say and bring them to Australia where their evidence could be adverse to Russian interests.

It is no answer that the court has power to stay proceedings if it is established that the defence is prejudiced in some way. The subtle, but most devastating prejudice is the inability to prove prejudice, by reason of an ability to produce any specific evidence of it, such as proof that there was some witness in fact who could have given some significant evidence, but could not be procured after diligent attempts to procure his attendance. This inability to prove specific prejudice leaves the trials with the dilemma that the true prejudice is what is known as general prejudice, ie to all trials, because of the great lapse of time and the remoteness of the subject matter of the trials. General prejudice is one where actual or specific prejudice cannot be demonstrated. If considered applicable to the proposed trials, courts could stay all trials individually. The dilemma is that the legislation had expressed the general intention of Parliament that there shall be trials.

Trial of these cases by juries, appropriate to the trial of an Australian citizen before a domestic court on any serious criminal charge, presents difficulties and highlights the problem. Basic to jury trials is that a jury of citizens is aware of the social circumstances of the community in which the crime is committed and represents the community conscience in this respect. The basic justification for there to be an acceptable jury trial is surely absent where, in 1989 or 1990, a jury is called on to try wartime events in a war before most potential jurors were even born, being events on the other side of the world committed by some people against other people with no connection to Australia. With clear guilt now the proclaimed justification for the selection of delayed prosecution of alleged war criminals, will not the trials be seen as little more than a formality given that jurors will be exposed to the horrors revealed in evidence, and everybody knows that only "watertight" cases will be brought to trial?

The problems of punishment to be imposed on those found guilty also highlight the difficulties. Changed circumstances during delays pending trial make the determination of punishment difficult, and in some cases the imposition of any punishment unjust. This is illustrated by the near impossible decision as to what to do in imposing sentence on a young man of eighteen who joins a pack rape where the trial is just three or four years delayed, and in the meantime the person to be sentenced has changed his company and his ways, is employed and leads a stable life. What is to be done after forty or fifty years? What is to be done if the man to be sentenced is seventy or eighty, perhaps now sick or near senile and has led a proper family life in this country for many years? Will not there be an injustice to his Australian family, some born after these events? What is hoped to be achieved by the trials and the punishment? Is it future deterrence of war crimes by others, or is it exposure, humiliation or retribution, or is it some other concept of justice? If this is done, why not do the same by vigorous inquiry into the conduct of others, perhaps Australian, American or Japanese?

In summary, looking back to the decisions of the London Conference in 1945, it appears that the immediate objectives were achieved and that the injunction that war crimes of the Second World War be fairly dealt with was substantially met. The short range objects of punishment were achieved. These included the important well recognised element of retribution judicially administered. I believe, however, that the long range objectives have failed. Those members of the War Crimes Commission who laboured in the period 1944–45 to establish the framework in which war crimes could be dealt with, were idealistic about the future when they laid the foundations for the decisions of the London Conference in 1945, and would now be disappointed with the controversy, misgivings and misunderstandings that have occurred in later years with respect to war crime trials. They would have been concerned that the hopes for future deterrence of war crimes has not been achieved in more recent wars and that instead there is some apprehension that the precedents created stand to be misused in future wars and themselves become an instrument for inhumanity.

11

SPECULATIONS AND REFLECTIONS

I have endeavoured to pry into the past and analyse some aspects of the Japanese at war, as they touched Borneo, Australia and beyond. I have sought to bring the events back to life a little, and so make them more understandable to the lay reader, by relating some of the intimate details of what occurred. The particular often speaks more clearly than the general. I do not profess to write of the past as some expert historian, as an investigative writer or journalist, but as one who saw, heard, felt and recorded, and who later tried his hand at a little investigation in order to fill in a few gaps in his stories.

As I have laboured at my task, I have asked myself many times whether I should rake over the embers of the past or whether, with Australia at peace with Japan and one of its trading partners and indeed beholden to its economic power, I should allow the past to lie buried. The force which prevailed on me to write what I knew and thought, was the overriding truth that history should not and cannot be shut out. Whatever it is, it explains the present, and its lessons and warnings are the guide to the future in the relations of people and nations.

Writing of and assessing some aspect of the past, as I have done, gave rise to speculations as to what the past and the present might have been and what the future may be. This, I maintain, is a legitimate and essential function of history.

AUSTRALIA AT RISK

Borneo, as I have shown, provided an example of what occurred, with variations, in every country occupied by the Japanese. Had Australia been invaded and occupied, even only in part, how different would it have been here? Does what happened in island Borneo provide a picture of what would have happened in island Australia? Had part of the US, such as Hawaii, been invaded, surely it would have been worse than in the Philippines.

The questions are far from academic because Australia and Hawaii were greatly at risk of attack and invasion in 1942. Each was included in early Japanese invasion plans and ambitions. There were Japanese aspirations and plans to bring Australia under its direct control and certainly to deny it as a base for the US. Japan undoubtedly had the will and interest to attack and occupy Australia. General Yamashita, the driving force in the Malayan and Philippines campaigns, had the early view that it was essential for Japan to occupy Australia. Whether Japan did depended greatly on its ability to maintain its initial headlong southward progress and the continued dominance of its navy and airforce. The very real possibility of what almost occurred it not negatived by post-war revelations that when the Japanese southward thrust slowed, a conflict arose between Japanese navy leaders in favour of the invasion of Australia and Japanese army leaders against it, and that it was resolved at the time on the army view. It was considered that Australia was of such a size that Japan could not afford to commit the number of troops required for an occupation. This view, it seems, was strengthened by the withdrawal of the Australian divisions from the Middle East on the insistence of Prime Minister Curtin against opposition from Churchill.

In early 1942, but in particular in April-May, Australia braced itself for possible attack or invasion, although it was not then aware of Japan's precise intentions. However, many Australians had little appreciation of the realities of an invasion, just as dwellers of Singapore did not appreciate these things in the early days of the Malayan campaign. What had already happened in Borneo and elsewhere was little known in 1942 and the worst which was to follow could not be anticipated. Even today, what really occurred is only known to Australians in a hazy way. Experience at first hand alone reveals the reality. In the tense days of 1942, Australia still had its strikes and race meetings and exemptions from military service on all sorts of grounds. What happened in Borneo and other places occupied by the Japanese serves in retrospect to show the reality of what the Australian people faced as individuals, if invasion had come in 1942.

A mere restatement of the course of notorious events to the end of April 1942 shows the reality of the peril in which Australia stood. Singapore, the British fortress of the East, had fallen, and a whole Australian division had been lost there. The British battleships the *Prince of Wales* and the *Repulse* had been sunk. The battles of the Java Sea and Macassar Straits, in which units of the Australian Navy had been sunk, had been lost and had failed to stop the Japanese southward advance. The US Navy had been crippled at Pearl Harbor and its Pacific airforce incapacitated by strikes at Pearl Harbor and the Philippines. The last US resistance at Corregidor in the Philippines had been overcome by the beginning of May 1942. The Netherlands East Indies, Timor and other islands close to Australia, Borneo, New Britain and the Solomons had been occupied, and the north coast of New Guinea invaded. Darwin, the most northern Australian capital city, had been heavily bombed and ships sunk in its harbour. A few token shells had been fired indiscriminately and harmlessly into Sydney and its harbour had been penetrated by midget submarines. A torpedo fired at the US cruiser *Chicago* as it put to sea missed, and hit a smaller vessel, in which Australian sailors were killed.

In late April-early May, there was some sort of Japanese invasion fleet moving south. It seemed obvious that the Japanese plans then were to occupy Australia or isolate her from the US. It is now known that the particular invasion force was intended to seize Port Moresby and so avoid having to attack it over the high mountains from the north coast of New Guinea. It was this fleet that was halted by the Battle of the Coral Sea.

I recall, that while I was an artillery and area intelligence officer in a heavy coastal battery on the east coast of Australia, an intelligence alert was received at about the time of the Battle of the Coral Sea, to the effect that it was considered that the invasion of Australia was imminent, probably with a feint attack on Darwin and the main attack on the east coast.

The Allied success in the Battle of the Coral Sea early in May 1942 was not a decisive victory so far as losses were concerned, but it halted for a time the Japanese southern progress. Although Japanese plans and ambitions, short and long range, in the years 1941–42 were then unknown, there have been considerable revelations about these matters in the years following the end of the war.

Just six weeks after Pearl Harbor, Premier Tojo Hideki in a speech concerning the Greater East Asia Co-Prosperity Sphere said:

> The cardinal point in the War of Greater East Asia, which our Empire is now prosecuting, is to secure strategic bases in Greater East Asia and to bring the regions with important resources under Japan's control, thereby augmenting our fighting strength and in close co-operation with Germany and Italy to extend increasingly vigorous operations to fight through until the United States and the British Empire are brought to their knees. The United States and the British Empire are, however, the countries which boast their wealth and power as the greatest in the world, having for many years consolidated the foundation for their domination of the world. Even although they have suffered overwhelming defeat in the opening stage of the War, it is not difficult to imagine that they will stubbornly resist us and try and turn the tide of war . . .
>
> It is a truly and unprecedently grand undertaking that our Empire should . . . establish an everlasting peace in

Greater East Asia with a new conception which will mark a new epoch in the annals of mankind and proceed to construct a new world order along with our allies and friendly powers in Europe . . .

The Imperial Army and Navy Forces have already occupied Hong Kong, secured the greater part of the Philippines, brought nearly all of the Malaya Peninsula under their control and recently occupied strategic points of the Netherlands East Indies. Of these regions, Hong Kong and the Malay Peninsula have for many years been the British possessions serving as vices for disrupting the peace of East Asia. Therefore, Japan will not only eradicate thoroughly the sources of such evil, but on the contrary intends to convert these places into bulwarks for the defence of Greater East Asia. As regards the Philippines, if the people of those islands will hereafter understand the real intentions of Japan and offer to co-operate with us as one of the partners for the establishment of the Greater East Asia Co-Prosperities Sphere, Japan will gladly enable them to enjoy the honour of independence. As for Burma, what Japan contemplates is not different from that relating to the Philippines.

As regards the Netherlands East Indies and Australia, if they continue as at present their attitude of resisting Japan, we will show no mercy in crushing them. But if their peoples come to understand Japan's real intentions and express willingness to co-operate with us, we will not hesitate to extend them our help with full understanding for their welfare and progress . . .

The constructive undertaking contemplated by Japan will in the early stages of the war, be commended under military administration, beginning with those which are essential for the prosecution of the war.[1]

One might interpose that elements in this speech are reminiscent of the speeches of Hitler and of his threats and false promises.

Dr Andrew Grajdanzei, a member of the staff of the Institute of Pacific Relations during the war, in an article published in *Pacific Affairs* in 1943, looked back to 1942, and commented:

> The term "Greater East Asia" lacks precision. For the time being it covers the Japanese Empire, Manchuria, China proper, the Philippines, the Netherlands East Indies, French Indo-China, Thailand, British Malaya and Burma . . . In respect of other we have more recent pronouncements.
>
> India, Australia and New Zealand are to be included in the sphere. In May 1942 the Japanese Minister of Agriculture and Forestry was not yet certain whether Australian wheat would be available in Greater East Asia during the war, but the Traffic Committee believe that large numbers of automobiles in use in Australia, New Zealand and India (808,500, 276,000 and 123,000 respectively) may be mobilised for the smooth transportation of materials in the co-prosperity sphere.[2]

The Japanese Minister said this in the same month as the Battle of the Coral Sea and just before the Battle of Midway in early June 1942.

In February 1943, when the tide of war in favour of Japan had ebbed owing in particular to the US victory at Midway (although the Japanese people had been told it was a Japanese victory), Tojo referred to the "supposition" of the war ending favourably to Japan in a speech to the Japanese Parliament. (It is likely that then, with the European war still in the balance, the Japanese were looking for a compromise peace with the US, leaving Japan in control of its Asian and Pacific acquisitions.) He said:

> I am not considering the reduction of the Japanese military preparations which form our kernel, even in post-war time. Consequently . . . I believe that there should be no hesitation in wartime management with dreams of the past and with thinking that there will be an immediate reduction (in armaments) if the war should end in the near future . . . The military preparations of Japan which are the pivot of Greater East Asia . . . will absolutely not be reduced.[3]

The dream referred to was that of a few pre-war civilian Japanese thinkers who had been in favour of a new co-operative group of nations in Asia. However, despite the propaganda and the lip service paid to the dream even by Tojo in the early stages of the war, the practice and policy of the Japanese Army and Navy, which were in control of all occupied countries, were stern domination with co-operative co-existence a pretence.

Whatever the significance at the time of what Tojo said in 1943, it demonstrates retrospectively that all along the truth was that Japanese occupation was intended to be a permanent military affair, by a permanent military-controlled establishment, with co-prosperity indeed a dream. Those who controlled the destinies of Japan were suitable partners for the Nazis. In Borneo, as elsewhere, there was no co-prosperity—only exploitation. If there had been any occupation of further countries by the Japanese then both during the war and afterwards. it would have been a military state enforced by kempei-tai police methods, with a seizure of resources for Japanese exploitation.

But what were the aspirations of the Japanese beyond the setback of the Port Moresby invasion and what were the perils which existed for Australia, despite the Coral Sea victory?

According to the post-war researches of Bergamini, Japanese navy and army commanders were in Bali just before the date of the Battle of the Coral Sea intending in the weeks ahead to occupy or isolate Australia, and the continuing Japanese plan, both before and after that battle, was to take Hawaii in August 1942, then seize the Panama Canal, terrorise California, and force America to abandon Australia. According again to these researches, the Japanese Emperor expected that the southern advance, halted in May in the Coral Sea, would resume in July, continuing to New Zealand and perhaps occupying French New Caledonia.

The first step in the great Japanese plan to move east, and incidentally isolate Australia, was to capture the Midway Islands. It was the US victory in the Midway naval and air battle that turned the tide of the war and removed the threat to Australia. Brilliantly, Admiral Nimitz anticipated the Japanese intentions and had, unknown to the Japanese, reinforced Midway with men and importantly a ground-based air fleet, and had secreted near Midway as many naval vessels as could then be mustered. This included the *Yorktown*, which was severely damaged in the Battle of the Coral Sea but was patched up and rushed to Midway. The Japanese battle fleet and fire power grossly outnumbered that of the US. The fleet was one of the most formidable in history, with ten battleships, eight aircraft carriers, twenty cruisers, as well as destroyers, submarines and other supply ships. The US had at Midway no battleships and only three aircraft carriers.

The story of the US victory at Midway has been told and I provide here only a brief account. Without a single torpedo or bomb-hit, flight after flight of US aircraft were almost totally wiped out by murderous and efficient Japanese defence, with many aircraft ditched into the sea, because they had to attack beyond the point of no return. By US persistence and some tactical Japanese errors, the tide was turned and the three spearhead Japanese carriers were directly hit, burned and sunk. As victory turned the American way, the Japanese fleet retired. As a consequence of Midway, the total Japanese carrier strength and naval and air power was about halved and the naval and air superiority gained at Pearl Harbor lost. Thereafter, Japan could not compete with the industrial might of the US, which had time on its side.

The tide of the Midway Battle had changed in just a few minutes. Australia was saved from the threat of invasion in those few minutes. If the Battle of Midway had gone the other way (and with Japanese air and naval superiority, it is surprising that it did not), the massive Japanese battle fleet would have commanded the South Pacific to the west and to the east. In this situation, the US would have been unable to prevent a Japanese attack or invasion of Australia, New Zealand or islands to the east of them. The limit of Britain's then stated and later revealed resolve was to devote its resources to Europe and send help to Australia only if actually attacked.[4] Despite post-war revelations of a Japanese decision in the end not to attempt to invade Australia, the decision could well have been different had the Coral Sea and Midway battles been Japanese victories.

It is clear from Tojo's earliest statements that even when flushed with initial success, he knew that the war against the might of the US would be a long and difficult affair. If after Midway, Japan had had sea and air superiority in the South Pacific, it would have wanted to deny Australia to the US as a base for later counter attack and would have wanted it as a source of supply for the long war ahead.

It serves no purpose to speculate precisely what might have happened if Australia had been invaded in 1942. However, looking back and recalling what occurred in Borneo and elsewhere, it is not idle for Australians to contemplate in a general way, based on events elsewhere, what they would have experienced had invasion come. We, in Australia, have never suffered invasion, but if we are to be a mature people appreciative of the real consequences of war, we should not shut our eyes to what invasion really means and what it would have meant if it had come in 1942.

In 1942 Australia appears to have made the obvious assessment that any Japanese attack would come in the north. It was on this basis that there was formulated the plan known as the "Brisbane Line" revealed after the war. This was a plan for the withdrawal of the line of defence of Australia to the Brisbane latitude if Japan invaded from the north. It was based on the tragic reality that, if invaded, Australia as a whole could not be defended and that partial defence would have to be undertaken by a concentration of limited resources.

If Australia had been invaded, three factors would probably have meant that brutalities and killings would have been beyond what occurred elsewhere. One factor was that the people of Australia were almost all of European origin, and as such the special object of Japanese hatred. The second was that any occupation would almost certainly have been only partial, so there would have been continuing resistance to the occupying forces, which would have been likely to produce mass reprisals. The third was that Japan had a supply problem in carrying on a long war, and Australia would have helped in providing produce, industrial output and slave labour. Other questions come to mind:

Would not the difficulties of the invader have resulted, as occurred in the Malayan operation, in no prisoners being taken during an invasion?

Would not Australia, as one quotation suggests, have been made the source of supply of food for Japanese operations in its East Asia and Pacific adventures? Would not Australians have provided slave labour forces, used not only within Australia but in the other occupied territories, as did the Javanese? Would not the Australian population have been denied the food resources turned over to other areas? Would there not have been repetitions of the conditions, including starvation, which occurred on the Burma Railway and at Sandakan?

Would there not have been policies of terrorism such as those implemented at Nanking, Chekiang, Jesselton and Bataan and elsewhere to induce whole populations not to resist and to co-operate?

In the event of individual resistance or a local uprising in response to some Japanese atrocity or otherwise, would there not have been far reaching retribution involving the killing of great numbers of people on suspicion, rumour or simply to terrorise? Would there not, in these circumstances, have been the massacres of men, women and children, as happened in Borneo, as the result of a limited uprising in Jesselton?

Would there have been an informer system, where one inhabitant was set against the other by inducements, threats or cruelty? Would not the kempei-tai and their methods be used within a police and justice system which employed torture as a means of gaining confessions and administering justice?

With a partial occupation and the war later turning against Japan, would not sections of the population have been at risk of suffering the same fate as the Sandakan POWs? In that situation, with the end of the war forced by the dropping of the bomb, would not the Australians of that day, as the prisoners who survived do, thank the atomic bomb?

It is the savage or criminal act, rather than the intention, which is remembered and colours future relations. This is why prisoners who knew cruelty at first hand cannot forget. The same would apply today to Australians if Australia had been invaded. It is only different today because the Japanese were unable to carry out their intentions.

These are the things that in reality Australia faced in the perilous months of April and May 1942. When we ponder on these matters, we should be thankful for the victories of Coral Sea, Kokoda Trail and Midway. We should never forget the debt we owe to our men who turned back the Japanese at Kokoda and prevented Japan from having a jumping off point at Port Moresby from which to attack Australia. We should never forget the debt we owe to the US airmen at Midway, who against overwhelming odds, flew knowingly to almost certain death. The airmen who died and the few who survived deserve to stand in history alongside the British and Dominion airmen who fought in the battle of Britain.

COULD IT HAPPEN AGAIN?

If involved again in war, would the Japanese act differently? Different people will give different answers. Many who suffered under the Japanese will give one answer, while many who have experienced the warmth and kindness of the modern Japanese will give an opposite answer.

Without a penetrating understanding of modern Japan and the Japanese people of today, no real opinion can be expressed. I do believe, however, that the question should remain an open one. The past must remain as a warning for the future and, as such, a matter for continuing concern.

Having written of the past, I can do no better than draw attention to the unknown future and point to some considerations and make some comments which point in opposite directions.

How Japanese act as individuals, their friendliness, kindness, courtesies and love of beauty, which are now evident, may not be indicative of how they would act under the stress and discipline of war. As earlier mentioned, the same kind of qualities appeared to exist in many Japanese in the Second World War who participated in atrocities. In the future, would there still not be the cruel—the Hoshijimas, the Babas, the Takakuwas—and the humane—the Takaharas?

There is a view that the disposition to commit atrocities in the Second World War existed because Japan grew up too rapidly from a primitive society to a modern nation. There is a further view that since then Japan has had time to mature. The quality, extent and relevance of Japan's post-war maturity themselves are open to different assessments. How these changes will in fact influence international conduct at times of stress is difficult to assess.

If one looks back to the history of Japan in the century leading up to the Second World War, it can be seen that it advanced from a primitive, feudal and isolated nation to a leading world military power. It was able to do so by catching up with the rest of the world, particularly in the field of technology, by its extraordinary ability to copy.

People, customs and national characteristics, however, cannot change as rapidly, and the revolution in Japanese technology and military might was not accompanied by similarly revolutionary changes in its people. As Eric Linklater put it:

> In their rapid progress, they had scarcely time to reconcile some contradictions in their national character. They were on the one side as clean and tidy and orderly, as fond of flowers and bright colours as the Dutch, on the other side they were apt to be hysterical, fanatic and curiously addicted to suicide.[5]

I believe that the rapid rise to military power, far in advance of changes in attitudes, was the basic reason for the Japanese atrocities. The community of nations took some centuries to evolve more humane attitudes in respect of behaviour in war than those that obtained twenty centuries ago. As a consequence, we have the various treaties established over the last century. The Japanese, however, were not in step with other nations and as a result the treatment of people in occupied territory and of prisoners of war, was much the same as that of centuries ago when conquerors brutalised the vanquished, made them slaves and regarded them as expendable. Japan acknowledged its inability and that of its armed forces to cope with these changing world attitudes by declining to ratify the 1929 Prisoners of War Geneva Convention.

The post-war rise of Japan as a world economic power is much different in character to its rise in military prowess, although it has been as surprising and rapid. Many countries are now dependent on its goodwill and on decisions made in Japan. The troublesome question, the answer to which is unclear, is whether the post-war rise has been accompanied by changes in attitude and character which will lead to the responsible exercise of that power. World interest is that power not be exercised in such a way as to cause international friction, the usual forerunner to military conflict.

It can be asked, has the Japanese character substantially changed from what it was in the Second World War, or from what it was last century? Have the Japanese thrown off their former insular, inwardlooking and group mentality? Has Japan set aside, in the political and military fields, that single-minded pursuit of conquest, unmindful of the consequences to others? There are some indications that a single-minded pursuit of domination, setting aside all other considerations, is still a characteristic of modern Japan.

Just the same, Japan today, at least outwardly, is undoubtedly a different Japan from that of 1941–45. The revolution of Japan aimed at and introduced during the US occupation under General MacArthur, has produced a more democratic Japan with many different outlooks and customs. The modern Japanese are more westernised, and although their leaders and businessmen have certain ways and adopt certain attitudes not always understood by us, they fit more comfortably into the international community. There have been fundamental changes to Japanese institutions and Japan has abandoned its isolation by moving to the front of the stage in the fields of trade and finance.

Critical to any question concerning the possible recurrence of past events is whether the two causes of the atrocities could again exist together. First, have the characteristics of the Japanese soldier earlier described changed? Second, could some extreme militarist group again seize control of Japan?

The attitude and actions of the Japanese, as soldiers thrown into war, depended greatly on the structure of Japanese culture, ideologies and concepts of what is right, wrong and acceptable. Part of this structure was dependence on the group, with an accompanying group mentality and resulting attitudes to outsiders. Has this structure changed as Japan has become more westernised and moved to its present position of world power? Has it changed to the extent that the Japanese in situations of war or international stress would now adopt different attitudes and act differently towards foreigners?

The wartime actions and attitudes of so many different Japanese, seen in the context of prior Japanese history, could only have been based on some fundamental features in the structure of Japanese society and culture. While, for my part, I have sought only to speak of the past up to 1946, later writings, observations and analyses of others, such as Tokyo professor Dr Doi Takeo and Mack Chrysler, a US journalist who lives in Japan, concerning the structures of Japanese society and Japanese ways and customs serve to explain most of what I observed at the time and have detailed earlier.

Dr Doi is an eminent Japanese scholar and psychiatrist. In *An Anatomy of Dependence*,[6] written in Japanese for Japanese readers and first published in 1973, he describes the group nature, mentality and dependence of the Japanese as basic to the structure of Japanese society. He describes, with all their nuances, concepts, little known to the West, which govern the group relations and group dependence of the Japanese. He demonstrates that the structure and functioning of Japanese society rest firmly on the group, with little individuality. He shows how the individual identifies with the group and confuses his own identity and interests with those of the group. Thus, when a Japanese resigns (or commits suicide) for something the group has done, he is not able to distinguish his own responsibility or lack of it from that of the group. If he appears to act on his own decision, he does what he believes to be what the group expects.

Doi acknowledges the absence in Japan of such Western characteristics as individual independence or freedom and guilt based on individual conscience, which he traces back to developments from earlier Christianity. As he puts it:

> Generally speaking, the Japanese like group action. It is extremely difficult for a Japanese to transcend the group and act individually.[7]

He acknowledges also that the sense of shame of a Japanese is due to a failure to meet group expectations. He contends that the individual may feel guilt, but says it is different from that of the Westerner, in that it is guilt because he has let the group down. He states that the fundamental difference between the Japanese and the West is Japanese group dependence and lack of independent action or a sense of guilt.

In analysing the forces underlying group activity, Doi refers in particular to what he calls *amae,* which is a continuance of the emotional parent-child bond into adult family and other relationships. The emotional element of this bond is *ninjo.* He refers also to *giri,* which is the bond arising from a social duty to the group. *Giri* does not depend on *ninjo,* but may include it. Conflict may arise from membership of different groups. As he quotes, "If I wish to be loyal to the Emperor, I can't be filial to my father".[8]

Doi discusses the Japanese in peace time and does not embark on the operation of group dependence and concepts during times of war or international stress. He does, however, deal with Japanese attitudes to foreigners. For example:

> The Japanese divide their lives into inner and outer sectors each with its own different standards of behaviour, no one feeling the slightest oddity in this discrepancy.[9]

and referring to those sectors:

> . . . strangers [are] in the outermost circle, being treated with indifference . . . This only applies, however, when the stranger presents no threat; once the threat occurs, the attitude abruptly changes. It is possible to see this attitude as an exaggerated reaction due to the fact that even at times of apparent coldness and indifference, a latent threat is in fact felt.[10]

He does not explain what a Japanese does otherwise when faced with a perceived threat, such as might apply when his attitude to a POW changes, from indifference to what occurs to the prisoner to a perceived danger from one who might escape and tell what has happened. Takakuwa met the danger by killing the Ranau POWs, just as in earlier centuries the perceived threat of intrusion from sailors shipwrecked in Japan was met by killing them. There was no rule, order or general moral precept against doing so.

> . . . the Japanese tend to ignore the world of strangers, but even this is far from meaning lack of interest. They ignore the outside world in so far as they judge this to be possible, but even when they appear to be indifferent they are in fact keeping a formidably watchful eye on their surroundings. And once they realize something cannot be ignored, they busily set about identifying with and adopting it.[11]

Significantly, he refers to the Japanese word for a foreigner being used in the same way as what he refers to as "the contemptuous Jewish term 'gentile' ".[12] He illustrates the Japanese attitude to foreigners by reference to the Japanese tourist, to whom the foreigner presents a kind of threat, inducing a feeling of inferiority for fear of not being accepted, so that he finds comfort and security in group travel.

In dealing with group dependence, Dr Doi explains how

the group way of life presents many beautiful, satisfying and human aspects, much to be admired as a way of living and not an aberration, as the West usually regards it. As his copious quotations from and references to the writings of other Japanese show, his general views concerning Japanese group ways appear to be generally accepted.

As indicated, Dr Doi does not explain how the structures of Japanese society outlined by him worked in relation to foreigners during war. However, they obviously operated to produce the attitudes displayed by Japanese soldiers to foreign POWs and foreign civilians in occupied countries, which attitudes, in turn, led to the atrocities. The soldiers were indifferent to what happened to these foreigners and to what they did to them, and there was no sense of guilt for what occurred.

Chrysler,[13] with some reliance on the work of Dr Doi and that of another Japanese, Dr Chie Nakare, refers to the Japanese living and dying in close reliance on multiple rules and customs which dictate duties and actions but are not subject to concepts of moral absolutes of right and wrong.

These post-war writings serve to explain the forces that produced the atrocities during war. Almost every aspect of what I observed and wrote about Japanese actions and attitudes in Borneo and elsewhere can be seen to be derived from and is explained by reference to the structures described by these writers.

As observed by Chrysler and as was apparent to me, Japanese behaviour was governed by rules which precisely covered all situations considered relevant. Some situations were irrelevant and were therefore devoid of rules, but the overriding and critical rule was that the individual acted as an unquestioning member of a group in accordance with the group's dictates and interests. Shame based on what others thought, not personal guilt, provided the sanction for observance of the rules. Above all else, the individual craved the security, acceptance and approval of the group—"face" within the group was the governing factor. The greatest punishment was openly to humiliate a person before others, as the Japanese often tried to do to Europeans and POWs.

Rarely could the individual rise above group action or escape from the group mentality. If he exercised some discretion or apparently acted as an individual, it was in ways which he conceived were in the group interest and acceptable to the group.

Action, backed in this way by rules and group sanctions, did not, as in the West under the influence of Christian and Judaic-based cultures, depend on individual conscience or the individual's sense of guilt derived from general concepts of what is right or wrong, humane or inhumane, true or false, just or unjust. Such general concepts did not exist for the Japanese.

The Japanese attitude to suicide, which to some degree still exists, illustrates the point. People did not commit suicide out of guilt for an action for which they felt personally responsible. They did it out of a sense of duty in circumstances in which the group had failed in some way. A soldier who had fought bravely to the end and then committed suicide did so not because of a sense of personal failure but because his honourable duty as a soldier, expressed as a duty to the Emperor, required it. Group failure brought dishonour on the group, and individual suicide was committed out of shame on the group's behalf. This action brought not shame but honour on the person, his family and his group. Death was less important than honour and duty. Suicide was often performed as a ceremony according to set customs, sometimes as a result of a superior giving the person an order or permission to commit "honourable suicide". Any death out of duty, whether in battle, by suicide or, according to Shinji, by execution as a war criminal, was honourable. The equivalent in the West was limited to the honour accorded a soldier, sailor or airman who "gave up his life" in defence of his country.

The field of operation of the rules and the area of group duty were limited. Duty was related to the group. Beyond the recognised group or groups there was indifference and no duty. Group relationships included those between superiors and subordinates in many different situations and within families and between persons accepted as friends. Loyalties, duties and rules were governed by a complex system of precedence. Foreigners regarded as friends would be treated accordingly. In wartime the Emperor and military superiors were in the inner circle of duty referred to by Doi, with family and friends in an outer circle. Foreigners were beyond any circle of duty. The rules, customs and orders of precedence were the product of a long past, many going back to feudal times. Part of that past was the exclusion by the Japanese of foreigners and strangers from their isolated island society. This was in contrast with most of the rest of the world, which for centuries had lived in association with other countries and peoples. Japan began its association with other countries only last century, when foreigners forced their way into Japanese territory and affairs. There have been great technological and other changes in Japan since then, but technology changes more easily than people and their ways. There are many indications that Japanese exclusiveness in relation to foreigners still continues substantially.

In all societies, customs and rules of conduct and peer and other approval play an important part in governing individual conduct. So far as Japan was concerned, compared with the West, the critical difference, which became important in the Second World War, was that in Japan there were no overriding standards and no individual sense of right and wrong to operate alongside and beyond the rules and independently of peer approval.

In wartime the Japanese soldier in his relations with foreigners, including POWs and civilians in occupied countries, was in a situation devoid of rules to direct or control his actions. Such foreigners were outside the sphere of his concern and rules. At best they were objects of indifference—it was a matter of no consequence what was done to them. In this situation, of course, there was the duty to the group, and, as earlier described, loyalty to superiors was more absolute and of a different quality from that of the dedicated soldier of the West. However, a few foreigners, even in war, might come to be regarded by Japanese as friends at some level—for example, as a result of long association between a guard and prisoner.

Japanese soldiers reflected the nationalistic spirit and the resentment of the people of opposing nations expressed by Japan's leaders. The rules of international law concerning prisoners and humanity were unknown to the Japanese soldiers and were not part of the rules governing their conduct, an attitude fostered by most superiors. As Hoshijima put it, "We know nothing of international conventions. You are under the Japanese army."

Not bound by any rules in relation to foreigners, the Japanese soldier on the spot was free to treat prisoners as he chose. Alternating fascination with and indifference to death and brutality and misconceptions concerning Samurai traditions led Japanese not constrained by any rules or superior orders to act as they did in committing widespread atrocities. As no rule was broken, there was no inquiry, no reprimand and no sense of shame or guilt for acts of brutality. It was as though what had been done did not occur. It seems that some Japanese in the Second World War were influenced to some extent by such Western ideas as a sense of right and wrong and broke away a little from the confinement of mere rules. This is probably true of Takahara. On the other hand, in the case of Suga, his considerable pre-war associations with the West had little effect. Consistent with the rules, he showed kindness, arising from friendly relationships, but this friendship, according to the rules, was at the bottom of the hierarchy.

Therefore, despite the great changes in modern Japan and its institutions and the appearances of westernisation, it seems there has been little change in the basic structure of its society. Doi's writings in regard to modern times support this view. These are the same structures that permitted the development of the attitudes that led to the atrocities. Other things appear not to have changed substantially. Some fascination with violence and beauty alongside each other remains, as evidenced in the fields of drama and the martial arts. There are indications that Japanese conduct is still governed by innumerable rules and customs without any separate philosophies of right and wrong, and that the foreigner is still remote from Japanese concern, as in the past. Japanese exclusiveness is still dominant. Thus, although Japan has exploited the current economic and commercial openness to acquire offshore interests and to control some activities within other countries, it has structured its own internal affairs in ways that have hindered or prevented the reverse happening. At a time when Japan has joined the great world powers as an international force, it has been able to regain, albeit in a somewhat different form, the island exclusiveness which it had geographically for centuries but lost with the hated intrusions by the West led by US Commodore Perry.

Then, could the second element that led to the atrocities recur—could militarists again seize power in Japan? Many factors are working against this, such as that Japan has no need to use military power to achieve what it has gained by other means. A recurrence of the past, however, cannot be ruled out. Japan, although economically strong, is still territorially weak, one of the principal reasons why it embarked on wars of expansion from 1931 onwards. The volatility of present Japanese politics and problems of corruption make Japan's political system vulnerable to takeover by pressure groups.

It was the recognition of the possible return of militarism that led to the prolonged MacArthur occupation, the restructuring of Japan and the provisions in the new Japanese constitution banning various actions which could lead to a return of Japan to military adventures. The Japanese people, at least originally, appeared to embrace the steps aimed at preventing Japan being again led into war. They had experienced the atomic bomb and otherwise had suffered greatly with an enormous number of soldiers and civilians killed and maimed. The appalling consequences of the war in its last year to the Japanese people, apart from the bomb, are not always appreciated.

However, with the coming of new generations, memories fade and circumstances, including national feelings, change. National interests change. In 1946 the concern of the US was to prevent its former enemy from repeating its past actions. As the years have passed, concern about its former enemy has switched to concern about its former ally, as the US and Russia confront each other as super powers. The US interest has now changed to have Japan ignore some of the constitutional prohibitions in respect of military capacity, in order to provide some of its own "defence" and provide a buffer to Russian expansion into South Asia and the Pacific.

Relevant to the principal question posed in this chapter, is the important subsidiary, but open question as to whether the Japanese people accept the full truth concerning the inhumanities and crimes for which they as a nation were responsible.

It is as fundamental to nations, as it is to people, that not repeating errors of the past is dependent on the recognition of those errors, their causes and the acceptance of responsibility for them. Those who fail to do this, preferring not to think about them or forgetting them or blaming others, are candidates to repeat them in the future in some new provocative situation. The West German President, Von Weizsacker, recognised this in relation to the atrocities of Nazi Germany in the Second World War in a recent address in which he was reported to have said:

> Is it a kind of embarrassment found impossible to bear? We cannot simply accept anyone wanting to look away and forget. But neither can we condemn anybody who withdraws in his distress. Instead we must be given courage to face the truth . . . [Germany] cannot make others responsible for what it and its neighbours endured under National Socialism. It was led by criminals and allowed itself to be led by them. It knows that this is true, especially when it would prefer not to know this. A path marked by violence, hardship and death led to the end of the war. Not until then, did many people feel the full extent of injustice and suffering. Only gradually did it become clear what had actually happened. It remains extremely hard to recognise these occurrences. And yet genuine liberation is achieved by facing the truth freely . . . The truth is inevitable

> and will not be forgotten . . . as historical responsibility means accepting one's own history. We must do so above all for the sake of the present. This is not changed by the passage of time . . .
>
> Of key importance is the search of young people for self-esteem for their place in today's world. They want to and have to know who they are, where they come from and with whom they are to share and shape this world. To them it is vitally important to know how the moral and political disaster came about in the days of their grandparents. Did their nation leave the civilised community of nations only temporarily and has it now returned to its natural position, albeit encumbered with that terrible aberration?[14]

The problem which in post-war years has faced the German people, so keenly perceived by the West German President, and the need for them to face up to the terrible conduct of their country in the war years, if they are to be liberated from it and prove it to be an aberration, applies equally well to post-war Japan.

Although Japan formally accepted the guilt of its war criminals in signing the peace treaty, it is far from clear that it has really come to terms with the truth. During the course of the war, the Japanese demonstrated what appeared to be a national characteristic of refusing or of being unable to admit, even to themselves, that criminal inhumanities were committed by their fellows. Significantly, it was these attitudes and the failure to inquire which fostered repetition and proliferation of atrocities during wartime. It is dangerous to do the same in peace time.

At the national level there has been a tendency to regard the accusations at the trials or elsewhere of Japanese atrocities, without further inquiry, as the fabrications of the victorious nations. This is illustrated by a memorial erected in recent years at Nagoya in honour of war criminals executed on the findings of war trials courts martial. Part of the inscription reads: "These trials were nothing more than vengeance, the proud victors exercising arbitrary judgment over the vanquished."[15] Could this be said, if there were an interest to know the objective facts such as were revealed at the trials of Hoshijima, Takakuwa, Watanabe and Baba? Erecting a national monument to war criminals as a group is disturbing. As already stated, failure to recognise past wrongs makes the repetition of them more likely in the future in some new provocative situation. It is a cause for alarm when it applies, as it appears to do, to a powerful nation such as Japan.

Is the Nagoya monument and its inscription symptomatic of a wider view in Japan, so that with the passing of time, the Tokyo trials have come to be seen, as Tojo labelled them, examples of "victor's justice"? Has it come to be accepted, as he claimed, that Japan had gone to war because of the oppressions of the US and its allies, and in consequence have the widespread atrocities now become taboo?

The comments I have made are intended to provoke thought in those with deep experience and an understanding of modern Japan, but who have limited knowledge of the past. I seek to show that quick perceptions cannot provide simple answers to complex questions. While we ought not to live in the past, later generations living in the present ought to know fully what occurred, and why it occurred, if they are to guard against its repetition in some form. They will pretend it did not happen or refuse to think about it at their peril. This applies with particular force to Japan itself, if it is to ensure, as we must hope it will, that the past was no more than a regrettable "aberration" in its history. It is to be hoped that books such as this, with all its shortcomings, will be read, criticised and thought about in Japan, and that its people may adopt a point of view similar to the one espoused by the West German President, Von Weizsacker.

12

PROJECT KINGFISHER —TOP SECRET

At the beginning of January 1945, there were 2100 prisoners at Sandakan. Four hundred and seventy left on the first march. At the beginning of March there were about 1500. At the end of May, before the second march left, there were 824. Only 6 were to survive to the end of the war. At this time the prisoners were obviously in peril, Sandakan was isolated and defended only by a small garrison, the Japanese everywhere were facing defeat and the Allies had sea and air superiority. Why was there no attempt to rescue them?

The question has often been asked[1] and still is being asked.[2] At the time of the Labuan trials, knowing these objective circumstances and a great deal more, I too wondered why no action had been taken to aid the prisoners at Sandakan or later at Ranau. I then knew from Rex Blow and his three men that well before the Borneo landings, Z Special Unit had been active operationally and on reconnaissance behind Japanese lines in many areas.

Why did the Allies attack Sandakan on 27 May by air and sea bombardments when there was no landing or rescue attempt? This attack led the Japanese to believe that a landing was imminent and hurled the ruthless Takakuwa, then the Sandakan prison commandant, into an accelerated flight on the second death march setting out on 29 May under the cover of night. There followed a rampage of killing, the burning of the compound and the abandoning of nearly 300 sick POWs.

Takakuwa, of course, had already received orders to evacuate the prisoners and take them on some kind of march and many prisoners would have died in any event, but this was not known to the Allies. The attack on 27 May, referred to by the Japanese at the Labuan trials, is confirmed in the official Australian war history[3] as a combined Australian and US air and torpedo boat attack causing considerable damage. It was a harassing attack and not in aid of the landing at nearby Tarakan, because that had been on 1 May. General Baba blamed the attack for causing Takakuwa to panic.

When I came to write this book, mainly based on what I learned in 1945–46, I determined to find, if I could, by some research, an answer to the questions which had troubled me back in 1946. Even stronger objective circumstances, which I found were well known at the time to the Australian Army, made it so clear that a rescue was practicable and would have substantially succeeded that, in the end, my research turned to why a rescue, which in fact had been planned, was never carried out.

The truth, I discovered, is that in early 1945 there were between 1000 and 1500 prisoners at Sandakan who could and should have been rescued and that the second death march could have been prevented. The truth is that in 1945 there was in fact a well advanced plan for a major rescue operation, which unjustifiably was not pursued. What occurred brings into further question the attitudes of General MacArthur revealed in the official Australian war history toward permitting and facilitating Australian operations and the use of Australian forces. It also raises the question why, following messages, including calls for help which it had received in 1944 from the Sandakan inmates via escaped prisoners, the Government did not insist on being kept informed of the plight of these prisoners and then exert its influence with Blamey, MacArthur and the US, in that order, to ask in 1945, when the Borneo operations were pending, what was to be done about the Sandakan POWs?

In order to piece together, as best I can, some forty-four years later what did or did not occur, I must go back to the beginning. I first set out in more detail the objective circumstances which raised the question posed.

By mid-February 1945, from which time onward the prisoners could have been rescued, it was clear that the Japanese had lost the war but would fight on. They had lost nearly all of their navy, shipping and air force, in or following their defeat in the great naval battles. Most of their island garrisons had been wiped out or by-passed. The Philippines and Iwo Jima operations were well on the way to US victory and the saturation bombing of Japan had commenced.

From late 1944 and throughout 1945, following the US victory at Leyte, the Allies had unchallenged air superiority over Sandakan, the route of the marches and Ranau. The Sandakan air strips had been severely bombed and the Japanese no longer used them. Virtually no Japanese aircraft were seen in Borneo after about February 1945. Sandakan was cut off by sea and US patrol boats roved along the nearby coast. There was Allied air reconnaissance and photography of Japanese positions.

The prison compound at Sandakan was then marked by a large "POW" sign. The Japanese garrison force at Sandakan was small and the prison compound was inland from it about eight miles. Combat units were being moved overland out of Sandakan to reinforce the north. This was observed by the Allies. An experienced unit was moved with the first death march and later the Kanno machine gun unit was transferred by this same route. As Baba said at his trial with apologies, the garrison troops were of poor quality and not well trained. From March to May there were very few Japanese at Sandakan itself and in the order of 1500 in the region. These included the "old" troops later sent on the second march. The number of guards at the compound initially had been 200, but was probably not much more than 100 by March 1945. Nearly half of them were Formosan civilians without military training.

It was known from aerial reconnaissance on 31 May that the prisoners had gone from the Sandakan compound and that it had been burned to the ground. On 27 June, after the second march arrived at Ranau, there were still 200 POWs alive at Ranau, who were the survivors of the two marches, incarcerated in a compound which had been moved away from the Japanese army posts. Intelligence systems, some using natives, had been set up by members of Z Force who by means of parachute or submarine had infiltrated many areas, including Sandakan, Tarakan, Brunei and Balikpapan and had been able to determine Japanese positions and strengths and identify targets. A combination of Australian and US intelligence revealed prisoner numbers and the starvation and deaths of hundreds of them at Sandakan. The marches were observed and it was known prisoners were being shot at least on the second march.

Back in Australia on the Atherton Tablelands were 800 paratroops ready and eager for action and trained for this very rescue operation. There could be no Japanese aerial defence against such an operation and no aerial or navy harassment of a sea pick up near the compound.

With all these circumstances well known at the time, why was there no rescue attempt? General MacArthur exercised, indeed had assumed, direct, detailed and absolute control of all operations and the use of all units, Australian and otherwise. This applied also to Borneo. Australian units stayed or went according to his decision and according to the availability of transport determined by him and his HQ. Why did he not do something about a rescue? Why did he not direct, permit or facilitate the use of the idle paratroops for a rescue? Why did not the Australian Army and Government insist that something be done?

I found from my researches that questions of this nature, but in particular in relation to a rescue using the Australian paratroops, had been raised in 1947 and reached the Australian Parliament, with a question being asked of the Prime Minister, Mr Chifley. The matter was disposed of politically after scant inquiry by a less than frank answer drafted by a Government department and the subject was then buried by a declaration by the Prime Minister that an enquiry or asking further questions would serve no purpose. The frailty of the Prime Minister's reply has since been concealed by the nonpreservation, loss and destruction of records from which the answer was derived.

A rescue operation would, of course, raise a number of questions and pose some problems. Some of these could dictate the nature and scale of the operation required, and this in turn would raise the question as to whether the resources required were available at the desired time. As some prisoners were sick, the operation would have to be a substantial one. A rescue might result in reprisals against prisoners elsewhere and, if it failed, against Sandakan prisoners or any sick left behind. The question of the resources available at the time to mount the rescue operation will be dealt with later. None of the other questions stood against a rescue operation, and a rescue plan (in fact made) dispensed with them.

Questions of danger to the prisoners, including the sick, were answered by the success of and revelations by the rescue of the Manila prisoners on 4 February 1945. MacArthur had been able to achieve this by a surprise operation. The prisoners rescued were emaciated and sick, and had endured torture and beatings over three years. Their condition was comparable to that of the Sandakan prisoners. The matter of reprisals elsewhere or against the prisoners to be rescued was irrelevant, for orders were found to kill them in any case. By March 1945, what had occurred at Palawan in December 1944 was known from the recovery of several of the prisoners who had escaped when all the other prisoners there were burned to death. Thus by February–March, the policy of disposing of prisoners upon threat of an invasion, which was likely to be applied in other similar situations, such as Sandakan, would have been known to US intelligence and to MacArthur. This would have been before the appropriate time, ie March or April, for any Sandakan rescue operation, and before the first Borneo landing on 1 May.

It is almost unthinkable that this information concerning what seemed to be Japanese policy was not passed on to combined Allied HQ and then to General Blamey and to those planning operations near where prisoners were held. If it was, it is difficult to understand why the combined Allied attack was made on Sandakan on 27 May. On any view, it is impossible to understand why MacArthur and his HQ allowed such a merely harassing operation to take place. It would be obvious that the Japanese would think, as indeed they did, that there would be an Allied landing, but this surely could be seen as likely to reproduce the Manila and Palawan situation, perhaps more so because of the small Japanese garrison there, cut off from assistance.

It might be said that the sick condition of the prisoners and the brutality at Sandakan would not have been known, as Warrant Officer Wallace, the only prisoner to escape from Sandakan compound and return to Australia, only knew the state of affairs there up to April 1943. It could be argued that the ultimate fate of the prisoners could not have been foreseen, so that to criticise now the absence of a rescue attempt is being wise after the event.

This is answered by my researches, which show that the condition of the prisoners and the dispositions of the Japanese at Sandakan were known in general terms to both US and Australian Intelligence and that in fact there was a rescue project which was not proceeded with for other reasons. Knowledge of what had occurred at Manila and Palawan denies any "wise after the event" argument to all who had that knowledge, which of course must have included MacArthur.

While it is true that Wallace's report, given directly by Major Steele to the Army Minister, Mr Forde, in 1944, and the other details Wallace gave to Army Intelligence could only provide information about Sandakan up to April 1943, and so could not cover the worst of the horrors, nevertheless there had always been a large number of sick at Sandakan and the pattern of brutality and cage atrocities and deaths had already emerged. This is confirmed by the circumstances that the brutality charge against Hoshijima was able to be established by the evidence of the officers who had been moved to Kuching shortly after the escape of Wallace. Blow, who escaped from Berhala with Wallace, had been able in June 1943 correctly to assess Hoshijima, and Hoshijima by then had made his Berhala speech of "welcome" about the rotting of bones under the tropical sun. Steele and Wallace also had access to the US guerilla intelligence about Sandakan, including the execution of Matthews and others.[5] However, the US and Australian Armies had much later intelligence concerning the Sandakan prisoners. From contemporary documents it appears that the Australian Army had intelligence reports dating back to 1943 from native intelligence, captured Japanese documents and Z Force (PYTHON and AGAS in the Sandakan area) which revealed the numbers and condition of the Sandakan prisoners. A captured document of the *37th Imperial Japanese Army* (the occupation force in Borneo) dated November 1944 revealed (correctly) that there were then 2400 prisoners at Sandakan. From some intelligence source not stated, it was known that 600 prisoners died before the second march left Sandakan. Other intelligence was that 300 prisoners were left behind when that march began. From this, it was deduced that just before the march there were 1800 prisoners still alive. This was the figure accepted after the war as accurate for that time. In fact, as revealed at the trials, the estimate of 600 deaths at Sandakan was wrong; the number of deaths was closer to 1100. It is curious that the number of deaths at the compound conceded by Hoshijima at his interrogation was 800, which included some, probably 200 or so, who died before November 1944. He conceded at his trial that the figure of 800 was too small. The circumstance, however, that is relevant is that the intelligence in early 1945 was that many hundreds had died at Sandakan. There was also US intelligence, before the second march, that the Sandakan prisoners were starved and weak and would not be able to travel far.

Even if the intelligence concerning the Manila and Palawan prisoners was unknown to the Australian Army and Government, it must have been obvious that the Sandakan prisoners in 1945 were in a position of great danger. There was a great number of them compared with the size of the Japanese Sandakan garrison, landings were pending at nearby Tarakan and there were proposals for ancillary activities at Sandakan itself. MacArthur was able to make an assessment of the danger to the Manila prisoners likely to arise from his operations there, sufficient to make an immediate surprise high-speed operation to rescue the Americans.

A lead to some answer to my question came from an undated press cutting kept by one of the Sandakan survivors (Nelson Short) of a speech made by General Sir Thomas Blamey after the war. It is clear now the report appeared on Friday, 21 November 1947 (probably in an afternoon Sydney newspaper), and that the speech was made in Melbourne on Wednesday, 19 November.

The press report of the speech under the heading "Melbourne Thursday" referred to a comment by the Victorian President of the RSL, Mr G. W. Holland, in these terms:

> He was commenting on General Sir Thomas Blamey's statement yesterday that the British and Australian soldiers who died on the march [Sandakan Death March] might have been saved if planes had been available for a special paratroop operation.

The report continued:

> Sir Thomas Blamey said that a "hush-hush" operation, which still could not be disclosed, was responsible for the abandonment of the plan to drop paratroops on Sandakan to rescue 1,800 prisoners of war, most of whom perished. It had been hoped to use Australian paratroops, but the planes and ships needed were required by the higher command for another operation.

The reference to "higher command" in relation to General Blamey could only refer to General MacArthur or his HQ virtually under his command. My searches have not uncovered any copy or record of the speech, if a copy was ever made.[6]

According to the press report, the RSL President had also said:

> Nothing less than an independent inquiry would satisfy relatives of men, who died during the Sandakan death march,

> that the loss of their menfolk was beyond human power to prevent.

There was no inquiry. He was reported to have added that:

> . . . if the aircraft were not available when they were wanted by the GOC for what must have been a more worthy purpose than the spectacular bombing of Japanese bases, the public should be told why.

Under the heading "Canberra Thursday", the press article referred to a question asked in the Australian Parliament about the failure to rescue the prisoners.

On Thursday, 20 November, the Melbourne *Argus* had made a report of the speech made "yesterday" in slightly different terms, under the heading "Disclosure by General Blamey. Lack of Planes Foiled Rescue Plan." The report stated:

> Australia just failed, through shortage of ships and planes to prevent the Sandakan "death march", in which all but 6 of 1,800 Australian and British POWs perished in Borneo, General Thomas Blamey said yesterday.
>
> Speaking at the Second Federal Conference of the Aust. Armoured Corps Association, he said an Australian paratroop regiment was specially trained on the Atherton tablelands to go in by air and rescue POWs in Borneo before Australian landings had taken place on the island.
>
> Maps and plans, based on first hand reports from Australian agents behind enemy lines and the specially selected and trained unit were ready, but the Allied counter offensive in the Pacific left Australia so short of planes and ships that it was never possible to carry out the daring rescue.
>
> Eventually the regiment was sent to Singapore when Japan surrendered, but until recently its members did not know the specialised role of mercy for which they had been trained and were prevented only by destiny from carrying out.
>
> Members of the regiment are part of the Armoured Corps Association.

The reference to the other "hush-hush" operation is put

differently and probably more accurately in the Melbourne *Sun* of 20 November. According to it, Blamey had said in his speech that the rescue operation was abandoned because the planes and ships were required by the Higher Command for "other purposes" and later that night, when questioned by the media, he had said, "I am not in a position to say anything about the 'other purposes' as it was a hush-hush operation." The *Sun* said that Blamey then added that some prisoners of war were released in other ways. The Americans were able to liberate service personnel and civilians in the Philippines. The report of his reply continued:

> We had high hopes of being able to use Australian paratroops. The paratroop regiment didn't know what we planned, of course. But at the moment we wanted to act, we couldn't get the necessary aircraft to take them in . . . We had completed plans for the paratroops . . .

The question asked in Parliament on 20 November, as reported in Hansard, was:

> Mr. FALKINDER.—Has the Prime Minister seen reports of a statement made by Sir Thomas Blamey to the effect that in 1945 the Australian Command prepared a plan the execution of which would have obviated the subsequent tragedy of the "death march" from Sandakan? That plan involved the employment of Australian paratroops, but, according to Sir Thomas Blamey, it had to be abandoned because aircraft were not available. Will the Prime Minister state the reason why aircraft could not be provided at that time, and obtain a full report for the information of honourable members?

The Prime Minister, Mr Chifley, said he would make inquiries, but made this observation:

> Operations in the Pacific campaign were carried out under the direction of General MacArthur, and I imagine that there were many instances in which sufficient aeroplanes were not available for the conduct of particular operations. As honourable members know, the number of aeroplanes

> available at times was extremely small, but because of American assistance it was possible at some later stages of the war to provide a very strong air force in the South-West Pacific. Whatever action was taken in the matter mentioned by the honourable member would, I presume, be decided upon only after consultation with General MacArthur or the Air Officer commanding in the South-West Pacific.[7]

On 3 December 1947 Mr Chifley made a prepared reply to the question in these terms:

> I have been informed by the Army authorities as follows:
>
> There is no record at Army Headquarters of the personal action taken by General Sir Thomas Blamey in this matter. The Army authorities state that the records held by them do not disclose any operational plan for the rescue of prisoners of war from Sandakan in 1945. Also, there is no record of any report or representations by General Blamey to the Prime Minister and Minister for Defence, to whom he had the right of direct access and communication on operation matters affecting the Australian Army. Similarly, no report or submission was made to the Advisory War Council by himself or his deputy. I mention this only to show that the matter did not receive consideration on a governmental level, nor was there any request for representations by the Government to the Commander-in-Chief, South-West Pacific Area in support of any plan. As I stated before, General MacArthur was responsible for the control of operations in the South-West Pacific Area in accordance with the overall strategy for the defeat of the Japanese, and I do not think that any useful purpose would be served by pursuing the matter further.[8]

There the matter has since rested. The reply left the impression that what Blamey had said at the service function was just something he must have had in his mind. The reference to the absence of any record and the use of the word "personal", which was curious in relation to the GOC, enhanced that impression. That was to be the end of the matter.

Mr Chifley used the occasion also to make the political response that, whatever had happened, it had nothing to do with the Government and in effect that responsibility rested outside Australia with General MacArthur and possibly General Blamey for not raising the matter with the Government. However, Blamey had been singularly unsuccessful in the past with his complaints to the Government concerning decisions of General MacArthur affecting the Australian armed services and the failure to use the 7th and 9th Divisions for the year or more before the Borneo operations, and concerning MacArthur, ignoring him or bypassing his agreed authority in the Pacific operations. Although he raised some questions with MacArthur, the then Prime Minister, Mr Curtin, in the end always took the view that MacArthur being in command, the Government should not interfere with his conduct of operations.[9] This soured relations between Blamey and Curtin and, later, Chifley. It is implicit in Chifley's reply that no inquiry had been made from Blamey. It is significant that in seeking a delayed answer concerning a serious wartime event, the Prime Minister did not seek to have some inquiry made by the Government from the man, who, at the time, had been the GOC of the Australian armed forces and who had made the speech.

The question asked was about a "plan", but as often happens in political responses, a word was added to make the denial one of an "operational" plan. The reply to the direct question about whether there was a rescue plan that had been abandoned because aircraft were not provided, appears in substance to deny the existence of any such plan. This illusion was achieved by a sleight-of-hand which used a play with words and omissions in the prepared response. The words used to conceal the reality were "*no record* of any *operational* plan" and "*no record* of any *personal* action *by Sir Thomas Blamey*" (my italics).

The truth is that Army records, now in the Archives,[10] show that there was what was code named KINGFISHER PROJECT, which by late 1944 had developed a plan for the rescue of Sandakan prisoners by a paratroop operation. As the extensive KINGFISHER record shows, what was done by early 1945 was not a feasibility study. It was an actual plan, which, however, could not become operational until some of the details and alternatives were decided. Some decisions necessarily had to be left until the eve of the operation. The plan depended on another plan to insert into Borneo a ground intelligence and operational party some six weeks before "D" Day of the rescue. The latter plan had been worked out in great and final detail. The truth is that the Australian Paratroop Battalion was, as Blamey said, trained for the rescue operation. The truth is that the plan could not proceed because Australia did not have the transport and drop planes for its paratroops and MacArthur's HQ declined to provide them. The truth is that the planning at the Australian end could not be completed until the availability of the planes, their number and the date they were to be provided were known. The same applied at the Sandakan end to the function of the ground party, which had in fact been landed in Borneo by a US submarine. That party had functions tied to "D" Day and "D-10" day which could not be fulfilled unless there was to be a "D" day. Not able to fulfil their planned function, they were diverted to other activity.

Thus it was true that there was no record of any "operational" plan in the sense of one ready to implement. It is true there was no record of what Blamey did in relation to the rescue plan. The true answer to the question to the Prime Minister, however, was that there was a plan to rescue the prisoners developed to a substantial extent and implemented in part and that it did not proceed because MacArthur's HQ did not provide the transport planes to drop the Australian paratroops. To have given that answer would have opened the controversial and embarrassing question of why the planes were not provided for a mission such as this. It is, of course, an entirely different question to ask who precisely were responsible for the unfrank answer drafted for the Prime Minister, which for the time buried the issue.

The Australian Paratroop Battalion, referred to by Blamey in his 1947 speech, was a unit independent of but intended to operate with the 1st Corps consisting of the 7th and 9th Divisions under General Sir Leslie Morshead. It, like the Divisions, undertook extensive training on the Atherton Tablelands in Queensland in 1944 and 1945. It was an elite unit with handpicked men, many with infantry battle experience in the Middle East. It was set up to give specialised aid in the Pacific counter-offensive, but as it happened, it never left Australia during the war. Its commander, who had been requested by Morshead, was a distinguished Middle East soldier, Lieutenant Colonel John Overall, decorated with an MC at Tobruk and a bar to it at Alamein—now Sir John Overall, distinguished in many fields. He will be remembered as the inspiration and leading force in the post-war development of Canberra and its suburbs.

The extensive training of this paratroop unit, of course, extended to infantry operations necessary following a unit drop. Some former members of the unit recalled training for a special unidentified unit operation, but did not know its purpose until after the war. One knew it was for an unidentified prisoner of war rescue and helped work out the number of planes required.

A former judicial colleague and former member of the unit put me in touch with Sir John Overall.

> Yes, there had been a plan to rescue the Sandakan prisoners. We were asked by Army HQ [Aust.] to undertake the rescue in the belief there were only third class Japanese troops there. I went to HQ, of which General Northcott was chief of general staff. General Morshead pressed the plan, and I understood General Blamey wanted it, but the US would not release the planes to make the drop. Certainly our HQ wanted it.

The unit trained for the mission, but for security reasons its members did not know what it was. The plan never became "operational", as the support and other details, although examined, were never finally worked out, because the drop planes required from the US were never provided. Morshead strongly favoured the plan and Overall's belief that Blamey supported it is confirmed by Blamey's 1947 speech. According to what Blamey said in 1947, the rescue plan reached MacArthur's HQ, but the necessary planes (and ships) were required by it for "other purposes".

The plan required a substantial number of drop planes for men, equipment and stores, some air force cover and some navy support and pick up. The planes which Overall sought were DC3s, or C47s as they were known when used for military purposes. The ideal number would have been 100 DC3s (C47s), 40 to carry the 800 paratroops, with about 23 in each plane, and the rest to carry equipment and stores. It was found there were just over 40 in Australia and that only 20 of these would be available. It was known that the US had a large number of C47s in each of the Asian-Pacific and Burma-India regions, as well as in Europe. Large numbers had been used in all these theatres, including the Normandy landing for troop and cargo transport. They had been used extensively for paratroops and to drop equipment and stores with or without parachutes. Their low speed capability made them ideal for drop work and landings in makeshift places.

The basic commercial DC3 had many military versions, the principal one, manufactured in the US in large numbers, being the C47. Some had been specially adapted, such as for carrying cargo and making paratroop and stores drops, but the C47 could be quickly adapted for any use. After the war the C47 was used commercially as the DC3 in Australia and elsewhere. It had landed in places such as on boulevards in the Philippines and on beaches in the Pacific. It had operated without air force cover. It was used for many mercy drops in jungle areas in the Pacific. It was affectionately called the "Gooney Bird".

On Overall's assessment, 80 US planes would be needed to supplement those available from Australia. He was told at the time his request for US planes was passed on but declined. In this, Blamey and Overall confirm each other. The operation could have been carried out with fewer C47s. Eighty DC3s, even 60, would have sufficed, but in the latter event some of the planes would have had to drop twice. This, with the delay, would have been less satisfactory. Thus the operation could have proceeded if the US had provided temporarily 40 C47s. Other larger planes, then in military use, could, it seems, have been used to carry men, stores and equipment at least part of the way. Distances to the drop presented no difficulties. There were ample airstrips, for example, for an operation starting from Australia. There were some airstrips well within range for a drop at Sandakan and return. Thus Morotai or Manila to Sandakan was only about the distance between Sydney and Melbourne. The airfield near Manila at that time was in constant use by C47s. A closer airstrip would have required fewer aircraft.

As Blamey said, the operation was intended to precede the first landing in Borneo. This would have put it between February and April 1945. Overall cannot now recall the precise month of the intended mission, except that it was to precede any Borneo landing and could have been in March or April. It can be inferred from the KINGFISHER records that early April or possibly the end of March was contemplated as the ideal "D" day. In fact, it could have been carried out after the Tarakan landing and up to and including the day of the attack on Sandakan on 27 May, just before the second march began on the night of 29 May.

Overall had been given direct access to combined operational HQ in Melbourne without having to go through Divisional Command. He made visits to Melbourne and was in touch with RAN and RAAF heads. Until the critical extra drop planes from the US were secured, no operational detailed planning with RAN or RAAF could proceed to finality, but Overall, from his discussions, was confident there would be no problem in getting the necessary RAN and RAAF support. The Allies had absolute air superiority over the approach route and drop area, so RAAF protective cover, although desirable, would not be a matter of any difficulty. Some support would have been necessary to provide diversions. The pick up contemplated, as Overall understood, was by landing barges and, with complete air and sea superiority, and with the Japanese without local artillery, naval assistance would present no problem. The KINGFISHER record shows that one option left open was evacuation by ship from the Sandakan wharf. The abandonment of Sandakan once the bombardment on 27 May had taken place, supports the view that this option could have turned out to be available. Although Overall did not mention it, if the operation had proceeded, one of the two nearby bomb damaged airstrips might in the end have provided an evacuation means using C47s. By March, the Japanese had abandoned the airstrips. Aerial reconnaissance on 31 May produced photographs which had only one airstrip labelled "unserviceable". Earlier there would have been less damage and the Japanese had no aircraft in the area.

The operation planned was not to be some daring drop onto the compound, but a proper infantry operation which would hold the area. The evacuation would be from the coast or a river very nearby. The rescue could have coped with any sick. There was intelligence covering the area. Overall had been shown aerial photographs, retained as secret, at Melbourne. As he put it to me, the Japanese forces were some distance away, were small and the troops "third class". This is confirmed by the KINGFISHER and AGAS records. I was able to confirm to him, which he did not know, that these same matters, and the fact that there were only 1500 Japanese in the Sandakan region spread out, had appeared from Japanese sources at the Labuan trials. As he responded, "The operation was absolutely ideal for us, we were trained for it, we had engineer and army support and would have succeeded if the U.S. had supplied the [drop] planes." He added that what happened was consistent with MacArthur's attitude not to use the Australian forces available. The same kind of thing occurred when a proposal to use the paratroop unit in the later Balikpapan landing was rejected. Many Australian servicemen, at the time, felt that MacArthur, in retaliation for his defeat at Corregidor, wanted his US troops to have the glory of the counter-offensive and not share it with the Australians. This view has support from the material revealed after the war and referred to in the official Australian war histories.[11]

The records of KINGFISHER, earlier referred to, reveal the extensive and detailed work which emerged as the rescue plan. Much of the intelligence concerning Sandakan, the prisoners and the Japanese activities there, had its origin in an intelligence network using local agents set up under the code name PYTHON (a Z Force operation). This was set up with W/T communications with Australia under Major Chester (who is now dead), in 1943, some two years before the first Borneo landing. It operated in the Sandakan region extending to Tarakan and nearby islands to give intelligence on shipping and other Japanese activities. The PYTHON force reached mainland Borneo via Tawi Tawi, where it liaised with Colonel Suarez, the US Filipino guerilla leader in the Sulu Archipelago. He provided, on attachment as a liaison officer, Lieutenant Valera, who previously had been a Sandakan Forestry Officer with the North Borneo Administration. He had extensive local contacts for intelligence purposes.[12]

The KINGFISHER record[13] shows detailed intelligence on very many matters relevant to the proposed operations. It extended to installations and Japanese dispositions at Sandakan, numbers, patrols and wireless communication points. The detailed intelligence was limited to Japanese posts near the compound, those at Sandakan eight miles away, and positions in between, presumably on the view that these were the primary areas to be dealt with in a surprise operation needing a rapid exit. Intelligence also covered places for paratroop drops and landing places for exit vessels. It included details of Sandakan harbour, beaches, inlets, rivers, etc. and beach compositions, water depths and access routes. Blamey was apparently referring to PYTHON and KINGFISHER when, in his speech, he said there were in respect of the rescue operation "first hand reports from Australian agents behind enemy lines." The KINGFISHER record was also supplemented by intelligence concerning the prison compound, prisoner routines, lay-out of buildings, etc. from the "Steele report" (originating from the escaped Steele and Wallace). The record shows that there were hundreds of hospital prisoner patients.

The KINGFISHER record put together relevant intelligence to late November 1944 at a time when the rescue date hoped for was January 1945. Intelligence was updated on some aspects in early 1945. The record at points refers to the "proposed (rescue) operation." It refers to the "Main Plan" (the actual rescue operation on what is referred to as "D" Day). This plan had three phases, firstly being dropped, secondly neutralising the enemy and releasing the prisoners, and finally the withdrawal. It indicated that information to be provided by an advance ground party was "essential before the operation could be planned in detail."

It was acknowledged that three matters had to be met, namely:

1. The physical condition of the POW which is likely to make evacuation difficult;
2. The attack must be timed to coincide with the concentration of POW in the camp;
3. The Japanese must be allowed as little time as possible to remove or massacre the POW.

These matters were proposed to be dealt with by various alternatives set out in some detail. However, it was accepted that in order to meet them, it was essential that there be last minute accurate intelligence from the ground party to confirm existing intelligence, add to it and bring it up to the moment of the operation. By way of example relevant to (1) would be the seizure of Japanese transport to carry the hospital patients. Relevant to (3) would be surprise and diversionary attacks. It was stated the complete paratroop battalion could be dropped by day in about eight minutes and would require three to five minutes to collect its arms and move off. In some conditions it might be longer. Surprise, speed and diversion made two drop zones desirable. By night, the whole operation in one drop zone would take one and a half hours. Diversion would be by attack on vulnerable non-compound points, such as the wireless station, the officers' and the CO's quarters and other points. Changes at the compound by March 1945 would have largely solved (2). The POW work at the airstrips was at an end and they were confined to the compound and the nearby garden.

In stating the problems to be met, there was no suggestion that enemy numbers in adjacent or other areas might cause a problem or frustrate the plan. The plan did not contemplate the need for or include any provision for reinforcement by troops landed by sea.

The main plan prepared in late 1944 and the final determination of its detail depended on the subsidiary plan, finalised and implemented in 1945. This was the insertion and operation of the ground intelligence party already referred to. It was to consist of two officers, two W/T operators and two natives. Its function was to obtain last minute intelligence and also to participate in the operation. The plan was to insert the party at least six weeks before "D" day in order to provide confirmatory intelligence by "D-10" day. The record added:

> It is considered that the party should contact a senior POW officer from whom information could be extracted, and who could organise selected POW within the compound to receive arms dropped from aircraft on "D" day. Further roles for the Intelligence Party on "D" day are as follows:
>
> 1. The placing of homing devices on the DZs [Drop Zones] to assist in the dropping of the Paratroop Bn.;
> 2. To act as guides from the DZ to objectives;
> 3. To mark out withdrawal points and assist with the evacuation.

The Party was to be evacuated with the prisoners.

The planning of this advance party operation was set out in complete detail, down to stores, the landing, concealment and the cover story. The insertion for security reasons was to be by submarine at night with landing by a rubber boat. The operations post was to be on an island in a river just north of Sandakan. It was stated that the party could not be landed until the end of February owing to the North-West monsoon.

Secrecy and surprise were stressed as top priority for the subsidiary and the main plan. As to the advance party, there were long and elaborate plans for a cover story in case of capture. The cover was to be of a paratroop landing by the advance party for objectives unconnected with the prisoners. Details, required to be learned perfectly, covered paratroop training in Australia, movement by air via the Philippines covering meals, times, etc.

Even without this further intelligence from the ground party, the existing intelligence covered most matters. There were three possible drop zones. The two most likely were one near the airstrip adjoining the compound and one at the golf course between the compound and the town. The airstrip, having been abandoned by the Japanese before March, made this an ideal drop zone. The golf course was close to a signal station and the army barracks and had uses for diversions. Both could be used. The Japanese numbers at the compound and at Sandakan were set out. It was said the numbers at Sandakan were small and the Japanese forces were dispersed. Those at Sandakan itself and nearby were less than 500 and were described as "B" class. The Japanese had no artillery, only machine guns and rifles.

Some matters recorded by intelligence up to November 1944 changed by February-March 1945 dramatically in favour of the operation. In late 1944 Japanese air defence based on Sandakan and elsewhere posed a major obstacle. The Sandakan airstrips were still operational and Japanese aircraft were based there. It was no longer in use by 1945 and there were no Japanese aircraft there. The KINGFISHER record indicates that the Japanese Air Force strength for all of Borneo was 119 on 4 January, 54 on 13 January and 39 on 21 January. Although not recorded, they were in effect none by February. The number of guards, recorded as 200 in November, was fewer after the march which left in January. In late 1944 requests to Allied HQ Air SWPA for US air reconnaissance photography of the compound were able to be met only by high level operations. However, KINGFISHER already had air photographs of the compound and Sandakan harbour installations. By early March, low level air photography of the compound was effected.

Apart from the KINGFISHER intelligence sources, there was intelligence sent to the US Eighth Army originating from Tawi Tawi via Colonel Suarez who had close links with many islands in the Sulus and with mainland Borneo in the Sandakan region. That this source existed is evidenced by intelligence reports to the Eighth Army in the Blamey papers now held at the War Memorial.[14] The source of these reports was Sulu Area Command (Suarez). One report shows that natives from the Borneo mainland were a continuing source of intelligence for Suarez. It indicated that Japanese brutality, tortures and killings led some 3000 to escape from Borneo to his command, many of them then acting as mainland intelligence agents for him. An Eighth Army report of April 1945 in the Blamey papers states:

> Lt. Col. Suarez believes there are about 1,000 white POW and, as lately they have been given little food, many are very weak and most of them would not be in a condition to do much work or marching.
>
> A most useful man in liberating these would be a Chinese, Sinyen . . . Sinyen has influence and contacts with the native police at Sandakan and has contacts with the POW through these native police. He has a plan for their liberation with Allied and native police aid. The plan involves landing on the coast North of the prison camp and a long withdrawal inland (no other details known).

Thus it is clear from the KINGFISHER material that at least up to early March 1945 there was current a paratroop rescue plan trained for and well under way, but not worked out in every operational detail. This could not be done until the availability of the drop planes, their number and date of availability were known. The last minute details and decisions dependent on the advance party could not be determined until "D" day was known, and whether there was to be one.

The term "PROJECT KINGFISHER", used in the records, meant, in Army language, a paratroop operation, code named KINGFISHER, to rescue the Sandakan POWs. Using the same language, AGAS had a number of "projects" under Z Force

"Project HQ". These were specific operations planned and carried out for intelligence, native recruitment and training and guerilla attacks in specific areas. In the case of KINGFISHER, the planning of the operation was not finalised, but was implemented to the extent of inserting the ground party and training the paratroops in this paratroop operation.

I have revealed details of the planning of KINGFISHER and the training and planning of the paratroops in Australia, because those details show that the rescue was not an "idea", but a plan. It makes it very hard to understand why the operation planned did not proceed. It is ever harder to understand because the importance of air force and navy cover had diminished, except for diversionary purposes. The capability of providing that diversionary function was demonstrated by the air and naval bombardment of Sandakan on 27 May, sufficient to cause the small Japanese garrison to retreat inland, leaving the prisoner compound, the most forward Japanese post, unprotected from 27 to 29 May.

The official history of AGAS I,[15] written after the war, records its object as:

> to establish a base on the East coast of British North Borneo with W/T communication with Australia; to set up a native intelligence network in BNB, particular importance being attached to detailed information of the POW camp at Sandakan [originally PROJECT KINGFISHER].

In the end, AGAS I did not fulfil its planned Kingfisher function in relation to the rescue. If no drop planes were to be provided for the paratroops, the only function of AGAS I would have to be otherwise, but could include some general intelligence concerning Sandakan. That is what occurred.

An aerial photograph of the compound dated 6 March 1945 is obviously in aid of a paratroop landing. The three photographs reproduced in this book include that of 6 March showing the compound in full operation when the rescue plan was current. The second, which is dated 31 May, has an endorsement on it that by that date the compound had been destroyed. A third photograph, taken later and undated, shows more clearly the burned out remains of the compound.

It is the photograph of 6 March that provides further support for my assertion that a rescue operation was under way in early March. The markings identify the Japanese areas ("P.O.W. Camp administrative area" and "Buildings probably used for administration") and the two prisoner areas ("Prisoners quarters, 20 buildings 45′ x 20′ each", "Quarters possibly prisoners" and "Prisoner quarters 16 buildings 52′ x 25′ each") and they identify the boundaries in a way relevant to a ground operation ("3-apron wire"—on top of an embankment described in another photograph as "low", "Prison gates", the various "guard towers" and their associated "guard sheds" nearby). Also located is "probably automatic weapons pit". It shows the nature of the immediate surroundings of the compound such as "clearance" and roads and to where they lead and information such as "single lane, light surface". It shows the road to and from the nearby airstrip and a "small bridge" on it. No doubt there would have been photographs of the airstrips close by, such as the photograph of 31 May. This photograph shows that each of the two airstrips by that date had considerable bomb damage, but only No. 1 strip is marked "unserviceable".

The photographs confirm that there were no Japanese army units nearby, that there were many cleared spaces in different locations, including the nearby damaged airstrips suitable for a paratroop drop, that there was an abundance of jungle cover and that there were access roads to the compound and exit roads.

A Z Force operation (AGAS I) inserted a party into North Borneo forty-five miles north of Sandakan in the exact manner and with a timing which complied with the subsidiary plan of KINGFISHER. The party left Darwin on 24 February 1945 in the US submarine *Tuna*. The seven members of the force, under Major Chester, reached the disembarkation point on 3 March 1945. Under cover of darkness, they went ashore in a rubber boat towing other boats, which carried supplies and equipment. They established W/T contact with Australia on 7 March from a base on a mangrove island in an unnamed river near Labuk Bay, the large inlet just to the north of Sandakan.

The official history of AGAS I[16] sets out its KINGFISHER objects in the terms earlier quoted. Then followed other objects in respect of other areas not connected with KINGFISHER. The history of AGAS I refers to guerilla activities with the recruited natives in other areas, with no reference to anything done to further the KINGFISHER plan, such as information about the proposed drop zones and attempted communication with the prisoners at the compound. The only information about the prisoners in the history was about those who had been later killed on the second and third marches.

It became obvious that at some early stage some decision must have been taken not to proceed with the paratroop rescue and hence not carry out the planned operations of its ground party. I went to the voluminous records and reports of AGAS I[17] (Sandakan) and AGAS III[18] (Ranau) to see if I could find out what had happened and why.

After PYTHON, which had been led by Major Chester, had had to be withdrawn, Chester had pressed to re-establish the operation on the east coast. His seeking to do so, which went back to late 1944, had no connection with KINGFISHER. His efforts succeeded and in consequence the AGAS projects (I to VI) eventuated, the first AGAS I, as already stated, being inserted on 3 March. The AGAS operations followed the SEMUT scheme, not only by providing intelligence, but also by arming the natives and by guerilla activities attacking Japanese outposts. This AGAS I did very successfully in the seven months it was in North Borneo. While AGAS was being planned, the KINGFISHER project arose, with the need for a ground party to provide up to date intelligence and participation on "D" day. High security and in the end a swift surprise operation required a separate party with no other operations, such as attacks on Japanese outposts in the Sandakan camp region. It was planned to have a separate operation, to be code named AGAS II.

A document of 5 February recorded that "AGAS II (KINGFISHER)" was to be inserted directly into its area by submarine.[19] AGAS I was to go in by submarine to a different location further north. KINGFISHER, as AGAS II, was to be independent of Z Force "Project HQ". AGAS I, with its original function, left Darwin on 16 January 1945 by submarine, with the party under Major Chester ready to land. A periscope reconnaissance revealed a Japanese presence, which showed the planned base to be unsatisfactory. The plan was aborted and the party returned to Darwin. It was then decided to combine the KINGFISHER PROJECT with AGAS I. The personnel, under Captain Sutcliffe, who had been trained for KINGFISHER, were transferred to AGAS I. The landing point and base for AGAS I then became that selected for AGAS II (KINGFISHER). AGAS II was later given a Z Force operation in the north. On 15 February there was an official addition to the AGAS I functions, which were now to include:

> To establish a party in the area of Sandakan BNB for the purpose of obtaining and relaying to Australia the detailed intelligence essential for the planning of a combined airborne naval operation on the POW camps in the area, aimed at effecting the rescue and withdrawal by sea of the prisoners therein, and such other information as is laid down under the project known as KINGFISHER.[20]

The same document fixed the date for the submarine to leave Darwin as 24 February.

The KINGFISHER ground party plan would have required urgent commencement of the KINGFISHER function as soon as the W/T post had been set up. This did not happen. The record shows that upon establishing W/T communications with Australia, other non-KINGFISHER operations were set about. What was done was inconsistent with any priority or "particular importance" being accorded to the KINGFISHER PROJECT. It is clear that, by early March, from outside AGAS I, a decision must have been made not to pursue the paratroop rescue operation. Most likely it was taken soon after W/T communication with Australia was established from the AGAS base on 7 March.

It is clear from the record of AGAS[21] and its reports

that nothing was found by AGAS intelligence which negatived earlier intelligence on which KINGFISHER was founded or which provided reasons against undertaking the rescue. If Army HQ had intelligence about Japanese numbers or dispositions at Sandakan which would operate against the KINGFISHER plan or contradict its intelligence, the only source could be a ground operation such as AGAS or PYTHON, as there was no other.

There is nothing in the AGAS official histories or in the voluminous AGAS I (Sandakan) or III (Ranau) papers which refer to any cancellation of the KINGFISHER function of the AGAS I earlier quoted. It is quite clear that this activity by AGAS was never commenced. As with the official history, there is not the slightest indication anywhere in the record of any attempt to get any, much less "detailed", information of the prison camp, about the drop zones or any of the other information or confirmations which the KINGFISHER plan required. The only information recorded concerning POWs relates to the later June–July period and to what occurred on the second and third death marches. It sets out native reports of the shooting of sick POWs and the plight of some escaped POWs who, having hidden in villages, were later revealed by informers. There follows an account of the subsequent torture and killing of the recaptured POWs and villagers, of the "reign of terror" in the villages and of the flight of some 1000 natives from Borneo. This is not what AGAS (KINGFISHER) was originally sent to find out. This is what KINGFISHER was intended to prevent, but tragically did not. The record describes in detail the other earlier intelligence and guerilla activities of AGAS; most in the opposite direction to Sandakan. The cancellation was probably just before 10 March. As the photography of 6 March shows, aerial reconnaissance for a KINGFISHER-style operation seems to have been then still current.

It is curious that there was no record of the cancellation or the reasons for it. It is beyond doubt it was cancelled at some date later than when the submarine left with the KINGFISHER trained personnel. All the KINGFISHER planning and the AGAS briefing for the KINGFISHER party of AGAS is recorded, as are variations in AGAS objectives, but there is a total absence of any record of the decision to cancel it, of the order to AGAS I or the reasons for so doing. The KINGFISHER ground operation just did not commence after the special party arrived in Borneo. This could not have occurred without some order and some cancellation of the already quoted function of AGAS I in relation to KINGFISHER. Such a cancellation without any record now in the papers is hard to understand having regard to what Overall said was done about the plan in Australia and the voluminous written material about the KINGFISHER planning. There could not have been any security reason to suppress the cancellation and the reason for it. The AGAS record shows that all sorts of top secret material was reported by it by W/T. The absence of record about the cancellation of the rescue plan and the reasons for it seems to have applied throughout in relation to the fate of the rescue project. In 1945, everyone appears to have avoided recording why the plan was dropped. By 1947, there was and hence still is a mysterious lack of records as to why the rescue was abandoned. There seems to have been a disinclination to face up to the fact that it did not go ahead because the drop planes were not made available. This became apparent when I tried to dig more deeply behind the Prime Minister's answer of December 1947. Facing up to the plan being cancelled owing to lack of planes, of course, raised the troublesome question of why they were not provided. Even Blamey shied off having to talk about the "other purposes" for which the planes were required.

What Blamey and Overall separately said makes it clear that the paratroop rescue plan was abandoned because Allied HQ SWPA declined to make the drop planes available. The KINGFISHER and AGAS I papers make it clear that the KINGFISHER ground party plan in aid of the rescue operation was abandoned for a reason unconnected with any intelligence found concerning Sandakan. That record shows that the decision to cancel the operation was not based on intelligence, which was no longer being gathered. If there had been doubt or concern about Japanese numbers and positions, AGAS I, KINGFISHER, could have been used to find the true position. It was not. KINGFISHER was cancelled without doing so. If the AGAS (KINGFISHER) ground party had been allowed to proceed with its function laid down on 15 February and earlier quoted, the drop planes would not have been required for some weeks, which unless the plan was accelerated would have been six weeks. The compelling inference is that it was determined many, perhaps six or more, weeks ahead of the period for the operation that the planes would not be made available. It was not just a last minute cancellation because of some sudden emergency requirement of the planes for some other special purpose. There were weeks available to bring forward or delay the rescue if the planes were not available on a particular "D" day planned. The strong inference is that MacArthur and his HQ did not really approve the rescue operation by the Australian Paratroop Battalion and, in advance, conveniently announced that the US planes would not be available. The KINGFISHER AGAS I records taken together point to this decision being taken by HQ SWPA at the time it was settling the plans in early March for the first Borneo landing.

The lack of US support or approval of these missions and the non-use of the Australian paratroops, is consistent with the non-use by MacArthur of the 7th and 9th Divisions and Australian forces in MacArthur's march to triumph over the Japanese in the Pacific counter-offensive. Testimony to this is now well documented and is evidenced by the disputes between Blamey and MacArthur into which Prime Minister Curtin was drawn. This included the non-use of the idle Australian Divisions in the Philippines operations. In response to protests by Blamey, through Curtin, MacArthur claimed that it had been planned to use the Australian Divisions in the Philippines but that this did not occur because a plan to use them in the initial assaults became non-operational. He also said that although it was then planned to hold them in reserve, his success with the US troops and the enemy weakness dispensed with the need to use them, and he further asserted that there were difficulties in providing the shipping to transport them.

Disputes over MacArthur's failure to use the Australian forces and his by-passing Blamey in his agreed position, was the subject of correspondence between Blamey and Curtin, and Curtin and MacArthur, in February, March and April 1945, being the time when the Sandakan rescue question arose. This correspondence is lengthy and is set out in part in the official Australian war history.[22] Some passages are relevant here. Curtin wrote a letter to MacArthur in February 1945 which reads in part:

> Elements of the 1st Aust Corp [7th and 9th Divisions] have been on the mainland for periods of up to 18 months and have taken no part in the war since 1943. You may have gathered from press reports that there has been considerable public criticism . . . I shall be confronted with a difficult situation if so many Australian troops are to be retained in an ineffective role . . .[23]

In response to MacArthur's claim, made in a letter dated 5 March 1945,[24] that he had had plans to use the 7th and 9th Divisions in the Philippines and to his reasons why he did not, which have already been referred to in general terms, Blamey, in a letter to Curtin of 5 April 1945,[25] challenged the "sincerity" of MacArthur's claims. He challenged lack of shipping as the reason for not moving the Australian Divisions from Australia to forward areas when there had been plenty of shipping to move US troops. He said that although he had talked with MacArthur about the Philippines operations, MacArthur did not mention any plan to use the Australian Divisions as a reserve and added:

> In spite of the fact he now claims the enemy weakness obviated the necessity for the use of the Australian divisions, nevertheless very large American forces have been and are being utilised still in the campaign.

Blamey then referred to what appears to be the real reason

for the non-use of the Australian Divisions. The US Chief of Staff, General Sutherland, had told General Blamey and General Berryman—and the latter entered it in his diary—that it was impossible, for political reasons, to use the Australian troops in the Philippines.[26] Whose politics it was he did not state. The 7th and 9th Divisions and their commanders had extensive battle experience in the Middle East extending back prior to the US entry into the war, being experience far superior to that in the US Divisions in the Philippines operations. The 1st Australian Paratroop Battalion had fifteen months extensive training and most had similar Middle East infantry battle experience.

The consequence of not using Australian troops and excusing this by plans it was found not necessary to implement, was that MacArthur was able to regain the Philippines in an exclusively US operation, and wade ashore in front of camera lenses and make his second most famous remark. The Borneo operation, principally undertaken by the Australian Army, with some US support, was offered after Curtin's protests as an operation for the 7th and 9th Divisions, but only in the dying stages of the war and, in the view of some, as a side show or mopping up operation after earlier US successes elsewhere.

Although Australia provided most of the Borneo invasion force, it was planned by MacArthur's GHQ and some US units were involved. The plans for the first landing, Tarakan, were settled by that GHQ on 17 March. Australian proposals for the operation would have been considered in the weeks preceding 17 March. As appears from the AGAS I record, the KINGFISHER ground party operation must have been stopped in the first weeks of March. Thus, by about 10 March it is likely that the KINGFISHER plan or the proposal to GHQ had been rejected in the course of decisions concerning the first landing. On 17 April, the date for the Tarakan operation was fixed by GHQ for 1 May, and on 19 April Morshead discussed the plans with MacArthur. MacArthur, as always, exerted, in relation to Borneo, the authority which he undoubtedly had. Thus later, when the oilfields of Tarakan and North Borneo had been recaptured, Curtin raised with MacArthur whether by then the Balikpapan operation fixed for 1 July was necessary. MacArthur tartly replied that the plan was in place and would go ahead and, if Curtin wished to withdraw the 7th Division, to advise him immediately, so he could substitute some other division.

It was against this background of conflict and non-use of Australian units that the question of the rescue of the Sandakan prisoners arose. Apart from the request from Australia, it raised itself as a special problem for any who planned offensive operations in the Sandakan region, because of the special and vulnerable situation of the large number of prisoners there. The proposed operations in the area should have made a particular impression on MacArthur, given his experience in the Manila prisoner rescue mission.

It was a matter of military necessity that one man be Commander-in-Chief of the counter-offensive and that he exercise his authority with resolution. In the end, Curtin always accepted that. MacArthur had the authority to decide or veto operational plans and determine the use of units for the Philippines, Borneo and elsewhere, and he did so.

Blamey, however, in February 1945, had complained to Curtin that MacArthur had exercised his authority so as to exclude Blamey and Australian commanders from any real say in operations. As he put it in relation to himself:

> You will recall that on the establishment of the South West Pacific Area, General MacArthur was appointed Commander-in-Chief. I was appointed Commander Allied Land Forces. I understand the appointment was made as part of the general agreement for the acceptance of the set up of the command of the SWP Area. Except during the offensive campaign in the field of New Guinea up to the end of 1943, I have never operated as such . . .
>
> GHQ, SWPA asserts its authority to exercise direct control over the 1st Australian Army and . . . intends to assume direct control of 1st Aust Corps in operations now under consideration . . . It is obvious to me that the intention

of GHQ SWPA is to treat my headquarters as a purely liaison element . . .[27]

The agreement made at government level when MacArthur was made Commander-in-Chief SWPA and how he later managed to subvert it, is set out in the official Australian war history.[28] Slight reference here will suffice. MacArthur and his HQ were given overall control, but on the basis that three commanders would individually control Navy, Air Force and Army. Blamey held the Army post as Commander Allied Land Forces. In Europe, Allied GHQ consisted of officers of different Allied countries. However, MacArthur selected for the senior posts at GHQ SWPA, eight American officers who had been associated with him in the 1942 Philippines operations. He explained the omission of an Australian on the basis that the Australian armed forces had expanded so rapidly that a senior officer could not be spared. The devices then used by MacArthur to exclude Blamey are well documented. They included GHQ dealing directly with local army commanders. Morshead, 1 Corps Commander (7th and 9th Division), in effect became beholden direct to MacArthur and his Philippines colleagues. Blamey protested to the Australian Government, but it did nothing effective to prevent the essence of the original agreement made at government level being subverted.

With the authority which MacArthur had procured and which he exercised with great zeal, largely excluding Blamey and other Australian commanders from the ultimate decisions, went responsibility as to what was planned and what was omitted. The US prisoners at Manila were rescued by a surprise land operation, but the Australian prisoners at Sandakan were not. In each case, there was a responsibility to consider the position of the prisoners. In any event, the Eighth US Army, through Sulu Area Command, had intelligence which raised the question of rescue of the Sandakan prisoners after the Manila and Palawan experiences were known. The Sulu report had indicated the need for Allied help in any rescue, the local co-operation available and a suitable place for a landing, which happened to be near where AGAS 1 had been landed by a US submarine in early March. All this was within the sphere of knowledge of the commander-in-chief and his staff before the first Allied landing in Borneo on 1 May and before the Allied attack on Sandakan on 27 May by Australian and US Air Force units, and by the US Navy. There was no attempt to rescue the prisoners then or earlier, and two days later the prisoners' compound was burned and the death march begun.

MacArthur had at his disposal the Australian Paratroop Battalion of seasoned and highly trained soldiers. They were a unit capable of spectacular operations in aid of the counter-offensive for which they had been formed under the influence of Morshead. They were capable of rescuing the Sandakan prisoners. They were not used for that or for any other operation. It was more than just not responding to a particular proposal emanating from Australia for the rescue mission. Of course, if it had gone ahead and succeeded, as Overall is sure it would, it would have been the first paratroop operation to rescue prisoners of war in advance of a seaborne attack. Such a rescue was possible because of the special and ideal circumstances at Sandakan already detailed. It would have used US transport planes for Australians to rescue Australians and British prisoners. The earlier MacArthur land rescue at Manila had been less spectacular.

The earlier non-use of the seasoned Middle East Australian Divisions and the entire non-use of the Australian paratroops in any spectacular mission, is at least consistent with the now well recorded conceit of MacArthur concerning the singular success of the US forces under his command. Until later Australian protests, news communiques were forbidden except by his HQ and these made almost no reference to the participation of the Australians in the counter-offensive. The Australian war history which sets out the details commented:

> Probably never in the history of modern war had so large a force [Australian], although in action, been hidden from public knowledge for so long.[29]

The Prime Minister's reply of 3 December 1947 and what it was apparently intended to convey in dismissing the matter as lacking substance, does not stand against the planning and preparation for the operation earlier referred to, yet it professed to be based on Army advice. It succeeded in closing the issue in the years which have followed.

I went to the Archives to find, if I could, the basis for the Prime Minister's reply. What has been confidential or secret should not now be so. I sought the file of the Prime Minister's Department to ascertain the advice he had from the Army and the corresponding Army file which ought to include the source of any Army advice. I met two blank walls.

The relevant file of the Prime Minister's Department had not been sent to the Archives. Apparently, "sensitive" files relating to Cabinet and the Prime Minister's Department from many years earlier are at times retained and not sent to Archives in case there might be some residual national security or like ground for not producing them. I made a formal written request with the assistance of Archives.[31] Section 40 of the *Archives Act* required the file to be produced promptly, and in any event within ninety days, or that a statement be issued in writing giving the reason for not producing it. Archives, which did not have the file, passed the request to the Prime Minister's Department, which indirectly was bound by Section 40. Despite further oral requests, ninety and more days passed without the file being produced. On my behalf a written reply was sought as required by Section 40. It came in the form of a polite reply from the appropriate officer in the Prime Minister's Department some four and a half months after the original formal request by me. There was an apology for the delay and a statement that following an extensive search, the file could not be located and that it was not possible to determine whether the file had been transferred to Archives (which it had not) "or to another Department, or top-numbered, cancelled or destroyed." It is clear the file is no longer with the Prime Minister's Department. It is quite likely that long ago it met the fate of destruction suffered by the file I am about to refer to.

I sought the corresponding Army file. It also had never been sent to Archives. An Army card with Archives in Victoria[31] led to an item in an Army registration booklet[32] which showed there had been an Army file entitled "The operational plan for the relief of Aust. POW in Borneo 1945" in relation to the Parliamentary question. The relevant item in the booklet showed a file number (206), opposite which was a stamp "Destroy", with some person's initials, later crossed out and now obliterated. There was no similar "Destroy" marking opposite other items, ie 207, 208, etc. The inference is that the file was destroyed by the Army before the booklet was transferred to Archives. The booklet entry shows the matter originated for the Army on 24 November 1947 with a request for information from the Defence Department and concluded the next day with a reference to the letter to the Defence Department.[33] This led me to a Defence Department file lodged with Archives in Canberra[34] in which was the Army letter[35] dated 25 November to the Defence Department, which was used in part for the Department to prepare the Prime Minister's reply to Parliament. It appeared from that file that the Prime Minister's Department had dealt with the matter and had made some inquiry from the Defence Department in a memorandum dated 24 November. This document is not in the Defence Department file. A copy of it most likely would have been in the missing Prime Minister's Department file.

The only matter of substance in the Defence Department's file was the Army letter (of 25 November) and the Defence Department's minute dated 27 November in respect of it to the Prime Minister.[36] There was also a copy of a formal request to the Secretary of the Army, dated 24 November, for information. The destruction of the Army file, however, meant that there was not available any documentation of any internal Army inquiry or report on which its reply, which was given one day after requested by the Defence Department, was founded. Having regard to what Blamey had said and some parts of the Army letter to be referred to, it seems impossible that such a reply could be satisfactorily given without some internal inquiry and documentation.

The Defence Department minute to the Prime Minister set out the Army letter in full and also submitted a draft reply for the Prime Mnister, which was that in fact given by him on 3 December.

The Army letter provides the source of the reply, but it has some curious aspects and raises more questions than it answers. Some parts of the Army statement, which it concedes are not based on any record, must certainly be wrong, but the source of these unsupported statements does not appear from any available internal Army document prepared in November 1947.

The letter[37] from the Secretary for the Army professing to report the observations of the then Chief of General Staff, made two very significant comments. One was:

> There is no record *at Army Headquarters* of the personal action taken by General Sir Thomas Blamey in this matter . . . [my italics]

and the other was:

> the possibility of carrying out an operation to rescue prisoners of war from Sandakan prior to the "Death March" was examined *at Advance Headquarters Allied Land Force* and was found to be quite impracticable from all aspects and therefore the idea *did not reach the stage at which a firm plan was prepared. There is no written record of the examination* . . . [my italics]

General Northcott, the Chief of Staff of HQ which had directed Overall to plan and train for the operation, had left that post at the end of 1945. The examination of the not "firm plan" for the 1945 rescue operation thus had been two and a half years before the Army letter was composed in 1947. Blamey, GOC Australian Military Forces in 1945, was also the General in charge of Advance HQ Allied Land Forces. He had directly said (in 1947) that there was a plan and that the only reason it did not go ahead, with the paratroops trained and ready, was the unavailability of the planes and ships.

Despite this, it was able to be said, two and a half years later in a letter composed in just one day and admittedly without any record to back it up, that Blamey's own HQ had rejected the "possibility" as "impracticable from all aspects" and that anything he had said referred to some "personal action". Later revelations, particularly those by Overall and those from the KINGFISHER AGAS records, make these assertions absolutely false.

The ambiguous word "personal" was incorporated into the Prime Minister's reply. Its convenient ambiguity carried the suggestion, when used in Parliament, that there really was no plan and it was just something which Blamey must have had in his mind or at best raised in some informal way. This became the inference from the Prime Minister's reply, when reference to the second passage from the Army letter was deliberately omitted. From the recent information supplied by Overall, Morshead, who was in charge of the 7th and 9th Divisions, did not think the proposed rescue was impracticable, nor apparently did the then Chief of Staff at the time Lieutenant Colonel Overall was instructed by his HQ to prepare the plan and his battalion trained for the operation. That same HQ told him that the plan could not go ahead because the US would not release the planes.

The Defence Department minute which was marked "Confidential" is that of its Secretary directed to the Prime Minister. After setting out in full the contents of the Army letter, the first comment in the minute was: "You may feel it inadvisable and likely to provoke unnecessary controversy to use the information in the form stated by the Chief of General Staff." Put bluntly, the advice was to suppress the fact that the Army had officially confirmed that Blamey's Advance HQ had considered a rescue proposal of the type referred to by Blamey and that there was a claim two years later, unsupported by any records, that the proposal was rejected for reasons (now shown to be false) which were in direct conflict with what the GOC of that HQ and of the Australian Army had said on one day and confirmed later. It was better to suppress the reference to the not "firm" plan and the questionable claims concerning it and leave the impression that there never was a rescue proposal and so avoid "unnecessary controversy".

The next advice given in the minute was that there should be no further inquiry (as the RSL and others had sought). On the same day as the minute was sent to the Prime Minister, a separate minute marked "Confidential"[38] was sent by the Secretary of that Department to the Prime Minister enclosing a copy of an article of some length on the issue published in the *Bulletin* dated 26 November (the day before). This article repeated its prior demands for an inquiry, saying that "The whole position had been a scandal" and that the gravest issues were raised by what Blamey said. It referred to many of the objective circumstances earlier stated in this chapter, including the weakness of the Japanese forces. It charged the Government with responsibility for not having done something, having regard to earlier messages from the Sandakan prisoners received through the Tawi Tawi escapees and said that if a special request had been made (by the Government) to MacArthur or to the US Government, something would have been done. In respect of the Prime Minister's comment on 20 November, when the question was raised, it challenged the Government by saying it fell back "on the Government's old whine" that the conduct of the Pacific campaign was under the command of General MacArthur who would have to approve of the operation.

It was in this climate that both the Army reply was given and the Defence Department minute was prepared in two days, the latter on the day following the *Bulletin* challenge. The advice in the minute that there should be no further inquiry was translated in the Prime Minister's reply as "No useful purpose [will] be served in pursuing the matter further." This answer was given on the basis that it was against Government policy to inquire into events during war years.

The suggested draft reply of the Prime Minister to Parliament set out in the minute, but not the other advices in the minute, has a signed note reading "Approved JBC". The draft reply, however, is based on the acceptance of the two advices referred to, including the suppression of part of what the Army had said.

The consequence of including the first and omitting the second passage of the Army reply quoted, was that absence of a record was used to cast doubt on what Blamey said, when, as the Army letter as a whole showed, the absence of a record proved nothing.

There are other parts of the Army reply reported in the minute which warrant some reference. These were presumably the alleged but unrecorded reasons arrived at in 1945 upon an unrecorded examination of the "idea" or "plan" which did not become "firm". In this respect the letter said:

> The strength of the Japanese garrison at Sandakan as known prior to 14th Feb. was 1,250. Their troops could have been reinforced by a further 2,250 who were located adjacent to Sandakan in the rescue of the prisoners of war from Sandakan. The rescue of the prisoners of war from Sandakan would have involved a much larger force than a paratroop battalion. If a paratroop battalion had been used, it would have been essential to support it by naval and air forces and reinforce it quickly by other troops landed from amphibious shipping. It will be seen, therefore, that the availability of aircraft was only one of a number of factors to be taken into account in considering an operation against Sandakan.

A rejection of the idea on this basis is quite inconsistent with what appeared to have been the attitude and hence assessments of Generals Blamey, Morshead and Northcott and with what Overall said he knew of what could be done by way of support, following discussions with Navy and Air Force heads at HQ and with the Army.

The Army letter and Defence Department minute fail to state the utter weakness of the Japanese forces at Sandakan, as stated by HQ in 1945 and confirmed in the KINGFISHER and AGAS records. It is inconsistent with the Japanese situation at Sandakan already outlined based on Army records, those of KINGFISHER and AGAS. The only reports in the AGAS I papers in relation to Japanese numbers and positions confirm that the Japanese in the region were widely dispersed, on the run, some "second class" and some of low morale. The only reports of significance which refer to Japanese numbers and dispositions in the Sandakan region are contained in AGAS I Intelligence Reports 1 and 2, being respectively "up to 20th May" (nine days before the second march set out) and "up to 27th June". No. 1 shows that there were 1000 Japanese at Sandakan. Some detail shows this included nearby outlying posts. No. 2 confirms KINGFISHER intelligence that there were less than 500 in Sandakan itself. It also stated that the Sandakan HQ and the Japanese civilian Governor of North Borneo had been moved to Khamansie. This is many days by trail from Sandakan. The June report shows that there were 2000 Japanese in the Sandakan region. An AGAS map attached to the report shows their locations and that most who could be described as "adjacent" troops were many days' march over trails from Sandakan. They would be irrelevant as reinforcements against a surprise paratroop rescue at Sandakan. Included in the 2000 were 500 at Boto. It took the Ranau marches ten days or more to reach Boto. There were 500 at Khamansie, a similar distance away from Sandakan, but more to the north. Other groups of 200 were some days' march away.

That the Japanese in fact were in a weak position is confirmed by the evidence at the trial of General Baba. Colonel Iwahaski, the HQ staff officer in charge of operations, gave evidence which in substance was that the Japanese force in the Sandakan area was a weak force with poorly trained soldiers, no artillery and a weak signal organisation. Other evidence at the trial shows that the Japanese were being moved out of that area to the north coast, the units being the better units, such as those which took the first march to Ranau and then moved on to Jesselton. Iwahaski gave evidence that there were only 1500 Japanese in Sandakan before the second march, which in its context meant the Sandakan region. His evidence was that the Japanese in the Sandakan area were strung out in a long line and were unable to cover the area. A Chinese doctor who had fled from Sandakan in the later period reported to AGAS that the Japanese at Sandakan were dispirited and, if attacked, would "run away". In substance, this occurred when Sandakan was bombed.

As stated, there was no specific intelligence on Japanese numbers for March and April. With the rescue abandoned, there was no need to confirm the KINGFISHER intelligence. Hence there was nothing in AGAS to contradict the Kingfisher figures, if there had been a rescue in, say, April. If, however, the May or June intelligence were applied to March or April, it would have caused no problem for the operation which was planned, even although it could be said there were about 2000 Japanese in the region or "adjacent". With Sandakan in the process of being abandoned, it is unlikely in any event that there would have been any interest to commit "adjacent" troops to difficult marches in order to resist a surprise paratroop operation in battalion strength which would only result in the release of sick and dying and cumbersome prisoners. The defence of Sandakan had been virtually abandoned. When the bombardment of Sandakan occurred on 27 May, the small Sandakan garrison retreated inland some miles beyond the compound, so the 300 POWs and the guards left behind were alone with no Japanese closer to the coast.

There is nothing in the KINGFISHER and AGAS papers which provide any reason why the rescue plan could not have gone ahead, provided the existing KINGFISHER intelligence was supplemented by critical last minute details just before "D" day. It seems clear from the KINGFISHER records and Overall's views that 800 well trained paratroops in a carefully planned surprise operation with exit areas nearby could have dealt with the Japanese forces which were well spread out and none of them close to the compound. The Australian paratroops could have coped with 1500 Japanese even if they were in or near Sandakan.

There must have been some oral or documentary source for the reference in the 1947 Army letter to 2250 Japanese "adjacent" to Sandakan. If it was documentary, I could not find it. Any lead to it was lost with the destruction of the Army file. Any worthwhile intelligence would need some ground party source or confirmation. The only such parties were PYTHON and AGAS, and the KINGFISHER plan was based on them. In any event, the statement in the Army letter that the rescue never got beyond an "idea" because of this intelligence *"as known prior to 14th February"* (my italics) does not stand up to examination, even if what Blamey and Overall said is set to one side. The claim that intelligence about Japanese numbers in February made the rescue "impracticable" is inconsistent with what occurred in February 1945 and later.

There is in the KINGFISHER papers a record dated 9 February which includes a later photograph of the Sandakan compound taken from the air. The KINGFISHER figures are earlier than February. With no Z Force in the area (PYTHON had been withdrawn), it is difficult to see how there could be any reliable intelligence concerning Japanese numbers and dispositions until the KINGFISHER (AGAS I) went in. If Japanese numbers before 14 February were as stated *and* had the relevance and consequences stated, why was AGAS II set up to provide the KINGFISHER ground party? Why was the ground party transferred to AGAS I *on 15 February*? Why, on the same date, did the Army formally pronounce the KINGFISHER plan as part of the AGAS I operation and the KINGFISHER ground party's part in it? Why was the party, which had been specially trained for the KINGFISHER operation, sent by submarine for Borneo leaving Darwin *on 24 February*? Why were the photographs of the compound taken *on 6 March* and marked with intelligence appropriate to the KINGFISHER plan? With the KINGFISHER party established in Borneo near Sandakan just after 3 March, with a brief which included obtaining up-to-date intelligence on Japanese precise dispositions relevant to a rescue at a date later than February, why would that activity be cancelled on stale intelligence? Why would that be done when the ground party was in place and when the mission was so important, in that there were believed to be 1800 POWs there, many of whom were known to be dying? Why do so on information concerning Japanese numbers up to mid-February, which was two months before a rescue then contemplated could have occurred? Was intelligence up to mid-February (supposedly relied on) so poor that it was not known that from early January the Japanese had been moving troops out of Sandakan overland to the north, which indicated that rescue prospects could only improve by the time it was planned to take place? Surely it would have been known that, with the impossible terrain and poor trails between Sandakan and "adjacent" areas, only current, on the spot ground assessments could be relied upon to establish the relevance of the dispositions of Japanese troops outside Sandakan to a swift surprise paratroop rescue eight miles from the town, with exits by sea nearby.

Against the background of the facts concerning February and March 1945, the assertion in the "one-day" letter referred to just does not make sense. The so-called examination in 1945 of the rescue "idea"—an examination, it was conceded, which was not backed by any record—obviously underwent some kind of a reconstruction in the 1947 "one-day" letter. It dredged up convenient reasons against the rescue proceeding. Some report that there were 2000 troops in the Sandakan region, could be seized on as a reason for non-action, if their location and the mud trails of the area were ignored.

The excusing nature of the "one-day" Army letter is further illustrated by including "support by air forces" (for the drop planes) as a possible factor relevant to not proceeding with the rescue "idea". The C47s had extensively dropped at Guadalcanal without cover at a time when the Japanese had considerable air power in the area. In Borneo from February, there was a total absence of Japanese aircraft. On 27 May, great numbers of US and Australian planes had been available to attack Sandakan without opposition in no more than a harassing operation. The same should be said of the suggestion in the letter that naval support was also a factor relevant to not proceeding with the rescue. The Japanese lacked aircraft, seacraft or artillery to prevent an exit by sea. The US Navy was able to have a presence at the May attack. The excuses set out in the letter avoided facing up to the true but embarrassing reason for the decision not to proceed with the rescue, revealed by General Blamey and later affirmed by him, and in later years further confirmed to be the truth by Lieutenant Colonel Overall.

The Army letter also says that there was *no record* of any request for planes by Blamey to MacArthur. This is of no consequence, because it is apparent that it was quite usual for proposals, plans and the like to be subject to direct discussion without record until they became "firm" or "operational". This was so even in respect of some large scale matters such as consideration and talks concerning the use of Australian divisions in the Philippines. The absence of records or at least any that could be found later does not go against what Overall or Blamey have said.

That Blamey had no doubt about what had occurred in 1945 about the rescue plan appears from press interviews with him after Chifley gave his reply in Parliament on 3 December 1947. His reported response[39] shows he did not resile from what he had said in November. He did not claim he had been misreported. As the press report put it,

> He had related all that was to be told about the scheme when he disclosed recently that the plan had to be dropped because insufficient aircraft were available . . . The rescue plan was prepared by Allied High Command.

It is clear, however, that the plan or proposal originated in Australia and that much planning and training were undertaken and much Australian intelligence gathered before the request was made for the planes. The practice, as appears in the case of the Borneo landings, was for the plans to be prepared by Allied High Command, even where preliminary plans or submissions originated elsewhere. Accepting that Blamey said to the press that the plan was "prepared" rather than merely "approved" by Allied High Commission, what Blamey said on 4 December, properly understood, can only mean that the proposed plan became an Allied HQ plan, but that the aircraft were found by that HQ not to be available. Presumably Blamey, wearing his hat as Commander Allied Land Forces, raised the matter directly with MacArthur's HQ. The plan was endorsed, but the reason given by that HQ for not proceeding was that the planes were required for "other purposes".

The reason for MacArthur's HQ not providing the drop planes and the "other purposes" for which they were required, of course, would have been secret at the time. Blamey may or may not have been informed of them or of their detail, but if he had known them they would not have been "hush-hush" still in 1947. It is more likely that the reason was one Blamey did not want to talk about. When, upon being interviewed by the press on the night following his speech in November, he declined on the grounds of secrecy to reveal the "other purposes" for which the aircraft were required, he added that some prisoners of war were released in other ways and that the Americans were able to liberate service personnel and civilians in the Philippines.[40]

On 1 March 1945, Blamey wrote:

> The allocation of Australian troops to operations is entirely the responsibility of General MacArthur . . . and I have no real say in the matter beyond carrying out the orders I receive. While I have pretty strong feelings on certain of these allocations, I have no right to criticise them.[41]

Although this was said at about the time when the Sandakan rescue plan was current, and almost on the very date that the KINGFISHER plan was abandoned, it was in a general context. In November–December 1947 he adopted the same approach as he had when he made the quoted statement in March 1945. He did not criticise the requirement of the drop planes for other purposes and avoided revealing those purposes. However, he did appear to reveal his feelings, as he did at times, when he added a reference to the rescue of the prisoners in the Philippines by the US. No doubt he knew, at least by then, of the orders to kill the prisoners found at Manila, which were not made public until later years by Bergamini's research and writing.

In 1947, Blamey was retired from the Army and probably did not wish to open up old wounds relating to his relationship with MacArthur.[42]

I could find no record of the "other purposes" or of the reasons, expressly stated or otherwise, for the unavailability of the C47s. None are in the Blamey papers. Some documents and correspondence, such as those which refer to discussions between MacArthur and Blamey concerning the Philippines operation, reveal that the details of proposals and plans were often dealt with orally.

In the absence of any archive record of why the C47s were not available, I determined to find, if I could, what was the likely availability of DC3s (C47s) in early 1945. Much was written after the war of the exploits of the DC3 in peace and in war.[43] It is not possible to point now to the precise dispositions, uses and availability of C47s in the Pacific theatre at times when the Sandakan operation should have been undertaken, in the period February to April 1945. It can be established, however, that the US had such great numbers of C47s engaged in or planned to be used in operations in regions near Borneo that it is difficult indeed to understand why 80 or even 60 or 40 US C47s could not have been made available for the relatively short time required for a drop operation at Sandakan, so close as it was to where the C47s were being used by the US in their hundreds.

In view of the total number of C47s in use, 80 was not a large requirement. From 1942 to the end of the war, just under 6000 C47s were delivered to the US Air Force for use in all theatres of war. Of these, 260 were delivered in the quarter January to March 1945. Of course, losses and demands of different theatres of war make this information of little use other than to provide an appreciation of the comparatively moderate requirement for Sandakan. After the Leyte naval and air victory in October 1944, and it seems at the very end of 1944, plans were laid for an airborne invasion of Mindanao for which 650 C47s were to be used towing 735 gliders.[44] However, in the event, Mindanao was by-passed. Luzon was invaded by sea on 9 January 1945, following which, using C47s, there was on 3 February a paratroop drop of 2000 paratroops without loss. In the same month 2000 men were dropped by C47s on the island fortress at Corregidor.

The fortress had been reduced to rubble by bombardment and the 2000 troops were dropped there in a number of waves over two days in order to wipe out, as they did, the Japanese hidden in the catacombs from which the US troops had surrendered in 1942. Thus the defeat at Corregidor and the Bataan death march were avenged.

There was only one other later paratroop operation recorded in the Pacific region. That was on 23 February, when ten C47s operating from Clark airfield near Manila (then recaptured) dropped 125 men onto a college in Luzon and released 2000 Allied internees.

For some substantial period (principally, it would appear, in late February and in March), the C47s were extensively used to and from Clark Field in Luzon to bring in 3000 troops and take out wounded and released prisoners to hospitals. They also brought in 7000 tons of cargo, including gasoline, which was used to fuel operations of US planes within the Philippine islands and beyond to Formosa and the Asian mainland. Some C47 missions ranged as far as the Netherlands East Indies beyond Borneo. The number of C47s used in this way is not available. There is not on record any Mindanao-type special "hush-hush" mission—say, in March and April 1945—which would have monopolised the C47s in the Asia-Pacific region.[45]

By early March, the Philippines operation was well under way to complete success. On 5 March, MacArthur had been able to write to Curtin explaining that his non-use in the Philippines of the Australian "reserve" divisions, was due to "the enemy weakness".[46]

The overwhelming inference is that the comparatively few US C47s temporarily required for the rescue operation could have been provided at some suitable time between March and April and even early May 1945, if there had been the will and interest to do so. It is difficult to understand why the impetus was not given to such a will by the discovery in February and March, from the Manila and Palawan events, of Japanese policies concerning the killing of prisoners. It is impossible to understand why there was no such will when the harassing strike at Sandakan was part of the agenda in the assault on Borneo.

There is a strong inference that there was no will to provide the planes because to do so would not have been consistent with MacArthur's cultivation of his personal image and the prestige of the US forces he commanded. Lack of transport by air and sea had been a convenient excuse for not using units or for not putting into operation plans which he did not favour. This, as Blamey suggested, indeed exposed, was the reason for not moving battle-seasoned divisions in Australia to forward areas. That MacArthur's reasons were only excuses, and that the plans said to have been made were not intended to be carried out, became clear when US General Sutherland revealed that the true reason for the non-use of the Australian divisions in the Philippines was "political". The politics, it seems, were those of MacArthur, driven by personal conceit and a desire to enhance his image in the US and on the world stage. In particular, he wanted to be seen as the leader, who with US forces alone, was able to avenge the humiliation he suffered in his defeat and retreat from the Philippines.

The compelling, but regrettable, conclusion that can be drawn is that the same politics dictated the decision and inaction which frustrated the projected Australian paratroop rescue at Sandakan using US aircraft. A spectacular success by non-American paratroops would have raised questions at home for MacArthur—why had there not been some similar rescue of Americans before the Philippines landings? If US aircraft were used to rescue British and Australian prisoners, why had they not been used to rescue Americans in a similar situation?

Blamey surely must have realised at the time that there were no legitimate "other purposes" which made unavailable for such a mission, not fighters or bombers, but transport planes, for a very short duration, at a time convenient to MacArthur, in March or April or even May 1945. He would have had little difficulty in perceiving that unavailability of transport again was probably MacArthur's excuse for avoiding an operation of which he could not otherwise disapprove.

Although Blamey contented himself at about the same time in 1945 with general complaints to his Government concerning MacArthur's failure to use Australian units, he, in the circumstances, appears to have been at fault for not positively raising MacArthur's response to this specific rescue issue with the Australian Government. When he made his 1947 speech on a semi-private occasion to console the unused paratroopers by the revelation of their important, formerly secret mission, the question as to why the planes were not provided arose, and he knew this would lead to questions of what he had done about it. He dismissed these issues by merely saying the aircraft were required for "other purposes". When what he had said reached the press, he resolutely refused to reveal what MacArthur's HQ had claimed to be the "other purposes" and hence to be drawn into awkward questions concerning the validity of those claims and the justification for refusing to make the C47s available. Instead he took refuge in the claim that the subject was still "hush-hush" in 1947. This avoided the ultimate question of his failure to seek the aid of the Australian Government, later raised by the Prime Minister.

I believe that Australian history should record that the Sandakan POWs could and should have been rescued in early 1945 by the Australian paratroops.

While responsibility (after the Japanese) for the fate of the prisoners appears to rest with those with ultimate authority, namely GHQ, SWPA and General MacArthur, some responsibility, it seems, rests also with the Australian Government and General Blamey. The 1947 *Bulletin* article was correct when it said that the Australian Government could not wash its hands of the affair by passing all responsibility to MacArthur, as the Prime Minister, Mr Chifley, had sought to do in 1947.

The failure to attempt any rescue of or to provide aid for the Sandakan prisoners, almost all of whom perished, was a delicate matter for the Government when the question was raised in 1947. The only man to escape from Sandakan prison camp, Warrant Office Wallace, who escaped with Major Steele from Berhala Island, was back in Australia in 1944. Steele was personally interviewed by Mr Forde, the Minister for the Army in the Curtin Government. Wallace defied death, the fate of his two fellow escapees, then hid for two months on the Borneo mainland, moved by night to Berhala Island, made a hazardous escape to Tawi Tawi and returned by submarine to Australia to bring a message from the prisoners as to their plight. He carried with him a letter from a prisoner, Sergeant Blain, reporting the condition of the prisoners and their need for medicines.[47] Blain was the independent member for the Northern Territory in the Australian Parliament. Blain was one of a group listed as being next to escape via the underground, but these escapes were shelved and none escaped from Sandakan after Wallace. When Blain could not go, he sent the letter by the underground to the escaped Wallace in hiding.[48] So far as has appeared, there was never any response initiated by the Government to the cries for help from the Sandakan prisoners via Wallace, Blain and Steele.

At the very time the question was asked on 20 November 1947 concerning the failure to rescue the Sandakan prisoners, another question concerning Sandakan, highly political and embarrassing to the Government, was current. It concerned Blain, the very person who had sent the letter to the Government in 1943. It was one of the sorriest incidents in the history of the Australian Parliament, in the form of a political wrangle concerning Blain's use of his parliamentary gold pass while a prisoner and led in January 1948 to an inquiry by the Privileges Committee of the House of Representatives. On 6 November, Mr Mulcahy, a Government member, responded to an interjection and unwisely said, in referring to another returned serviceman member:

> . . . this man who went away to fight for his country was a member of Parliament, but unlike Mr. Blain, he didn't show his gold pass to the Japs to gain special treatment.

I interpose that Blain's involvement with the escape plans was discovered when the underground collapsed and he with many others was tried at the same time as Captain Matthews. He faced the same terrors of the interrogations and prospect of death in fact suffered by others, including Matthews. He was convicted, but only given a sentence of eighteen months, as were some others. He served the sentence at Singapore and this saved him from death at Sandakan.

Blain demanded an inquiry as to whether he had breached parliamentary privilege. Some members on either side said they would use their pass to save their lives. Chifley endeavoured to subdue the affair, but the Opposition made the incident into a major political issue. Mulcahy avoided giving an unqualified withdrawal and apology. On 7 November, the Opposition moved a motion for an inquiry by the Privileges Committee. On 18 November the *Sydney Morning Herald* published a leading article on the issue. This was the background against which the question was asked on 20 November concerning the rescue of the prisoners, although no direct attempt was made to link it with the Blain-Wallace incident. The Blain letter, however, and the Steele interview could have been raised if the rescue question had been allowed to run on or if the inquiry sought had taken place.

The Blain affair continued into 1948. The Government managed to have the inquiry heard in camera. Some of the declarations of fellow prisoners were given publicly before the inquiry was heard. One was from Blain's commanding officer, Major Fleming, who commended Blain for his fortitude and help to other prisoners. Another from Captain Wood revealed that after Blain was arrested and in custody elsewhere, the kit bags of the men charged were emptied out in front of Hoshijima and the gold pass fell out. Hoshijima was suspicious of it, but Wood explained its use and Hoshijima put it in his pocket. Hoshijima must have given the pass back because another prisoner charged with Blain said that when threatened with death, Blain produced the pass to save his life. It should be recalled that many people interrogated lost their lives under torture. The report of the inquiry dated 8 April 1948 unanimously cleared Blain.

It was in this political climate in November and December 1947 that the Government closed for the years to come the

Sandakan prisoner issue by a quick political answer. The question which the *Bulletin* asked still remained—having been alerted by Steele, Wallace and Blain in 1944 of the dire state of the Sandakan POWs, why did not the Government itself initiate some action by raising the question of what could be done for the Sandakan POWs when the Borneo operations were pending? This question could have been directed to Blamey and MacArthur and, if necessary, the US Government.

If the Government did not have the 1945 intelligence concerning the prisoners, it had been alerted as to their predicament in 1944, and surely, through the Minister for the Army or for Defence, it should have sought to be told the position in 1945, when the Borneo landings were contemplated using Australian divisions. While Steele was being interviewed by Forde, Wallace was interviewed by Army intelligence. He asked that something be done for the prisoners.[49]

It seems inconceivable after being alerted by the 1944 message to Forde that, at the time when Generals Blamey, Northcott and Morshead were involved in the paratroop rescue plan and the paratroop battalion was training for the rescue, the Defence and Army Departments knew nothing about the rescue project, even if Blamey did not complain to the Government about MacArthur's decision.

The Government does not appear to have protested to the US Government at Blamey being by-passed by MacArthur, contrary to the original inter-Government agreement. But surely after the 1944 alert it should have sought to know from the Australian Army what was being done, and then, with knowledge of the facts, in the end have asked the US Government that something be done about the Borneo prisoners, who were likely to be caught up in the projected Borneo operations.

When the plan for a full-scale paratroop rescue of the prisoners before the first landing failed to proceed, the rescue or recovery of the prisoners after the Borneo landings by other means came under consideration, but again nothing effective was done, either by the US or by the Australian forces in Borneo.

The question of rescue of the Sandakan prisoners was raised with General Blamey at Morotai by Major Rex Blow, DSO, and Captain Jock McLaren, MC and bar. The account, given by McLaren before his death in 1956, appears in *One Man War* by Hal Richardson, published just after McLaren's death. The exploits of Blow and McLaren were considerably intertwined, particularly in their escapes as POWs and their guerilla activities. My source for what follows is principally conversations with Rex Blow in 1988. Although his memory is hazy about dates and some details, he confirmed the substance of McLaren's account.

In April 1945, the US Command, following successful operations in the Philippines, was proposing to use Blow and McLaren on a new mission, when a request came from the Australian Army for their release so that they could be used in connection with the Borneo operations then under preparation. They saw Blamey on 23 April, at Morotai, having arrived there the day before. Blamey showed great interest in having them detail their guerilla activities in the Philippines and discussed with them using their experience by having them assigned to SRD (Z Force).

The two men then raised the question of the rescue of the Sandakan POWs. Although neither had been in the mainland Sandakan compound, their 500 companions in "E" force on Berhala Island, from where they escaped, had been moved there the day after their escape. They asked Blamey what could be done to rescue the prisoners and volunteered to participate. They offered to go in with any paratroops used and suggested the prisoners could be taken out by landing barges from a spot on the coast only a few miles from the compound. Having been under Colonel Suarez, they would have had some knowledge of later conditions in the Sandakan area, which they discussed. Blamey showed an awareness of the condition of the prisoners and other circumstances concerning the compound's location and discussed the proposal in some detail. Finally, he said that if the operation could be fitted in, it would be done and that Blow and McLaren would be in it. Blamey then suggested that they go to Australia and have some leave. They had been in the Malayan campaign, then prisoners of war for sixteen months, and for just under two years had engaged in guerilla activities without a break. The date of the interview was just a week before the first Borneo landing and many weeks after MacArthur's HQ had fixed the final plans for it. It is clear now from the then top secret KINGFISHER and AGAS I records that, by then, the proposal for a unit paratroop operation had been abandoned. This is confirmed, in any event, by Blamey's suggestion, made just a week before the first Borneo landing, that Blow and McLaren should have leave before their promised participation in what would have had to be some fresh, smaller scale plan. Blamey, of course, would not have disclosed to them past or future plans.

After their return to Australia, and some leave, the two joined the Z Special Unit, but thereafter went their separate ways. As appears from Richardson's book, McLaren was involved in undercover work in connection first with the Brunei and then the Balikpapan operations. Blow was directed to Melbourne, where it was arranged that he go to the Sandakan area and endeavour to enter the Sandakan compound or otherwise communicate with the POWs. He was to provide information for some possible but unspecified plan, to explore possibilities of escape and to alert the prisoners as to what could happen. This, of course, had been part of the function of the KINGFISHER ground party of AGAS I which did not proceed.

On a date of which Blow is now unsure, but which must have been near the end of May or in very early June, he was landed by a US patrol boat in the vicinity of Sandakan, where he picked up a native canoe and a native. The plan was to go by river and then walk to the compound. The patrol boat was to come back at twenty-four hour intervals at a rendezvous. With his native assistant, Blow went inland and came upon the trail of what must have been the second death march. There were indications it had recently passed through. They followed the trail back towards the compound and on the way met natives who told them the prisoners had gone.

It was too late! Blow believes he missed the end of the march by only a few days. He returned to the rendezvous and was picked up by the patrol boat and then returned to Australia to report what he had found.

After his return, Blow was put in charge of another undercover Z Special Unit operation known as AGAS IV in the general Sandakan region. In the meantime, another operation, AGAS III, had been planned. From aerial and other intelligence, the Japanese and prisoner movements to Ranau were known. AGAS III was directed to the Ranau region. Its purposes included reconnaissance "for the rescue of POWs at Ranau."[50] The original party consisted of two Australians, Flight Lieutenant Ripley, Sergeant Hayward and four native "agents". Travelling from an island off the coast, first by native boat and then on foot for some weeks on a long and difficult journey through the jungle and over the mountains, they avoided Japanese locations and reached the Ranau area. They set out on the land journey in early July and it was not until 7 August, eight days before the war ended, that they reached that area. It was here that they heard news of the escapes from Ranau. The escaped Sticpewich was recovered on 10 August. On the same day a native attempted to smuggle food and medicines into the compound. According to the AGAS record of 10 August, there were only twenty POWs alive, who were all very sick, and there were eighty Japanese. The source of this report is not shown. The information could have come from Sticpewich, who was picked up on that date. However, there is later confirmation from other sources that POWs were still alive on and after 10 August. Rescue by the tiny force of six, of course, was impossible. The official report of AGAS III concludes on this aspect:

> The party was unable to rescue the remaining 20 odd POWs at Ranau. They were all known to be in a very weak condition, many were actually dying and all were entirely dependent upon each other for food, sanitation, etc. Any attempt at rescue necessitated the removal of all survivors, as rescue of the fittest would have meant death of the remainder.

Arrangements were made, however, for a large white arrow to be placed on the hillside in a jungle clearing to indicate the camp for possible rescue by paratroops.[51]

On 18 August, which was after Sticpewich had been picked up and three days after the general Japanese surrender, AGAS III was reinforced by parachute by seven extra soldiers, including a medical officer. Sticpewich had told Ripley that four others had escaped and might still be in the jungle. The function of AGAS III was now to set up a field medical post, search for surviving POWs and evacuate them.

The AGAS III record[52] positively confirms the inference drawn in Chapter 1 that the last of the Ranau prisoners were shot after the Japanese general surrender on 15 August and not on 1 August, as claimed by the Japanese at the Labuan trials. This confirmation is provided by the AGAS III chronology of reported sightings of POWs. It states that on 25 August there were about twenty POWs closely guarded (at Ranau) and on 28 August that the POWs had left Ranau the day before (the 27th) for Tambunan and that on 1 September a native policeman coming along the Tambunan trail to Ranau had not encountered any POWs. Then, on the same day (1 September), it was recorded: "POW moved from Ranau [on] 27th Aug. have all been murdered and buried [on] 30th August." This was thirteen days after the general surrender. Australian hats were found at a place along the trail and nearby there were graves. At the trials, the Japanese admitted that two of the three groups of the POWs last shot were taken along the Tambunan trail and then killed. Their claim that this was two weeks before the surrender was false. The truth is that it was two weeks after the war ended. The only possible motive for killing the last of the prisoners then was to destroy all evidence of the Japanese treatment of the Sandakan POWs. The Japanese at Ranau surrendered shortly after the last of the POWs were killed.

Whatever may have happened earlier, a handful of men were left to do what was obviously an impossibility in view of the timing and their numbers. The men of Z Force are

A Chronology of Project KINGFISHER

4 February	Plans to kill prisoners discovered upon rescue of 5000 prisoners at Manila by MacArthur's forces.
24 February	KINGFISHER ground party leaves Darwin in US submarine *Tuna*.
3 March	KINGFISHER party lands in Borneo 45 miles north of Sandakan.
7 March	KINGFISHER party establishes W/T communication with Australia.
10 March	Approximate and presumed date of decision not to proceed with KINGFISHER (on MacArthur's claim that transport drop aeroplanes not available for Australian paratroops).
17 March	MacArthur's HQ finalises plans for first Borneo landing (Tarakan).
5 April	Blamey's letter alleging lack of sincerity in MacArthur's excuse that lack of transport prevented Australian divisions being earlier used in counter-offensive.
23 April	Blow and McLaren urge Blamey to rescue Sandakan POWs.
1 May	First Allied Borneo landing (Tarakan).
27 May	Allied air and sea bombardment of Sandakan—no landing.
29 May	Second POW death march leaves Sandakan at night for Ranau—compound destroyed.
June	Blow attempts to get into Sandakan POW compound but turns back when discovers POWs gone.
June	AGAS I obtains intelligence of death march and shootings of POWs.
21 June	AGAS III lands in Borneo—intelligence mission for Ranau POW rescue.
26 June	Survivors of second march reach Ranau and find only six survivors of first march.
7 July	Short, Botterill, Moxham and Anderson escape from Ranau into jungle.
15 July	AGAS III at Melinson slowed by difficult mountain journey.
28 July	Sticpewich escapes from Ranau into jungle.
4 August	Morshead I/C 7th and 9th Divisions proposes to MacArthur's HQ a plan to persuade Japanese to release Borneo POWs.
6 August	Atomic bomb dropped on Hiroshima.
7 August	AGAS III reaches Lansat, just short of Ranau.
8 August	AGAS III picks up Sticpewich, very weak, and brings him to Narawong.
15 August	Japanese agree to general surrender.
18 August	AGAS III reinforced at Lansat by paratroops.
24 August	Botterill and Moxham (on stretchers) and Short brought to Lansat, after seven weeks in jungle.
27 August	Last POW at Ranau massacred.
10 September	General Baba I/C Japanese Borneo forces surrenders to General Wootten.

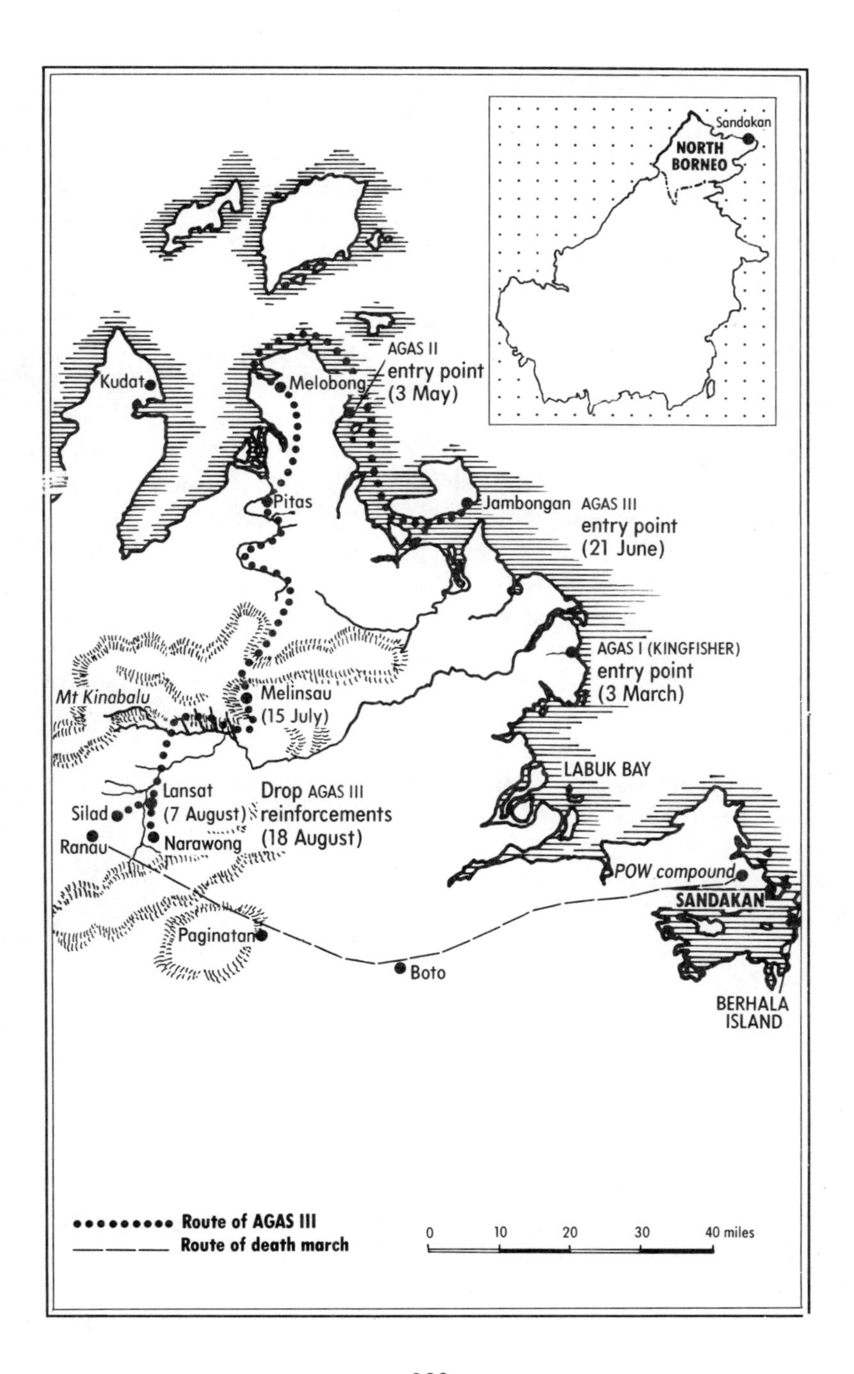
Sandakan
NORTH BORNEO
AGAS II
entry point
(3 May)
Kudat
Melobong
Pitas
Jambongan
AGAS III
entry point
(21 June)
AGAS I (KINGFISHER)
entry point
(3 March)
Mt Kinabalu
Melinsau
(15 July)
LABUK BAY
Lansat
(7 August)
Drop AGAS III
reinforcements
(18 August)
Silad
Ranau
Narawong
POW compound
SANDAKAN
Paginatan
Boto
BERHALA
ISLAND
Route of AGAS III
Route of death march
0
10
20
30
40 miles

to be commended for what they did in impossible terrain and with the cards stacked against them. But for the presence of the two men and their four native agents in the AGAS III operation, aided by the reinforcements dropped in, the four prisoners who escaped from Ranau and were picked up by them would certainly have died. But for this, little would have been known about the fate and experiences of the Sandakan POWs and the Japanese responsible could not have been effectively tried and perhaps not even brought to trial.

General Morshead, Corps Commander covering the 7th and 9th Divisions' operation in Borneo, had always been concerned at the plight of the prisoners in Borneo and their known decline and deaths. Despite his support for the proposals to rescue the prisoners at Sandakan by Australian paratroops, they had been abandoned. By late July and early August, his divisions were in control of key areas of Borneo. The Japanese, although in a hopeless position there, were still retreating and resisting and were in control of areas where prisoners were held. Morshead realised that with the Japanese in this desperate position but still holding prisoners many more prisoners would die. If the war dragged on, as appeared likely, the death rate of prisoners would escalate. Morshead conceived a plan to endeavour to have the Japanese in Borneo release the prisoners while the war continued. The difficulty was to persuade the Japanese to hand over the prisoners and to find an acceptable scheme for doing so while the Japanese were still fighting fiercely. Questions of "face" and other psychological considerations were involved. However, with the danger to the prisoners now obvious, it was worth doing something. Morshead's plan emerges from papers formerly marked "Top Secret" and now held in the "Morshead papers"[53] at the Australian War Memorial.

In those papers in aid of the plan were summaries made of earlier intelligence concerning the number of prisoners held by the Japanese at various locations. Some reference has already been made to the part relating to the Sandakan POWs. The captured *37th Imperial Japanese Army* document of November 1944 earlier referred to, also revealed that at that date there were 2600 prisoners at Kuching. As to Sandakan, the summary also said:

> Taking the 37 Army report of 2,400 as correct in Nov. 44, and allowing for 600 who are reported to have died through sickness and ill treatment, it would appear that 1,800 remained at the time of movement from Sandakan in Mar/Apr. 45. It is known that many died or were killed during this movement . . . it is assumed that an additional 6/700 were lost during this period.[54]

It then concluded that taking the initial 2400 less those thought to have died, there were still 1200 alive at Ranau and at various points of the march right back to Sandakan. This and some detail are wrong. Other information put the second march at its correct date (May 1945, confirmed by the aerial photograph). The 1200 was wrong because of the higher death toll at Sandakan and at Ranau. The summary was made before AGAS III found on 10 August that only twenty remained at Ranau. The summary refers to other areas. As to Kuching, it says:

> The figure of 2,600 in Nov. 44 seems to have remained fairly constant although transfer of labour and some losses through sickness etc. may have reduced the total to the vicinity of 2,000. From all reports the POW have been divided into three groups—British, NEI and Indian POW and women and civilians.[55]

The assistance was sought and given by an intelligent, co-operative Japanese officer held prisoner at Morotai. As Morshead summed it up, the officer made these points:

> (a) The appeal should be a direct one as from one Commander to another and should be in the best formal style of Japanese etiquette.
> (b) There should be no "psychological nonsense" (as he expressed it) included.
> (c) The appeal should treat the Japanese Commander as a gentlemen, fully appreciative of the normal humanitarian qualities.

(d) There should definitely be no bargaining, and negotiations or a truce should be avoided at all costs as these will place too great a responsibility on the Japanese Commander, and he would be almost certain to refer it to higher command.

(e) The appeal should imply that we consider the Japanese Commander of adequate importance to decide the question.

(f) The appeal should be made in the form of several identical letters formally addressed to the Japanese Commander, dropped at several different places, stating where they were dropped, to eliminate the possibility of a subordinate destroying the letter and not forwarding it.

(g) The whole proposition and the implementing of it should be made in the one letter to reduce to a minimum the necessity for inter-communication, from which it is considered the Japanese Commander would fight shy.

(h) The proposal should require the minimum and simplest action on the part of the Japanese Commander and should merely request the Japanese to leave the PW at some point or points near the coast where we could go in and take them out without interfering or affecting the tactical situation in any way.[56]

On 4 August 1945, Morshead sent a letter (a signed copy is with the Morshead papers) to GHQ SWPA (MacArthur's Headquarters) outlining the proposal. After revealing the prisoner situation in some detail it proposed:

> It is suggested that a personal letter be addressed to the GOC 37th Army by GOC 1 Aust Corps, and that several identical letters in English with Japanese translation be dropped by aircraft at different places, these letters to be marked "Personal and Confidential. To be delivered to HQ 37th Army".
>
> It is thought that the text of the letter should be in the form of a frank request for the compassionate release of PW and internees who, in account of sickness and poor physical condition, are of little use to the Japanese Commander for labour and whose part in the war is over.

These matters were then enlarged upon. The letter concluded:

> I should be glad to have your approval of the proposal in which case I should welcome your guidance generally, and particularly on the procedure and on the composition of the letter.

It was a consequence of the command structure which MacArthur had set up that it was necessary for the Australian Commander of the forces in Borneo to obtain MacArthur's consent to a plan such as this and in doing so by-pass the Australian GOC, Blamey. This was necessary, even though it involved Australian units attempting to release what were principally Australian prisoners in Borneo, because it would have involved aircraft to drop letters and supplies and ships to pick up prisoners. It highlights MacArthur's position of authority and responsibility in relation to the earlier question of a paratroop rescue of the Sandakan prisoners.

Also in Morshead's papers is an undated and unsigned form of letter to the Japanese Commander, Lieutenant-General Baba, in these terms:

> 37 Army Commander TOP SECRET
> BABA Masao
> Lieutenant-General
>
> On my instructions as commander of all allied forces in BORNEO, one copy of this letter addressed to you is being dropped today at each of the following places:
>
> RANAU airfield
> KENINGAU airfield
> SAPONG ESTATE
>
> Further copies of the letter will be dropped at these places on each successive day for 10 days unless an acknowledgement that the letter has actually reached your hands is made before the expiration of this time. It is suggested that this acknowledgement might take the form of a large white cross displayed for at least 24 hours on the ground in the centre of the KENINGAU airfield. If no acknowledgement is made in the first ten days then reconnaissance aircraft of my command will observe the

KENINGAU airfield daily for a further ten days or until your acknowledgement is made, whichever is the sooner.

This acknowledgement in itself will not constitute a rejection or acceptance of the request which I wish to make to you.

I ask you to release into my care the Allied prisoners of war and civilian internees at present in your keeping.

I ask this because, as a soldier, I believe they are no longer capable of bearing arms against your forces. I further believe that their usefulness to you as labourers has been impaired by illness to such an extent that you may be willing to adopt this humane course in preference to permitting the death of further of their number, not on the field of honour but as unhappy captives.

On the seventh day after the day upon which you acknowledge receipt of this communication, an allied vessel carrying my representative and flying the Australian flag and a white flag of truce will anchor a mile off the JESSELTON wharf at 0300 hrs. GMT. For a period of one hour this vessel will endeavour to communicate with your shore station by visual signals using the International Morse Code.

In the event of failure to enter into communication with your shore station, the Allied vessel will return at the same time each day for a week and renew the attempt. If no reply is received during this period, then I will understand that you are not willing to grant my request.

If however you answer that you will release these prisoners then it will be necessary that your message should also contain your decisions on the following points:

(a) Places at which PW should be picked up by Allied vessels.
(b) Dates on which PW will be assembled at these embarkation points.
(c) Numbers of PW to be picked up.
(d) Points at which supplies of food, medical stores and clothing should be dropped from Allied aircraft to provide for PW during movement from PW camps to embarkation points.

I appeal to you to give this request the full benefit of your mature deliberation.[58]

Events overcame the proposal. The letter to MacArthur's HQ of 4 August was just two days before the atomic bomb was dropped on Hiroshima and eleven days before the general surrender. The Morshead papers have no indication of any reply or whether the letter to Baba was ever dropped. The lack of any reference in type at the end of the letter to Morshead's position and ink alterations suggest it was not. There was no copy in Japanese.

In any event, although Morshead would then not have known, the later revelations at Baba's trial of his actions and attitudes and his failure to surrender his forces on the general Japanese surrender, make it unlikely that he would have released any prisoners if the war had continued. The direction from Japan on 17 March 1945 concerning prisoners and their posssible use for propaganda, if freed, would certainly have discouraged him. In any event the view that over 1000 POWs from Sandakan were alive along the trail and at Ranau was wrong by 4 August, the date of Morshead's letter to HQ. At most, only twenty or thirty were alive in captivity at Ranau and possibly one or two in the Sandakan area. However, he was correct in respect of the large numbers still alive at Kuching.

Morshead realised the position was desperate and he must be given the credit for initiating a plan at a time when it had the best chance of succeeding—a plan which was aimed at avoiding further prisoner deaths, which could certainly have occurred in other prison compounds such as Kuching, but for the unexpected end of the war.

As the war ended, there was on a plateau in a range of mountains in Borneo an arrow, erected just days before, pointing the way for a paratroop rescue of the last handful of the Sandakan prisoners. On a plateau in a range of mountains in another country, the Great Dividing Range of Australia, were 800 paratroops whose unit saw out the war without action, and who, four or five months earlier, could and should have been allowed and enabled to fulfil a function for which they had been trained in an operation which would have rescued more than 1000 prisoners at Sandakan. By this action the hell of the second death march and that of the last days at Ranau would have been prevented.

On the day the war ended, there lay in Borneo far from their homelands the bodies of young Australian and British prisoners of war, most in rough or mass graves, some alongside the burned out compound at Sandakan and at the edge of the jungle at Ranau, and hundreds of others strewn unburied beside the jungle trails of the marches of death. In all, there were about 2400.

On the day the war ended, the same number lay entombed in sunken ships or otherwise buried or missing as a result of the Japanese attack on Pearl Harbor. In all, including civilians, they numbered 2403.[59]

NOTES

Chapter 2

[1] Keith, *Three Came Back*, pp. 276-71. The husbands were in Kuching prison compound, where Agnes Keith and her husband were also imprisoned. These events, with some additions, were confirmed to me by a member of Z Force.

Chapter 3

[1] More intimate and at times horrifying details are set out in *From Hell to Eternity* by Firkins and *Sandakan* by Wall. The most shocking incident, described on pp. 227-9 and 119 of these books respectively and derived from an account given by a native boy in hiding, was of the crucifixion at Sandakan of a British officer, with nails hammered into his hands, feet and head while he was still alive, followed by a disembowelling and dissection, his remains then being left displayed as an example to others.

Chapter 4

[1] See bibliography and acknowledgements.

[2] Sticpewich told me of the diary, and later, in his evidence, Hoshijima referred to finding it.

Chapter 5

[1] For greater detail, see Firkins, *From Hell to Eternity*, and Wall, *Sandakan.*

Chapter 8

[1] Shinji, *The Account of the Legal Proceedings of the Court for War Criminal Suspects*, which gives a Japanese account of the Ambon war crimes trials.

[2]. Quoted in Russell, *The Knights of Bushido*, p. 58.

[3] ibid.

[4] Bergamini, *Japan's Imperial Conspiracy*, p. 1033.

[5] Quoted: ibid., p. 1035.

[6] Hudson, *The Rats of Rangoon*, pp. 167-212, 204, 208.

[7] Bergamini, pp. 1033-4.

8 *Australian Encyclopaedia*, p. 488.

Chapter 9

[1] Russell, *The Knights of Bushido*, p. 57; *Australian Encyclopaedia*, p. 156

[2] Bergamini, *Japan's Imperial Conspiracy*, pp. 912-13.

[3] ibid.

[4] Williams and Wallace, *Unit 731, the Japanese Secret of Secrets.*

[5] *Australian Encyclopaedia*, p. 156.

[6] Shinji, *The Account of the Legal Proceedings of the Court for War Criminal Suspects*, p. 1.

[7] ibid.

[8] ibid., p. 3.

[9] Storry, *A History of Modern Japan*, p. 80.

[10] Maraini, *Meeting with Japan*, p. 428.

[11] ibid., p. 429.

[12] Keith, *Three Came Back*—summed up on pp. 274–5 but detailed in course of book.

[13] Sleeman, *Trial of Gozawa Sadaichi and Nine Others*, foreword, pp. xiii–xiv.

[14] The Japanese characteristic of dependence on the group, discussed by psychiatrist Dr Doi Takeo in *An Anatomy of Dependence*, is consistent with the behaviour of the Japanese described in this chapter.

[15] Storry, p. 141.

[16] An English translation is in the Mitchell Library, Sydney.

Chapter 10

[1] Minear, *Victor's Justice*.

[2] Foreword to Sleeman, *Trial of Gozawa Sadaichi and Nine Others*, pp. xiii–xiv.

[3] A detailed bibliography is given by Ward and Shulman in *The Allied Occupation of Japan*.

[4] Foreword to Sleeman, pp. xiii–xiv.

[5] Minear, p. 6.

[6] Bergamini, *Japan's Imperial Conspiracy*, p. 1048.

[7] ibid.

[8] ibid., pp. x–xi.

[9] *Ex parte* Quinn (1942) 317 U.S. (Reports) 30.

[10] *Law Quarterly Review*, no. 62, p. 45.

[11] ibid., pp. 44–5.

[12] ibid., pp. 40–52.

[13] ibid., p. 50.

[14] Bergamini, introduction, pp. xi–xiii.

[15] ibid., pp. 1049–54, where Bergamini argues convincingly that Yamashita was not responsible for most of the atrocities proved in evidence and that the trial was pursued by MacArthur for his political reasons.

[16] ibid., introduction, p. x.

[17] Shinji, *The Account of the Legal Proceedings of the Court for War Criminal Suspects*, p. 37.

[18] ibid., pp. 37–8.

[19] Hudson, *The Rats of Rangoon*, pp. 57–60.

[20] *Menzies Report*, Australian Government Publishing Service, 1987, p. 11.

[21] ibid.

Chapter 11

[1] Lebra, *Japan's Greater East Asia Co-Prosperity Sphere*, pp. 78–81.

[2] ibid., p. 95.

[3] ibid., p. 97.

[4] Day, *The Great Betrayal* (generally).

[5] Linklater, *Juan in China*, p. 37.

[6] An English translation is in the Library of New South Wales.

[7] Doi, *An Anatomy of Dependence*, p. 54.

[8] ibid., p. 34.

[9] ibid., pp. 42–3.

[10] ibid., pp. 44-5.
[11] ibid., pp. 46-7.
[12] ibid., p. 37.
[13] Chrysler, Mack, "For most, shame is the spur", *Sydney Morning Herald*, 20 June 1989.
[14] Quoted in *Sydney Morning Herald*, 30 October 1988.
[15] ibid., 15 October 1988.

Chapter 12

A = Archives (ACT or Victoria)
AWM = Australian War Memorial

[1] *Bulletin*, 26 November 1947.
[2] ibid., 31 January 1989.
[3] *Australia in the War 1939-45—Air*, vol. 2, p. 459.
[4] Bergamini, *Japan's Imperial Conspiracy*, p. 1034.
[5] Wallace, *Escape from Hell*, p. 169.
[6] There is none in the Blamey papers at AWM.
[7] Hansard—Australian Parliament.
[8] ibid.
[9] *Australia in the War 1939-45—Army*, vol. 7, pp. 40-50.
[10] A3269/A22/1 and 2 (ACT).
[11] *Australia in the War 1939-45—Army*, vol. 7, pp. 40-50.
[12] CRS A3270, vol. 11, part 3, PYTHON (ACT).
[13] A3269, Item 22, part 1 and 2, KINGFISHER Project (ACT).
[14] AWM 3 DRL 6643.
[15] CRS A3270, vol. 11, part 3, AGAS I.
[16] ibid.
[17] A3269, Item A1, AGAS I (ACT).
[18] A3269, Item A3, AGAS III (ACT).
[19] A3269, Item A1, AGAS I (ACT).
[20] ibid.
[21] A3269, Items 1 and 3, and CRS A3270.
[22] *Australia in the War 1939-45—Army*, vol. 7, pp. 40ff.
[23] ibid., p. 42.
[24] ibid., p. 45-6.
[25] ibid., pp. 47-9.
[26] ibid., p. 48.
[27] ibid., p. 43.
[28] ibid., pp. 43-4, and see General Berryman's comments on p. 45.
[29] ibid., pp. 37-9.
[30] A461, item Q350/1/1, Parts 1 to 5, "War in the Pacific Policy", Access Job No. 1128/88.
[31] Aust. POW and I, No. 255/1.
[32] 246/1 Military Operations (Archives, Vic.).
[33] SM1007, referred to in 246/1 Military Operations and being the Army letter included in Defence Department file 0148/2/470.
[34] 0148/2/470 (Archives, ACT).
[35] SM1007 (see note 33).
[36] Unnumbered minute dated 27/11/47 headed "Operational Plan for Relief of Australian Prisoners of War in Borneo—1945" in file 0148/2/470.
[37] SM1007 (see note 33).
[38] Source as for note 36.
[39] *Sun*, Melbourne, 4 December 1947.
[40] ibid.
[41] *Australia in the War 1939-45—Army*, vol. 7, p. 58.
[42] ibid., pp. 56-72.
[43] Grandridge, *The Douglas DC3 and its Predecessors*, and Glines, *The DC3* and *The Grand Old Lady*.
[44] Grandridge, p. 89.

[45] The basis for these comments is provided by the three books referred to in note 43.
[46] *Australia in the War 1939–45—Army*, vol. 7, p. 45.
[47] Firkins, *From Hell to Eternity*, p. 131.
[48] Wallace, *Escape from Hell*, p. 69.
[49] ibid., p. 173.
[50] CRS 3270, part 3, AGAS.
[51] ibid.
[52] ibid.
[53] AWM 3DRL 2632(5).
[54] ibid.
[55] ibid.
[56] ibid.
[57] ibid.
[58] ibid.
[59] *The History of U.S. Naval Operations in World War II*, vol. III, by Morison, p. 126. The numbers of those killed or missing or who died of wounds were: Navy 2008, Marines Corps 109, Army 218, civilians 68—a total of 2403.

BIBLIOGRAPHY

Bergamini, David, *Japan's Imperial Conspiracy*, Morrow, New York, 1971

Browne, Courtney, *Tojo: The Last Banzai*, Angus & Robertson, Sydney, 1967

Butow, Robert, *Tojo and the Coming of the War*, Princeton University Press, Princeton, NJ, 1961

Day, David, *The Great Betrayal: Britain, Australia and the Onset of the Pacific War 1939–42*, Angus & Robertson, Sydney, 1988

Doi, Takeo (Dr), *An Anatomy of Dependence*, trans. John Bester, 2nd edn, Kodansha International, Tokyo, 1981

Firkins, Peter, *From Hell to Eternity*, Panther, London, 1985

Hall, William L., *International Law*, 8th edn, Oxford University Press, London, 1924

Glines, C. V., and Moseley, W. F., *The DC3: The Story of the Dakota*, Deutsch, London, 1967

—— *The Grand Old Lady: The Story of the DC3*, Pennington Press, Cleveland, Ohio, 1959

Grandridge, J. M. G., *The Douglas DC3 and its Predecessors*, Air Britain Publications, UK, 1984

Hudson, Lionel, *The Rats of Rangoon*, Leo Cooper/Heinemann, London, 1987

Jessy, Joginder Singh, *Malaysia, Singapore and Brunei 1400–1965*, 2nd edn, Longman Malaysia, Singapore, 1974

Jones, Frances Clifford, *Japan's New Order in East Asia and its Fall 1937–45*, Royal Institute of International Affairs, Oxford University Press, London, 1954

Keith, Agnes Newton, *Three Came Back*, Michael Joseph, London, 1948

Lebra, Joyce E., *Japan's Greater East Asia Co-Prosperity Sphere in World War II* (selected documents), Oxford University Press, London, 1975

Linklater, Eric, *Juan in China*, Cape, London, 1937

Long, Bob, *Operation Semut 1: Z Special Unit's Secret War*, published by author, Australia, 1989

Maraini, Fosco, *Meeting with Japan*, Hutchinson, London, 1959

Minear, Richard Hoffman, *Victor's Justice: The Tokyo War Crimes Trial*, Princeton University Press, Princeton, NJ, 1971

Mountbatten, Rear Admiral (Earl), Foreword to Sleeman, *Trial of Gozawa Sadaichi and Nine Others* (see below)

Nelson, Hank, *Prisoners of War: Australians under Nippon*, ABC, Sydney, 1985

Rawlings, Joan, *Sarawak 1836–1963*, Macmillan, London, 1965

Richardson, Hal, *One Man War: The Jock McLaren Story*, Angus & Robertson, Sydney, 1957

Russell, Edward, F. L. (Lord of Liverpool), *The Knights of Bushido: A Short History of Japanese War Crimes*, Cassell, London, and Dutton, New York, 1958

Shinji, Munemija, *The Account of the Legal Proceedings of the Court for War Criminal Suspects*, trans. Kaguo Yoshioka, Manunouche Press, Horitzu Shimpo Press, Japan, 1946

Sleeman, Colin (ed.), *Trial of Gozawa Sadaichi and Nine Others*, William Hodge, London, 1948

Storry, Richard, *A History of Modern Japan*, Penguin, Harmondsworth, 1960

Wall, Don, *Sandakan: The Last March*, published by author, Australia, 1988

—— *Singapore and Beyond*, published by author, Australia, 1985

Wallace, Walter, *Escape from Hell: The Sandakan Story*, Robert Hale, London, 1958

Ward, Robert Edward, *The Allied Occupation of Japan 1945–1952*, Chicago American Library Association, Chicago, 1974 (includes an annotated bibliography by author and F. J. Schulman of the judgments and proceedings at the Tokyo trial and the writings in Western language countries concerning Japanese atrocities and the Japanese war crimes trials in Tokyo and elsewhere)

Webb, Sir William, introduction to Bergamini, *Japan's Imperial Conspiracy* (see above)

—— *Summary of facts and findings from the report on Japanese atrocities and breaches of the rules of warfare in the neighbourhood of the territory of New Guinea and Papua—Australian War Crimes Commission*, Australian Government Publishing Service

Williams, Peter, and Wallace, David, *Unit 731, the Japanese Secret of Secrets*, Hodder & Stoughton, London, 1989

Wright, Lord, "War Crime under International Law", *Law Quarterly Review*, no. 62, 1946, p. 40

Official Histories

Australia in the War 1939-45—Army, vol. 7, *The Final Campaigns*, by Gavin Long, Australian War Memorial, Canberra, 1963

Australia in the War 1939-45—Air, vol. 2, *Air War against Japan 1943-45* by George Odgers, Australian War Memorial, Canberra, 1957

Australian Encyclopaedia, under "Prisoners of War" and "War Crimes"

History of U.S. Naval Operations in World War II, vol. III, by Morison; Little, Brown, Boston, 1950

Official Histories of Z Special Unit (Z Force or SRD) in Borneo—Python, Semut, Agas, Stallion and Platypus, Australian Archives CRS A 3270, vol. II

INDEX

Prisoners of War

Japanese

OTHERS

General Index